DRAWING THE DREAM OF THE WOLVES

Theories of Representation and Difference

General Editor, Teresa de Lauretis

DRAWING THE DREAM
OF THE WOLVES

Homosexuality, Interpretation, and
Freud's "Wolf Man"

WHITNEY DAVIS

INDIANA UNIVERSITY PRESS

Bloomington and Indianapolis

Library of Congress Cataloging-in-Publication Data
Davis, Whitney.
Drawing the dream of the wolves : homosexuality, interpretation,
and Freud's "Wolf Man"/Whitney Davis.
p. cm.—(Theories of representation and difference)
Includes bibliographical references and index.
ISBN 0-253-32919-1 (alk. paper).—ISBN 0-253-20988-9 (pbk. : alk. paper)
1. Freud, Sigmund, 1856–1939. Aus der Geschichte einer infantilen
Neurose. 2. Pankejeff, Sergius, 1887–1979. 3. Homosexuality—
Psychological aspects—Case studies. 4. Psychoanalytic
interpretation—Case studies. 5. Intersubjectivity—Case studies.
6. Freud, Sigmund, 1856–1939—Psychology. I. Title. II. Series.
RC509.8.D385 1995
155.3—dc20
95-4117

1 2 3 4 5 00 99 98 97 96 95

CONTENTS

LIST OF ILLUSTRATIONS

PREFACE

This book was drafted in 1989–90, when I held a Humanities Research Award from Northwestern University. I was able to complete it in 1994 with the assistance of funds from the Arthur Andersen Professorship of Teaching and Research in the College of Arts and Sciences at Northwestern. Russell Maylone and Helmut Müller-Sievers at Northwestern, Stephen Teitsworth at Duke, and Mark Micale at Yale suggested important references at crucial points. Presenting aspects of the book to audiences at the University of Chicago, the Association of Art Historians (U.K.), the University of California at Berkeley, the University of North Carolina at Chapel Hill, the University of Western Ontario, and Harvard University, as well as to students in my graduate seminars at Northwestern, stimulated much rethinking.

I thank Erica Davies and the staff of the Freud Museum, London, the staff of the Library of the Wellcome Institute for the History of Medicine, the staff of the Library of the New York Academy of Medicine, the staff of the Health Sciences Library at Columbia University, Ronald S. Wilkinson of the Manuscript Division, Library of Congress, Todd Smith and other staff members at the Kinsey Institute for the Study of Sex, Gender, and Reproduction at Indiana University, Russell Maylone of the Special Collections Department at Northwestern University Library, and Dr. K. R. Eissler of New York for assisting my research on materials in their care and for answering various inquiries. Sigmund Freud Copyrights, The Institute for Psycho-Analysis, and The Hogarth Press extended permission to quote text and to reproduce graphics from *The Standard Edition of the Complete Psychological Works of Sigmund Freud.*

I am especially grateful to Teresa de Lauretis, editor of Theories of Representation and Difference, for her interest in and comments on this project and for her enthusiastic support of its publication.

This evening I saw Leonardo, standing under the rain in a narrow, dirty and stinking alley, attentively contemplating a wall of stone, with spots of dampness— apparently one with nothing curious about it. This lasted for a long while. Urchins were pointing their fingers at him and laughing. I asked what he had found in this wall.

"Look, Giovanni, what a splendid monster—a chimera with gaping maw; while here, alongside, is an angel with a gentle face and waving locks, who is fleeing from the monster. The whim of chance has there created images worthy of a great master."

He drew the outlines of the spots with his fingers, and, to my amazement, I did actually perceive in them that of which he spake.

"It may be that many would consider such power of invention absurd," the master went on, "but I, by my own experience, know how useful it is for arousing the mind to discoveries and projects. Not infrequently on walls, in the confusion of different stones, in cracks, in the designs made by scum on stagnant water, in dying embers, covered over with a thin layer of ashes, in the outlines of clouds— it has happened to me to find a likeness of the most beautiful localities, with mountains, crags, rivers, plains and trees; also splendid battles, strange faces, full of inexplicable beauty; curious devils, monsters, and many other astounding images. I chose from them what I needed, and supplied the rest. Thus, in listening closely to the distant ringing of bells, thou canst find in their mingled pealing, at thy wish, every name and word that thou mayst be thinking of."

—Dmitri Merezhkovsky, *The Romance of Leonardo da Vinci*

No other work has been so completely my own, my own dung heap, my seedling and a *nova species mihi* on top of it.

—Sigmund Freud to Wilhelm Fliess (Freud 1985: 353 [May 28, 1899])

INTRODUCTION

In this book, I consider the emergence of subjective sexuality in the relationship between Sigmund Freud (1856–1939) and his patient Sergius Konstantinovitch Pankejeff (1887–1979), the "Wolf Man," so called after a childhood dream involving wolves (Fig. 1). Although Freud's famous "case history" of the Wolf Man, *From the History of an Infantile Neurosis* (Freud 1918b), will provide my principal materials—this book is conceived as a reading and interpretation of that text—I will also focus on the analysis itself, completed four years before Freud published his account.

As an explanation of the Wolf Man's striking childhood neuroses and troubled adolescent and adult experience, Freud offered a complex analysis of Pankejeff's "latent homosexuality." This account was based in part on the materials of the analysis itself, in part on Freud's more general theories of "sexuality" and homosexuality, and in part, and most important for my purposes, on Freud's imagination—it achieves only partial expression in Freud's explicit discussions of sexuality—of his own sexual or subjective position, of his own "homosexuality," in relation to that of his young male patient. Though I will not explore the topic here, the Freudian conception of latent homosexuality presented in *From the History of an Infantile Neurosis* has had a tremendous influence on all twentieth-century approaches to human sexuality and gender—from medical clinics or psychiatric hospitals to law courts and military institutions to kindergarten classrooms and academic disciplines such as history or literary criticism.

Later on, Freud sometimes seems to have used a diagnosis of latent homosexuality as a stick to beat a man, or his female partner, back toward what he regarded as a more fulfilling, expressive, or appropriate heterosexual existence. He would suggest that if a man did not actively grasp his heterosexual ideal, he could become an *actual* or practicing—not merely a "latent"—homosexual (see especially Edmunds 1988). But in principle the concept could also be used to help a man explain his heterosexual anxieties or failures, whether or not the next step—typically it was not—would be to encourage him to express his hitherto unacknowl-

Figure 1. Serge Pankejeff,
self-portrait, 1920
(Pankejeff Papers, LC)

edged homosexual potential. In Freudian therapy, the concept essentially instructed a patient, with the analyst's help, to rescue an actualizable heterosexuality from an unactualized homosexuality.

Of course, this plan turned out to be largely impossible for men whose "homosexuality" had *already been* actualized—who were not latent but blatant. The concept of "latent" homosexuality, then, must be accompanied by a further account of its *realization* in some cases for some men— "homosexuals" in the ordinary, non-Freudian sense of the term. Later I will explore how Freud hoped to draw the crucial line between the latent and the manifest homosexual. It is no surprise that the terminology itself played a variation on fundamental Freudian views about psychic processes and the production and location of meaning. But we should beware assuming that a latent homosexual is like a latent dream-thought.

In the case of manifest, practicing, or overt homosexuals, or "inverts," Freud sensibly took the view that analysis could not "cure"; the cure, if it was attainable at all, would have had to have happened at the preceding stage of latency. But analysis could help a homosexual man to cope with his situation, which was often quite a miserable one (see especially Lewes 1988). The concept of "latency" is fundamental, then, to the psychoanalytic possibility of "curing" or "overcoming" homosexuality—so long as the potentially homosexual individual is caught by the therapeutic net *before* he reaches blatancy. Still, the concept of latent homosexuality could function intelligibly for practicing or self-acknowledged homosexual men and women. However peculiar, it provided some kind of explanation for the historical emergence of their "inversion," and in particular for its neurotic configuration as a set of sometimes unhappy erotic and social relations with *other* men and women understood to be "latent" homosexuals as well.

In sum, the Freudian concept of latent homosexuality has an integral role to play in many registers of the Freudian theoretical and therapeutic system. But, of course, it would not really have occurred to observers before Freud that male—and female—"homosexuality" is a universal intrapsychic (or psychological) but frequently unrealized interpersonal (or social) possibility. For such observers, including many self-acknowledged "homosexuals" participating in homoerotic social networks, homoeroticism was either a fully actualized social institution, as in ancient Greece, certain "primitive" societies, or (to a much lesser extent) the subcultures of modern European and American cities, or it was an individual peculiarity, even an abnormality, as in the modern Euro-American world outside a few delicately self-sustaining homosexualist milieux. This dichotomy is readily visible, for example, in the way many Victorian intellectuals idealized the social and ethical institutions of the Athenians and even the Spartans at the same time as they vehemently condemned sodomy and, later, "homosexuality." But after Freud, the idea that very often homoerotic interests, attachments, or values are in themselves *neither* actualized *nor* peculiar—but instead subsist as a universal potentiality waiting, as it were, for actualization among some people or in certain institutions—became a commonplace. Though the idea, in certain specific versions, has been very useful to homosexualist emancipation movements and even to the latest generation of gay and lesbian activists or "queer" theorists, it is, in my judgment, substantially or even wholly false. On the whole, I believe, it has proved to be a pernicious concept. It is one of the most popular and powerful ways by which ideologies for the management and improvement of human intrapsychic teleologies, on both the right and the left of the political spectrum, identify human malleability or adaptability in such a way as to suggest that some form of ethical and cultural policy ought to be instituted—that latency ought, in fact, to be cultivated. Whether this process, as a point of ethical and cultural policy, should involve the winnowing or the fertilizing of the latent potentiality hardly matters to me as a point of principle, though in practice and if forced to choose, I would, of course, prefer to fertilize rather than to winnow.

In this book I try to lay a few elements of the groundwork for a thorough and in particular a historically grounded critique of Freud's conceptualization. At the same time, however, I try to suggest why it has seemed, and probably will continue to seem, to be plausible or necessary—to be true at some level of our experience of ourselves as subjects and of other subjects, despite its logical flaws and its complicity with nonlibertarian social philosophies. One way to do this, I am convinced, is to show that the intellectual origins of the concept are rooted in a specific interpersonal, argumentative, and textual situation which does, in fact, display some of the properties the concept attempts to represent and—here it goes wrong—to universalize. I freely acknowledge that this approach involves some sleight of hand. The reader will not fail to note that I have found myself in the awkward position of writing a historical and textual analysis and criticism of a concept which I simultaneously, and in ways about which I am probably not even fully aware, must depend on. I do not, for example, have any kind of alternate explanation or account—what Freud would have called an "etiology"—of homosexuality that covers the phenomena mapped by Freud's term "latent homosexuality" in more depth or with greater accuracy.

The case history of the Wolf Man, of course, is not the only place in Freud's work and writing where this idea was developed. Freud's *Three Essays on the Theory of Sexuality* (1905d), for example, presents the elements of a general sexology, tied in turn to the general psychology presented in *Die Traumdeutung* (1900a) and elsewhere, which provided a basis for his work with and published discussion of the Wolf Man. Indeed, we sometimes associate the thesis of primordial human "bisexuality," or undifferentiated sexual potential, including "homosexual" potential, with Freudianism as such. The emphasis should be placed here on the notion of erotic *potentiality*. Although other observers had identified "bisexual" attitudes and practices in human emotional and social life, and specifically homoerotic attachments had long been acknowledged as one form of male and female eroticism, Freud formulated the most complete account of the way in which the mind can be "predisposed" or (to use one of the languages he deployed) of the way in which it must be "statically charged" to become "homosexual" without ever manifesting any overtly homoerotic attitude, practice, or attachment whatsoever. In addition, he provided an account of the actual *realization* of erotic potential—of the development or transfer, for example, *from* the primordial bisexual potentiality *to* an individual homoerotic (or any other sexually specific) practice.

These are large topics simply to try to explicate. To do justice to them would require an extensive analysis of many Freudian, pre-Freudian, and non-Freudian texts—not my intention here. For my purposes, the case history of the Wolf Man purported to offer one of the supports which the broad sexological and psychological approach desperately required. *From the History of an Infantile Neurosis* provided a particular but supposedly exemplary "case"—a highly differentiated and detailed (if sometimes compressed or implicit) history of the "latent" and the manifested homoeroticism or "homosexuality" of a man from his very birth (even, as we will see, *before* his birth) to his full maturity.

In this regard, the case history was unique in Freud's and possibly in any contemporary or later representation of the modern "homosexual" life-historical possibility. Its resolution depended, at least in part, on the text's extraordinary species of historical narrative imagination. As we will see, Freud links the evidence of the most "present" time, his relationship with the Wolf Man in the psychoanalytic encounter itself, to the most "past" time, the descent of both parties from their ancestors, from prehistoric human beings, and, ultimately, from animals. I will stress that no one stage of this long history of "homosexuality" was theoretically privileged by Freud, despite the fact that the case history explicitly concerned itself with the Wolf Man's infancy and childhood and that, following Freud, there has been a tendency to see homosexual "latency" as a fairly well-defined stage of human development. Instead, at least according to the principle or theory which Freud attempted to express in the case history, the most remote phylogenetic and the most immediate intersubjective histories should not be detached, though they might—in fact, must—be narratively disentangled.

All of these remarks might suggest that my focus in this book will be the Freudian concept of homosexual latency as such. But in fact I will not be exclusively or even very actively concerned with this or any other *explicit* Freudian theory of, or model for, human sexuality or subjectivity.

I will assume their presence in Freud's work, their influence on later thought, sometimes even their possible logical coherence—which charitable analysis, if it is sufficiently willing to go along with ideas such as the founding Freudian thesis of "bisexuality" or originally undifferentiated eroticism, can sometimes succeed in suggesting. A number of careful expositions have already concentrated on extracting them (e.g., Lewes 1988: 24–47; Birken 1988: 92–112; Silverman 1992: 339–88).

The sheer variety of these commentaries, however, suggests that a good deal always remained unsaid in Freud's explicit theoretical discussions of sex or sexuality, in his narrative portrayals of life histories, and in his abstract metaphysical (so-called metapsychological) investigations of mental processes. Freud's most immediate students and colleagues in the early institutionalization and publication of psychoanalysis were extremely alert to this pattern of gaps and to what some of them came to see as the incoherent, unnecessary, or implausible commitments which disguised it. They saw—this is to oversimplify for the moment—that Freudian sexology and metapsychology, including their theories of or models for "homosexuality," were substantially determined and disturbed by Freud's own imaginary sense of his homoerotic positions in relation to those of his friends, students, and patients. At points, Freud readily acknowledged this fact. But his most broad-based and useful theoretical and empirical typology of "homosexuality"—completed between 1908 and 1914, it identified the sublimated, the regressed, and the "latent" homosexual in terms of their different Oedipal histories—did not and probably could not represent his own homosexuality, neither sublimated nor regressed nor latent, *as* a type. Thus his theory, at any level of articulation, remained very obviously incomplete.

The dynamic of Freud's homoeroticism comes to at least one of its heads or crises—a very productive one, to be sure—in the analysis and in the case history of the Wolf Man. In this social encounter and in the text which represents it, we will not find a complete resolution of Freud's "homosexuality" or a fully manifest historical or theoretical portrayal of it. But the theory of homosexual latency and the narrative of the Wolf Man's latent homosexuality afforded an imagination of homosexual position that for the first time probably did enable Freud to register his homosexuality as such—to symbolize and to some extent, as he himself put it, to "overcome" its neurotic (that is, its partial) realization. This transformation was literally a *transference*, as we will see, from one "homosexuality" to another and, indeed, from one "homosexual" to another. It could be achieved in part precisely because the conceptualization of "latent homo-sexuality" is more or most fundamentally a recognition of the irreducibly intersubjective nature of sexuality and thus of any conceivable homosexuality. The Freudian theory of latent homosexuality is simultaneously and by definition *also* a theory of the specific intersubjective history of ac-quaintance, address, solicitation, seduction, and frustration in which the merely "latent" becomes the socially realized—an actual interpersonal eroticism or, in the strict sense of the term, a sexuality. At the level of theory, the Freudian theory of sexuality is, at root, an acknowledgment of human intersubjectivity. But at the level of *method,* as well as in the historical emergence of this theory of sexuality itself, it was the experience of a particular human intersubjectivity—the relationship between Freud and the Wolf Man—that afforded the most comprehensive "case" of and for this very theory, this very model or picture of eroticism in or as the mind.

It is not surprising, then, that much of the discussion of the Wolf Man case since the publication of the case history in 1918, both inside and outside psychoanalysis, takes up the relation of interpretive and narrative "subjectivity" to theoretical and historical "objectivity." I will refocus this concern to consider intersubjectivity in the case. It will be essential here to investigate the *temporality* of the case and the case history, from the first meetings of Freud and the Wolf Man in 1910 (as well as some earlier events) to the final writing out and publication of the case history in 1918 (as well as some later events). We cannot possibly grasp the theory of intersubjectivity—of human sexuality—addressed by the published case history without setting it in the intersubjective context of its emergence, its historically determined identity, *as* a text. We will see, for example, that the case and case history have what might be called an emergent, and very specific, intersubjective form—namely, an exchange of objects in and through which the two principal parties to the exchange, Freud and the Wolf Man, rescue one another from their existing "homosexuality." This mutual "overcoming" of homosexuality happens, I will argue, to be the emergent form of homoeroticism, the sexuality, of and between Freud and the Wolf Man; it is not necessarily, and in its fine particulars can-not be, the historically emergent homosexuality of and between anyone else.

The burden of my interest, it follows, will be the historical dynamic and more specifically the actual psychological and social *mechanism* of the intersubjective emergence and transformation of homosexuality in the case and case history of the Wolf Man. It is easy enough to assert that some such temporality must characterize the case—for it must characterize all human relations. But it is more difficult to say exactly *how* this intersubjectivity was resolved or relayed in its fine particulars, which, as I have already suggested, must be the real interest of a Freudian theory of sexuality. And it is most difficult of all to say how its mechanisms, whatever they might have been, ultimately coordinated the whole encounter, from first meeting to final writing, as the "case" of and for precisely that view of human relations—as the very particular and possibly exemplary "case" *for* the psychoanalytic concept of human sexuality as emergent intersubjective eroticism.

To address this last problem, I will examine the history of *visual interpretation,* or more broadly of visuality, in the case and case history. In fact, in this instance intersubjective significance is especially palpable in the visual domain precisely because images, broadly defined to include all tactile, acoustic, and visual impressions, are the medium of fantasy and desire. (It would take a differently conceived book, however, to examine Freud's or related theories of visuality and desire as such. I will simply assume rather than explicate their relation, although I do hope to provide a suggestive "case.") I do not hold and will not propose essential distinctions between visual and verbal, or between depiction and script, or between viewing another's face and reading another's book. But even the most rough-and-ready distinctions here will introduce a new perspective on what might seem to be quite familiar territory. Despite the great diversity of commentaries on Freud's *From the History of an Infantile Neurosis* and more generally on Freud's histories and theories of sexuality, there has been a tendency to focus exclusively on the published case history itself and on other Freudian texts as specimens of Freud's expository German prose.

The case history is, of course, writing—writing which has a complex internal stratigraphy of composition, revision, and dissemination. But this writing should not be conceived as taking place solely in German (a point to which I will give brief attention) or solely in prose, in script, or in natural language (speech) at all. The case history substantially rests, as we will see, on the production and propagation of significance in graphic media, depending on several conventions of graphic notation apart from script and relying on visual and to a lesser extent tactile perception and understanding. Freud's approach to the case presented to him by the Wolf Man derived in part from an iconography that had set up and continued to provide a representation of the historical development of minds and persons. The history of this iconography itself must take us through domains of graphic imagination, conception, and notation as diverse as psychoanalytic metapsychology and narrative, histology and neurology, Darwin's evolutionary theory and Haeckel's comparative embryology, and Freud's own personal artifacts and image making—to mention only a few of the relevant materials. The bulk of my exposition and interpretation, in fact, will be concerned with this element of the case and case history— not only because it has received no attention but also because it is, almost by definition, the site of what we could call the *manifestation* of latency: a picture is the formation in which mental memory- and fantasy-images become, at the moment of production and observation, nominations or predications, symbols or "meanings." I have not written a book about the theory of this process, though I am extremely interested in the topic (Davis 1995a), but I do hope to provide a good example of it and in particular of its sexual, and hence intersubjective, status. In a very important way, although the graphic dimension or notation emerged and was published *in* Freud's text, it was not wholly derived *from* and made *by* Freud. Instead, in substantial measure it included the *Wolf Man's* contribution to his history and to what, I believe, we should conclude became the joint or intersubjective writing of its origin and meaning *for* both of the participants and *as* their mutually determined sexuality.

Anyone working on Sigmund Freud and the Wolf Man owes a great debt to several translators and editors: James Strachey, the chief editor of the *Standard Edition* of Freud's works translated into English (24 vols., 1953–74); Muriel Gardiner, the American editor of the Wolf Man's *Memoirs* (1971); William McGuire, the editor of the Freud/Jung letters, translated by Ralph Manheim and R. F. C. Hull (1974); Jeffrey M. Masson, the editor of Freud's letters to Fliess (1985, 1986); R. Andrew Paskauskas, the editor of the Freud/Jones letters (1993); and Eva Brabant, Ernst Falzeder, and Patrizia Giampieri-Deutsch, the editors of the Freud/Ferenczi letters (1993). It will be obvious throughout that I have depended on their work.

Still, much basic work remains to be done. In one area of particular interest to me, for example, virtually nothing is known: Isidor Sadger, one of Freud's lesser-known early students, should probably be credited with fundamental aspects of the psychoanalytic theory of homosexuality, such as its emphasis on "narcissism." Among all the early analysts, it was almost certainly Sadger who acquired the most extensive "clinical" experience with manifest or practicing homosexuals (as opposed to the "impotent" married men who consulted many psychotherapists or the "latent" homosexuals the Freudians later identified). But as far as I know, Sadger's biography has not been attempted, and his work has not been systematically studied.

To take another example, the early psychoanalysts' knowledge of homosexuality was shaped by their interaction with the homosexual sexologist and emancipationist Magnus Hirschfeld. Though the psychoanalysts accepted "homosexual" patients referred by Hirschfeld, Freud reacted strongly against Hirschfeld's essentially nonpsychological theories. We can now see Hirschfeld's practice as extremely forward-looking in several respects: it was an early model of a nonjudgmental and noninterventionist venereal-disease and sexual-counseling clinic, and Hirschfeld's "therapy" concentrated on helping homosexual men and women cope with hostile environments. But the prestige of the Freudian metaphysics of "sexuality" remains so great that Hirschfeld's approach, despite the careful work of several historians (see especially Herzer 1992), has not been fully appreciated. Elsewhere I hope to explore these and related questions in greater detail (see further Davis 1995c).

In writing this book, I have continually referred to the work of Didier Anzieu (1986), Lisa Appignanesi and John Forrester (1992), Albrecht Hirshmüller (1991), John Kerr (1993), Marianne Krüll (1986), William McGrath (1986), Saul Rosenzweig (1992), and Frank Sulloway (1979), the authors of essential books on Freud's personal and intellectual development and the cultural and historical context of his thought, and to the work of Mikkel Borch-Jacobsen (1988, 1993), Jean Laplanche (1976, 1989), Malcolm Macmillan (1990), Paul Ricoeur (1970), and Samuel Weber (1982), the authors of stunning interpretations and critiques of Freudian metapsychology. Unlike all of these writers, however, I do not offer a general historical or theoretical inquiry or attempt to excavate the deep psychological or conceptual structures of Freud's thought.

Instead, I offer a focused reading of a single text and use historical and theoretical materials in order to reveal one aspect of its identity *as* a text. Some of these materials are familiar, and some perhaps less so. I have, for example, placed some stress on Freud's histological and neurological work from 1878 to 1897. This emphasis may strike some readers as unusual. But apart from the fact that Freudian metapsychology is, I believe, unintelligible without its biology, I hope to identify the specifically textual place of Freud's biological interests in his psychoanalytic writing—one specimen of it, at any rate. In fact, I hope that some perhaps superficially surprising juxtapositions will make sense at another level ("in another scene"). Needless to say, I have learned a great deal from focused interpretations of Freud's study of the Wolf Man written by a number of psychoanalysts and literary critics, cited where appropriate, though I have pursued some questions which I believe to be novel ones.

Quotations from the works and correspondence of Freud are as exact as possible; where the present author has abbreviated the text, the ellipses appear in square brackets (i.e., [. . .]) to distinguish them from Freud or his correspondents' own ellipses. A note on the citation of Freud's scientific and psychoanalytic works appears at the beginning of the first section of the References Cited at the end of the book. In general, for translations of Freud's psychoanalytic works into English, this book uses the versions published under the general editorship of James Strachey in *The Standard Edition of the Complete Psychological Works of Sigmund Freud*. Note, however, that this multivolume work, though indispensable, does not include the "scientific" and in some cases arguably protopsychoanalytic works of Freud and does not, of course, include Freud's fascinating "Overview of the Transference Neuroses" (Freud 1987), written in 1917 and discovered only recently. (As we will see, this text contains material of great interest for the interpretation of Freud's case study of the Wolf Man.) For Freud's works in German, the various German editions used here are cited as appropriate. The unpublished material quoted here has been drawn from the Muriel Gardiner Papers and the Serge Pankejeff Papers in the unrestricted access collections of the Manuscript Division of the Library of Congress; these collections are cited in the body of the text as Gardiner Papers and Pankejeff Papers respectively.

DRAWING THE DREAM OF THE WOLVES

I

FREUD AND THE WOLF MAN

> Transference arises spontaneously in all human relationships. [. . .] The less its presence is suspected, the more powerfully it operates. [. . .] It plays a decisive part in bringing conviction [*Übertragung*] not only to the patient but also to the physician.
>
> —Freud, "Five Lectures on Psychoanalysis" (1910a: 51–52)

> I am the most famous case.
>
> —The Wolf Man, about 1975 (Obholzer 1982: 175)

Sigmund Freud and Serge Pankejeff saw and spoke with one another fairly constantly for three and a half years in a psychoanalysis that lasted from late January or early February 1910 until July 1914. The principal interruptions were caused by Freud's vacations and trips, chiefly in the summers. In 1910, for example, Freud went to the Netherlands with family members for the second half of July and the whole of August and traveled in Italy with Sandor Ferenczi for most of September. After 1914, Freud and the Wolf Man encountered or communicated with one another intermittently, though still substantially—including another brief period of psychoanalysis in 1919. In 1926, for example, Freud corresponded with the Wolf Man about certain details of the first analysis (Lewin 1957). (For the most recent—and a finely balanced—account of Freud's treatment of the Wolf Man, see Gay 1988: 285–92.)

1

Freud and the Wolf Man Represent One Another

Freud immediately represented Serge Pankejeff in the session notes he took during the analysis itself. Unfortunately, these do not survive. Probably they resembled the notes Freud kept from October 1, 1907, to January 20, 1908, during his analysis of the "Rat Man" (1909d: 251–317). These records are notably discrepant from Freud's final published case history of the patient and suggest that the published case histories—as many readers and historians of psychoanalysis have come to recognize—should always be considered in the light of the human intercourse from which they sprang and which they partly portrayed.

In 1913, while the analysis of the Wolf Man was still under way, Freud published a brief essay describing the patient's childhood dream. It formed his contribution to the first volume of the new international psychoanalytic journal (Freud 1913d). In addition, in the same year his presentation to the Munich Psychoanalytic Congress, "The Predisposition to Obsessional Neurosis," addressed issues raised in and by the case (Freud 1913i), as do elements of later essays such as "Lines of Advance in Psycho-Analytic Therapy" (Freud 1919a).

The text of the case history itself was titled *Aus der Geschichte einer infantilen Neurose* ("From the History of an Infantile Neurosis"). It was written in the months of October and November 1914, after the termination of the analysis in July 1914. The text was published, however, only after the war, in 1918; it was included in the fourth volume of Freud's *Sammlung kleiner Schriften zur Neurosenlehre,* with two very important additions written that year (Freud 1918b). (Hereafter, page numbers in parentheses are to the *Standard Edition* translation; the German text is quoted from Freud 1924: 439–567.) After the case history was drafted but before it was published, the twenty-third "introductory lecture" on psychoanalysis, "Paths to the Formation of Symptoms"—probably delivered in April 1917 (Freud 1916x: 358–77)—continued the speculations on the subject of the "primal scene" broached in the case history.

Freud represented the Wolf Man's analysis more indirectly—but nonetheless quite obviously—in his polemical refutation of Alfred Adler and Carl G. Jung, *On the History of the Psycho-Analytic Movement,* completed in the middle of February 1914 (Freud 1914d). Sometime in the late winter or early spring of 1914, Freud imposed a time limit on the analysis in order to hasten it to a conclusion, which it reached in July. Although fruitful results were obtained in the final months of the analysis, it may be that when Freud had completed the *History,* he began to lose interest in his patient. (A suggestion that Freud might have foreseen the outbreak of war is implausible; although the geopolitical situation in July was very tense, a few months earlier—when Freud imposed the termination date— the summer crisis could not have been predicted.) At any rate, the arguments of the *History* (Freud 1914d) and the questions Freud pursued in the analysis and wrote up in the case history (Freud 1918b) were intimately linked.

Later on, the results of the analysis and case study made themselves felt in a great many of Freud's theoretical and speculative writings. Among these we should probably include his famous discussion of the fantasies of the unnamed "male child" in his paper "A Child Is Being Beaten" of 1919 (Freud 1919e) and several additions on bisexuality, castration, and anality written in 1914 for the third edition of the *Three Essays on the Theory of Sexuality,* which was being prepared as "hack work" while Freud labored on writing the case history itself (Freud 1905d: 123–24; Freud/ Abraham 1965: 199 [November 18, 1914]). (A catalogue of additions to the *Three Essays* derived from the Wolf Man work has been proposed by Mahony 1984: 47 n. 63.) Other writings of 1914 were deeply influenced by the case—particularly the essay "Remembering, Repeating and Working-Through" (Freud 1914g), which evaluated patients' recollections during analysis, and the metapsychological reflections "On Narcissism" (Freud 1914c), a text which has generally been seen as arising out of the case, ongoing debates with Jung, and related aspects of Freud's work (see Steele 1982: 271–74; Segal and Bell 1991: 149–74).

Such later works as *Inhibitions, Symptoms, and Anxiety* (1926d), "Analysis Terminable and Interminable" (1937c), and "The Splitting of the Ego in the Process of Defence," Freud's very last, incomplete project (1940e), reflect his continuing preoccupation with his "most famous case" and the further questions it had raised. The patient displaying *Ichspaltung im Abwehrvorgang* may have been Mark Brunswick (the husband of the Wolf-Man's second analyst, Ruth Mack Brunswick) rather than the Wolf Man himself, at least according to the Brunswicks (Roazen 1975: 425). But for various reasons—not least the Brunswicks' own peculiar relation with Freud (see Roazen 1992: 294–304)—this opinion need not be taken as definitive. Freud's last study contains recognizable echoes of the Wolf Man's case. Probably, then, Freud's picture of psychic "splitting"—one of his most productive and influential speculations—is an amalgamation of material derived from several clinical sources reaching as far back as the analysis of 1910–14.

For his part, Serge Pankejeff represented "the Professor," his analyst Freud, to his second analyst, Freud's American student Ruth Mack Brunswick, who treated him from October 1926 to February 1927. Brunswick interpreted this opportunity as a sign of Freud's special favor and published her representation of the patient's story in her own account of the Wolf Man, published in 1928 as "A Supplement to Freud's 'History of an Infantile Neurosis' " (quoted here in the edition of Gardiner 1971; see also Brunswick 1929, 1940).

Brunswick treated the Wolf Man again, probably sporadically, for several years beginning in 1929, and yet again in 1938. In a very brief note updating her 1928 "Supplement" published when the essay was anthologized in 1945, she claimed that her later work had "revealed new material and important, hitherto forgotten memories" (Brunswick 1945). Apparently she intended to publish a more extensive discussion of these "hitherto forgotten memories," revolving—she believed—around the Wolf Man's supposed genital seduction by his older, "pre-schizophrenic" sister Anna and an earlier and even more defining "anal-masturbatory" seduction by his old nurse. Certain draft work for this presentation—what would have been Brunswick's "Supplement" to her "Supplement"—is published here for the first time (see Appendix); it consists of a brief conceptual outline and a fragmentary text. Internal evidence suggests that the text may have been prepared for oral presentation as a preview of the publication she did not bring to completion; it was apparently begun in 1930, soon after the first of Brunswick's supplementary blocks of analysis of the Wolf Man. We do not, however, have any record of its having been delivered to an audience.

It is not fully clear why Brunswick did not publicly report immediately on her work with the Wolf Man in 1929 and later. In 1937, some members of the psychoanalytic community apparently expected her to do so (Roazen 1975: 434), perhaps aware of the fact that she had been writing. As her draft suggests, however, her new results—or constructions—must alter our conception of Freud's results and interpretations substantially. Brunswick's investigation would seem strongly to imply, for example, that Freud had not succeeded in unraveling the story of an important, perhaps determining, event in the little Wolf Man's sexual history—namely, the boy's "seduction" into "anal masturbation" by his nursemaid, his old Nanya (see Appendix). By now it is widely appreciated that Freud's account in "From the History of an Infantile Neurosis" was, in large measure, the narrative construction of the analyst himself—a perspective Freud himself took toward the end of his life, as "Constructions in Analysis" suggests (Freud 1937d). But in the 1930s, Brunswick's presentation, had she published it, might well have been construed as a direct and overly ambitious attempt to revise some of the essential historical conclusions of Freud's case study—to challenge her aged and ailing teacher and benefactor. Perhaps, then, she refrained from publishing her essay to avoid controversy; her relations with Freud had always been troubled (see Roazen 1975: 156; Appignanesi and Forrester 1992: 374–77). Other explanations for Brunswick's delay, however, are quite possible, including the fact that the draft is obviously very rough and partial and perhaps simply could not be completed to her satisfaction.

The Wolf Man himself wrote seven "autobiographical" essays, solicited from him by Muriel Gardiner, a wealthy American Freudian who had known Ruth Mack Brunswick and had been referred by her to the Wolf Man for Russian lessons. These essays were published in the 1950s in an American psychoanalytic bulletin and republished with minor changes in 1971, with an eighth essay, initially published in 1958 under the title "My Recollections of Sigmund Freud" (they are collected in Gardiner 1971: 3–152; see Kanzer 1972). Following common practice, here these eight essays collectively will be called the Wolf Man's *Memoirs*. In publishing them, Serge accepted the name that Freud had given him, "Wolf Man" (see Rycroft 1971), in part, probably, because he hoped to retain his anonymity. Living as he did in Vienna until his death at the age of ninety-two, on May 7, 1979, he may have wanted to avoid being pestered by visiting psychoanalysts and historians.

In addition, the Wolf Man wrote at least two essays sketching his general views of the relation between human identity or freedom, on the one hand, and the psychoanalytic account of the mind, on the other ("Eine Parallele," possibly c. 1925, and "Psychoanalysis and Freedom of the Will," probably 1948; now in the Gardiner Papers). The matter seems to have been on his mind continually as Freud's "most famous case" (Obholzer 1982: 175). Finally, he drafted at least two essays on topics in the history of art and culture ("Poe, Baudelaire, and Hölderlin" and "In Memoriam Aubrey Beardsley," both possibly c. 1925 or earlier; now in the Gardiner Papers). These texts manifest his interest (difficult to document from the strictly Freudian sources) in species of nineteenth-century Romanticism, aestheticism, and "decadence," including those aspects, such as the art of

Aubrey Beardsley, which had been popularly as well as historically equated with late-nineteenth-century homosexualities. These interests would have been fairly typical for an educated, relatively liberal Viennese gentleman in the early part of this century. But the Wolf Man was originally Russian; he self-consciously understood himself to display "Russian" character traits. As we will see, in fact, his strong identification with European (particularly German) Romanticism has a great deal to do with his representations to Freud in the analysis itself, whether Freud—whose cultural interests were generally more classical—fully apprehended and appreciated them or not.

Always dependent on analysis, in 1926 the Wolf Man asked Freud's opinion about publishing these or other essays that apparently do not survive, including a "motion picture piece"—and, on Freud's advice, refrained from doing so (Lewin 1957). The matter deserves further exploration; although I have not been able to track them down, some essays above and beyond the "autobiographies" and "recollections" may have been published after all (see Jones 1955: 273). According to notes made by Muriel Gardiner, the Wolf Man did "deliver one lecture on political economy, which was quite a success"; "like all Russians," he told her, "he wanted to prove to himself and others that he could do *everything* and do it well" (Gardiner Papers). (The lecture was probably part of the project on the legal foundations of social-security insurance, the Wolf Man's professional specialty, represented by two versions of a text [Pankejeff 1939] on the subject now in the Pankejeff Papers.) The philosophical and critical essays that survive are not especially original. But neither are they incompetent; they display a clear intelligence and distinctive sensibility as well as the wide-ranging interests which we can also document in the Wolf Man's reading notes on astrology, Wittgenstein, Proust, linguistics, and other topics (Pankjeff Papers). They could well have been published in a literary review. But it is conceivable that Freud was reluctant to see his "case" assume such an independent public identity.

In the mid- and late seventies, the Wolf Man—still residing in Vienna—granted an important series of tape-recorded interviews to a West German journalist, Karin Obholzer, who had succeeding in locating and meeting him in 1973. Obholzer has published an edited transcript of these "conversations" (Obholzer 1982; see Masson 1982). Although this document is interesting and important, it must be treated with great caution. Obholzer does not clearly explain her editorial principles, and it is difficult to determine from the published transcript what proportion of all the "conversations" have actually been published.

In the Obholzer interviews, at the same time as he regarded himself as the "most famous case," the elderly Wolf Man was quite critical of psychoanalysts and psychoanalysis. According to Muriel Gardiner (1983b), the editor of the Wolf Man's *Memoirs,* he had made negative remarks to her about Obholzer. For Gardiner, then, the Wolf Man's highly critical comments in the interviews about psychoanalysis and psychoanalysts should be understood as part of an overall pattern; such hostility was, she claimed, "automatically aroused [in him] toward most people who were kind to him, to whom he owed and often felt and expressed gratitude, whom he liked or loved" (Gardiner 1983b: 885). Nonetheless, as Paul Roazen has put it, "Gardiner had her own ideological agenda which could cause her to tailor the truth. [. . .] Whatever the Wolf Man himself may have said [to Obholzer], Gardiner always did her best to put Freud's handling of the case into the best possible light" (Roazen 1993: 54). The Wolf Man had an extensive correspondence with Gardiner, now in the Gardiner Papers housed in the Manuscript Division, Library of Congress (a few excerpts appear in Gardiner 1971, 1983b). His correspondence with and visits from other psychoanalysts and scholars are briefly recounted in her introduction to the *Memoirs* (Gardiner 1971) and Obholzer's introduction to her interviews (Obholzer 1982). The factual discrepancies between these two accounts, as well as the quite different attitudes of the authors, underscore the fact that the Wolf Man's long-term involvement with, not to say dependence on, psychoanalysis has been intrinsically controversial. Psychoanalysis needs a complete "case"; as we will see, Freud probably seized on the Wolf Man for just this reason. But the more thoroughgoing the case, the more pathetic, sinister, or unreliable it might seem.

Exchanges between Freud and the Wolf Man

In addition to voluminous verbal and written representation of each other's experience of the other, and even more striking, Freud and the Wolf Man exchanged—or withheld exchanging—several objects, including other persons. During the first psychoanalysis in 1910–14, for example, Sigmund required Serge to delay marrying his fiancée, Therese, whom he had met in 1909 at Emil Kraepelin's sanatorium in Munich the year before seeking Freud's treatment in Vienna. (This episode is outlined clearly by Kanzer 1972: 421.) For his part, in 1922, well after the analysis had ended, Serge did not inform Freud that he had received an inheritance of jewels from his family in Russia. Thus he allowed Freud to continue in the belief that his former patient was poverty-stricken (and thus could barely maintain his wife Therese and their household) partly as a direct result of following Freud's advice not to return to Russia (the Wolf Man had thought, during the 1918 revolution, to try to protect the Pankejeff family's property).

After its 1918 publication, Freud presented Serge with an autographed copy of the history and interpretation of Serge's analysis. The Wolf Man was still quoting from this volume, sometimes by page number, toward the very end of his life. And for several years in the 1920s, Freud supplied Serge with small amounts of cash—apparently raised as a collection among Viennese analysts and even among his patients—to help support Serge and Therese in a flat in Vienna, where the couple had finally settled. Freud conducted the 1919 reanalysis free of charge.

For his part, on the termination of the analysis, Serge presented his analyst Freud—following Freud's advice that the transference needed a symbolic resolution—with an Egyptian statuette of a female divinity. He knew that the object would greatly please Freud, an enthusiastic collector of small antiquities. As many commentators on clinical technique have remarked, Freud's solicitation of this gift, along with other actions, may actually have interfered with his ability to resolve the Wolf Man's troubles, particularly his strong attachment to Freud himself. In a sense, in fact, it kept the analysis alive after its ostensible conclusion. In his *Memoirs*, the Wolf Man claimed that Freud kept the Egyptian figurine on his desk (Gardiner 1971: 149–50; see further Mahony 1984: 34). Freud's collection of antiquities is now well published (Gamwell and Wells 1989). He owned many similar pieces, purchased or presented to him at various times. Although he probably associated each object with its circumstances of acquisition—on June 30, 1912, for example, he accepted another Egyptian figurine as a personal "totem" from Ernest Jones's mistress Loe Kann (Grosskurth 1991: 60)—he apparently did not keep detailed records of all of these transactions. I have been unable to identify the Wolf Man's gift.

Such complex interchanges ramified extensively. In 1919, for example, in order to take the Wolf Man back as a patient, Freud suddenly terminated his patient and student Helene Deutsch. Deutsch later developed depressions, understood by her to be a result of this disappointment and other perceived injuries, not least Freud's 1928 referral of the Wolf Man to her rival Ruth Mack Brunswick (Deutsch 1973: 132; see Roazen 1975: 464–66, 1985: 157–58, 251). Brunswick sent Muriel Gardiner, one of her own patients and also referred by Freud (Gardiner 1983a: 32), to the Wolf Man; later, Gardiner solicited and edited the Wolf Man's *Memoirs* and passed the royalties on to him as well as sending him "regular funds" (Roazen 1993: 54).

These interchanges continued into very recent times. In the latter part of the Wolf Man's life, the Freud Archives (based in New York) regularly provided him with a supplement to his pension in Austria. Although the evidence is ambiguous, it would seem that at least tacitly, the Wolf Man was expected to be accessible to favored analysts associated with the archives (see Obholzer 1982). After the Wolf Man's death in 1979, Freud's family—presumably his daughter Anna Freud—somehow arranged for a death mask of "the most famous case" to be displayed in Freud's study in his (later Anna Freud's) house in Maresfield Gardens (now the Freud Museum) (Roazen 1993: 57; see Roazen 1990: 183–86), where it apparently continues to be displayed intermittently.

The Wolf Man's Paintings

Most interesting for my purposes, the Wolf Man, a good amateur painter, presented or sold more than forty paintings to psychoanalysts in Vienna and elsewhere. One such sale was made, for example, as late as the late 1960s, when the Chicago Psychoanalytic Institute and New Orleans Psychoanalytic Institute purchased "Wolf Mans" through Muriel Gardiner, who had received a number of them from the Wolf Man himself (Gardiner Papers). We do not know whether any of the paintings were made *directly* in exchange for the financial assistance of Freud's circle, but some of these sales did bring in a little money for the Wolf Man. Some of them were apparently intended as gifts from the Wolf Man to his Freudian friends, such as a small painting of trees inscribed by Pankejeff "for Frau Dr. Gardiner" (now in the Pankejeff Papers). At least some of the paintings would have been fully intelligible only to viewers who knew Freud's published case history of the artist. In turn, as we will see, his pictorial works reflect his own understanding of what Freud had written about him.

In his adolescence, the Wolf Man had formally studied with a Russian painter hired by his father to spend time ("a few summers") on the family's estate. This man offered lessons in drawing and painting to the Pankejeff children, Serge and Anna. Apparently for some time he was a close companion of the young man, at this point a military cadet in his later teens.

The Wolf Man's published description of his painting teacher is somewhat sketchy (Gardiner 1971: 66–67), and the information he provides is not necessarily accurate in all details. It has not been possible to identify this man with absolute certainty. Called "Painter G" in the *Memoirs*, he may have been the Russian landscapist Victor Elpidiforovitch Borisov-Musatov (1870–1905) (see Gray 1962: 60–64; Rusakova 1975; Kolchik 1980; Sarab'ianov 1990: 241–42; Raeburn 1991: Figs. 62–67, 71). Borisov-Musatov certainly offers a revealing parallel for the Wolf Man's teacher as he describes him. The Wolf Man tells us, for example, that his teacher "was elected a member of the Paris Salon d'Automne"; Borisov-Musatov's works were shown in the Troisième Exposition of the Salon d'Automne of 1905, and the famous Quatrième Exposition, "L'Art Russe," in 1906 (see Société du Salon d'Automne 1910), and he was elected a member of the Salon national de la société des arts plastiques. The Wolf Man notes that his teacher "was a follower of the then prevailing *art nouveau* style"; Borisov-Musatov is generally regarded as one of the principal exponents of *art nouveau* (or *style moderne*) in Russia. He had been influenced by Gustave Moreau (with whom he had worked in Paris) and Pierre Puvis de Chavannes and on his return to Russia became the godfather of the "Blue Rose," a loose group of Moscow painters who evolved their own species of Symbolist painting (see Bowlt 1973; Borisova and Sternin 1988; Minkina 1991). The avant-garde nature of the Wolf Man's instruction in painting was consistent with the Pankejeff family's cultural and political interests; despite his inherited landed wealth, the Wolf Man's father was a left-leaning, "freethinking" liberal lawyer who owned two Kandinskys (Obholzer 1982: 77). In Borisov-Musatov's *Autumn Evening* (1904–1905), a study for a fresco decoration intended for another wealthy landowner's house, the building in the background closely resembles the vast main house on the Pankejeffs' principal estate (Figs. 2, 3). A contemporary photograph of the Wolf Man's sister Anna sitting beside a large pond on the estate captures the kind of leisuretime torpor evidently depicted in Borisov-Musatov's most well known painting, *The Reservoir* (1902) (Figs. 4, 5).

The Wolf Man tells us that he was never strongly directed by his teacher; he found Painter G's trendy *art nouveau* style "too contrived." But he did learn "to catch a certain moment in the ever-changing light of the landscape" (Gardiner 1971: 67), an apt characterization of Borisov-Musatov's

Figure 2. V. E. Borisov-Musatov, *Autumn Evening,* 1904–1905 (photo Northwestern University Library)

Figure 3. Photograph of "Painter G" and the Wolf Man on the Pankejeff estate, 1903 (Pankejeff Papers, LC)

Figure 4. V. E. Borisov-Musatov, *The Reservoir,* 1902 (photo Northwestern University Library)

Figure 5. Photograph of the Wolf Man's sister Anna, c. 1900 (Pankejeff Papers, LC)

most impressionist canvases, which present dappled or dusky landscapes peopled by withdrawn, mysterious female figures (Figs. 2, 6, 7). The Wolf Man's own paintings, however, are relatively conservative works (Figs. 8, 9, 10) most closely related—despite the bright color and broad brushwork— to the traditions of nineteenth-century Romantic landscape painting. As his *Memoirs* indicate, throughout his life, painting continued to be one of his deepest interests, which he regarded as quite different from his professional and other intellectual activities; for example, at one point he told Muriel Gardiner, as she recorded in her notes, that the "only field" in which he did not experience his "Russian" drive to excel was painting—"this is something he does for love of the work" (Gardiner Papers). All the evidence suggests that he was very knowledgeable about art and art history; the Pankejeff Papers in the Library of Congress, for example, contain painstakingly written hand copies of a standard handbook on human anatomy for artists as well as many notes on geometrical optics, perspective, and colors. As we will see, the point is not a trivial one in understanding the nature of his representations to Freud.

The Analysis

The Wolf Man's most important gift to or exchange with Freud, of course, was the psychoanalysis itself. The relationship afforded an intersubjective environment in which the patient's—but also, we will see, the analyst's—"bisexual" and "homosexual" wishes and conflicts could supposedly be resolved by interpretively deriving them from an archaic context, transposing subjective, contemporary desires into an objective analysis of their very origin in the deep past. The transposition supposedly permitted the symbolic "overcoming" (or "cure") of subjective, "homosexual" desires—a transformation symbolized most succinctly, perhaps, by the exchange of final gifts, Serge's presentation of the Egyptian statuette to Freud and Freud's presentation of his publication to Serge. But the transposition was also mediated by the production of a representation during the analysis itself. This whole complex dynamic will be the principal topic throughout this book, but a few preliminary points should be made here.

By now the published case history of the Wolf Man has acquired canonical status. It is widely recognized as the best example of Freud's powers of historical and narrative realization. Required reading in many

Figure 6. V. E. Borisov-Musatov, *Spring,* 1898 (photo Northwestern University Library)

Figure 7. V. E. Borisov-Musatov, *Tree in Sunlight,* 1897 (photo Northwestern University Library)

Figure 8. Serge Pankejeff
(the Wolf Man), untitled
landscape (Gardiner Papers,
LC)

Figure 9. Serge Pankejeff
(the Wolf Man), untitled
landscape (Gardiner Papers,
LC)

Figure 10. Serge Pankejeff
(the Wolf Man), untitled
landscape (Gardiner Papers,
LC)

psychoanalytic institutes and in universities around the world, it has been and remains the object of many commentaries inside and outside the institutions of psychoanalysis. The case history is indeed an advanced but readily intelligible introduction to psychoanalysis as such. It established or extended many of Freud's principal theoretical interests—for example, in the determining place of infantile fantasies and childhood neuroses in adult neurosis; in the "primal scene"; in primary "bisexuality" or "homosexuality," a subject's cognitively first-order or temporally archaic belief in "one sex only" which does not distinguish between the sexes or between self and others and thus serves the subject's primary "narcissism"; in polymorphous perversity, the ability and desire of the child to assume many kinds of stimulating positions; in conflict between identifications; in "castration threat" and resulting anxiety in the normative psychic development of neurotic male heterosexuality; in the genesis and function of "latent" or "shackled" homosexuality; in *Nachträglichkeit,* the "deferred action" of events and fantasies; in the evolution and inheritance of "phylogenetic" dispositions and memories grounding the vicissitudes of "individual experience." We will examine many of these ideas as they emerged in or, by contrast, helped to determine the course of the analysis and its later textual representation by Freud.

The psychoanalysis itself, however, was a failure—acknowledged as such to a greater or lesser degree both by Sigmund and by Serge. For Freud, the analysis required his later tinkering in 1919. More important, he explicitly presented the case history as "fragmentary" (7), even though it was certainly the longest and most complex of his case studies and even though his critics had been demanding a "complete" illustration of his procedures. In particular, Freud offered his additions to the 1914 draft of the case history, prepared for the 1918 publication, as a "supplement and rectification" (*erganz und berichtig*) (57) of the draft. But, as he well knew, in some places these additions actually amount to retractions and outright contradictions. Probably the analysis was incomplete for Freud in a productive way; ultimately, for example, it stimulated his creative reflections on the "interminability" of analysis (Freud 1937c). In fact, the case probably permitted him a partial resolution of conflicts of his own—a resolution that required some degree of indeterminacy in his interpretive position and conclusions.

By contrast, the analysis evidently crippled Serge—or, at any rate and not quite the same thing, permitted him to continue to cripple himself. It cast him as a perennial ward of psychoanalysis. Although symptoms of this dependence were apparently attacked by Freud in the corrective analysis of 1919, the Wolf Man developed both an unrealistic grandiosity and a debilitating masochism and passivity as Freud's "favorite," "most famous" patient. In her first (re)analysis of the patient, Brunswick (1928) discovered that she needed to investigate this complex of fantasies and symptoms in considerable detail.

With the important exception of the doctors personally involved in his ongoing psychoanalytic and psychiatric treatment, psychoanalysts and psychiatrists who have reviewed the case history have tended to conclude that the Wolf Man must have been, in current jargon, a "borderline patient." He probably suffered, according to them, from a "narcissistic personality disorder" largely out of the reach of psychoanalytic intervention, especially as it could have been accomplished in 1914. We might see such judgments, of course, merely as a transparent excuse for Freud's lapses: if the Wolf Man was not curable, and probably not even analyzable, then Freud's obvious failures might actually be praised as efforts to chart the outermost frontiers of psychoanalytic therapy and theory. On this view, Freud's work with the Wolf Man was doomed to fail as a full cure or a final analysis, but it should nonetheless be regarded as heroic. In fact, the Wolf Man's own *Memoirs* vividly describe at least one and possibly several episodes of psychotic break. In 1951, for example, he somehow "wandered" into the Russian zone of occupied Vienna to paint the sights, only to be arrested by the secret police as a spy. According to him, he was totally unaware of what he was doing (Gardiner 1971: 325–33; see Greenacre 1973). On evidence such as this, it would indeed appear that virtually no psychoanalytic technique or theory—at least to the extent that it was in fact a specifically psychoanalytic one—could have enabled Freud to alleviate the Wolf Man's suffering.[1]

These rediagnoses have been offered, of course, from the vantage point of contemporary clinical psychiatry and psychoanalysis and on the basis of a privileged hindsight. Since we will focus here on certain historical, intersubjective, and textual conditions of the analysis itself and Freud's initial representations of it, we can set them aside. But it is entirely possible, as some of the rediagnoses implicitly or explicitly suggest, that the Wolf Man's unconscious world remained at least partly beyond Freud's historical and interpretive observation because Freud did not know—or grossly misunderstood—some crucial facts about the Wolf Man's earliest childhood.

In a remarkable study, for example, Nicolas Abraham and Maria Torok

(1986) have suggested that the Wolf Man's German speech to Freud was inflected by the connotations and homophonic associations of words both in Russian, his native tongue, and in English, a language he supposedly acquired from his first governess. Abraham and Torok's book is one of the few serious reexaminations of the actual text of Freud's case history as opposed to its ostensible content—which many other commentators have felt free to rearrange and summarize in their own words—and as such warrants notice here. In the psychoanalysis of 1910–14, as the case history of 1918 shows, Freud pursued German homophones—such as the important resemblance between the Wolf Man's initials, "S. P." (*Es Pay*), and the German word for "wasp," *Wespe*—but he did not know Russian. (The missing *W* has been ingeniously, even playfully, explored by Friedrich Kittler [1990: 273–88] in a study focusing on the technique, even the technology, of Freud's text that has affinities with Abraham and Torok's.) And indeed, in the case history Freud never explains the relationship between the Wolf Man's adult, German-language representations in Freud's consulting room in Vienna and his childhood linguistic experiences in Russia; because Freud never directly raises the question, the reader more or less forgets to ask it. The Wolf Man's second analyst, Ruth Mack Brunswick, recognized the linguistic and cultural differences between herself and her patient. But she acknowledged her inability to handle the problem: "I had never been able to understand a single word of the Russian phrases which he occasionally interjected into his German sentences" (Brunswick 1928: 285).

Abraham and Torok are surely correct that Freud was unable fully to work out this complex dimension of the Wolf Man's subjectivity; they rightly suppose it was part of the *inter*subjective history of the analysis. In what amounts to a separate, further thesis, they suppose that the Wolf Man's unconscious mind somehow spoke a "polyglot" Russian/English speech which supposedly reveals the deepest determinations of his neurosis for those listeners (or readers) who can understand it: for them, the Wolf Man saying (in German) "white wolves" (*weisse Wölfen*) was unconsciously saying (in Russian/English) "*wide goulfik,*" or "open flies," referring (they propose) to his father's open trousers in a reconstructed scene of the father's sexual seduction of the little boy's older sister. According to Abraham and Torok, although Freud could hear and transcribe this speech as it was presented to him orally in German, he could not understand it.

Abraham and Torok's thesis has some extraordinary attractions. Among other things, what the patient said and what Freud heard were clearly two very different things—despite Freud's temptation, followed by most commentators, to take his transcription of the Wolf Man's representations at face value as a "clear and life-like picture" (29) of the Wolf Man's psychic condition and history. In turn, this feature of the analysis (we will come back to it in a way somewhat different from that of Abraham and Torok) can support a larger but fundamentally independent thesis: Freud's construction of the meaning of his patient's history was one of the products of a subjective object of his own.

But Abraham and Torok's account rests on an astonishingly close scrutiny of Freud's text, and it would seem to stand or fall partly on the accuracy of that scrutiny—textual and historical. It is worth noting, then, that in his own independent and explicit testimony, the Wolf Man later asserted that he never learned English from his governess or anyone else (Obholzer 1982: 26, 73). Abraham and Torok must suppose, then, that the patient's "English" comprehension was always entirely unconscious— a much more extreme, less plausible hypothesis than the possibility that during the psychoanalysis he unconsciously remembered some English words or phrases he had *once* understood as a child. Indeed, Abraham and Torok do not extend to the Wolf Man the very principle they apply so convincingly to Freud: Freud hears but cannot understand Russian/English, but the little Wolf Man both heard *and* supposedly understood English/ Russian.

Along similar revisionary lines, Jeffrey M. Masson has written that among "Muriel Gardiner's papers" (namely, the Gardiner Papers now in the Manuscript Division of the Library of Congress) he found notes for an unpublished paper by Ruth Mack Brunswick. Evidently this document was the outline and fragmentary text published here (see Appendix). According to Masson's reading of this text, Brunswick "was astonished to learn that as a child [the Wolf Man] had been anally seduced by a member of his family—and that Freud did not know this" (Masson 1985: xxvii). (This "member of his family" was actually his nurse—but for all intents and purposes she was a mother to him.) This finding is not quite consistent with Masson's controversial thesis that Freud suppressed empirical evidence for actual sexual abuse in the childhoods of his patients (see generally Robinson 1993). In this case, Freud could hardly have deliberately ignored information if he failed to discover it or if the Wolf Man had completely withheld it from him. But the information does suggest, as Masson intends that it should, that Freud's evidence on and approach to the phenomena of the sexual abuse of children were partial and skewed.

A more orthodox Freudian analyst than Masson, however, might see

Brunswick's material as a fantasy projected *by* the Wolf Man *for* his second analyst: both Brunswick and Serge had already assimilated Freud's published reconstructions in the case history and, in their own ways, desired to confirm them as well as their overall relationship with the master. In fact, there is a major distinction to be drawn between Brunswick's conclusion that the young Wolf Man had been treated erotically enough to seduce him into a certain emergent sexuality—*this* point had been made, about different events, by Freud himself, so Masson can hardly claim that Freud ignored or suppressed it—and Masson's view that she had abused him. (The difference would seem to be that seduction lures a subject further along a path emergent in or native to him, whereas "abuse" implants a formation that has no grounding in the subject's being.) In his *Memoirs* and interviews, the elderly Wolf Man gave no hint that he had been sexually abused. In his conversations with Obholzer (1982), in fact, he claimed to disbelieve Freud's preferred interpretation of his earliest childhood, the famous reconstruction of the "primal scene" published in the case history. If he had actually been sexually abused in childhood, and his neurosis had derived from a purely external trauma imposed by others, he could certainly have used the information to demolish Freud's case. But instead his reservations about Freud's construction are based on other, much more circumstantial grounds—for example, that he could not recollect the real event which Freud had reconstructed from his remembered fantasies. On balance, then, Brunswick's information has to be treated skeptically as the basis for a redescription of the Wolf Man's actual life history, along Masson's lines, although it is certainly evidence for his psychic and intersubjective history.

There have been many other attempts to redescribe or rediagnose the Wolf Man's psychic condition and life history. A number of them offer substantial extensions of or revisions to Freud's interpretations; some of them are highly critical of Freud's procedures and conclusions (for a review, see Mahony 1984). Finally, however, all redescriptions and rediagnoses *depend on Freud's case study's being taken as documentary evidence for the Wolf Man's history,* a clear window through which we can look—at least accompanying if not always agreeing with Freud—at the sometimes shadowy landscape of the Wolf Man's life. In fact, as an analysis of the Wolf Man's discourse becomes more and more subtle—like that offered by Abraham and Torok (1986)—it becomes all the more necessary to take Freud's case history as a faithful transcript of the patient's speech and ideas: the case history must be regarded as the trace or imprint of the Wolf

Man's subjective objects, identifications, symbolic performances, and so forth. As Cynthia Chase has noted, Abraham and Torok's "reconstruction of a specific, contingent episode at the origin of the illness keeps faith with the profound historiographic imperative of Freudian analysis"; "the 'fact' of a dream . . . , the fact of the existence of a dream text: these *words* are the event from which Freud's interpretation starts, and Abraham and Torok start there too" (Chase 1992: 109). But the dynamics of intersubjective representation and exchange between Freud and the Wolf Man, as they have already been sketched here, suggest that this confidence has been misplaced. We require some "supplement and rectification" before we can really use Freud's case history to describe or interpret the Wolf Man's unconscious history in one way or another. Whether or not the Wolf Man offered Freud an *Ebenbild,* a "perfect likeness," of *his* past, the "clear and lifelike picture" he did offer was an *Ebenbild for Freud.*

II

THE WOLF DREAM

> It is never the aim of discussions like this
> to create conviction. They are only in-
> tended to bring the repressed complexes
> into consciousness, to set the conflict go-
> ing in the field of conscious mental activ-
> ity and to facilitate the emergence of
> fresh material from the unconscious.
>
> —Freud, "Notes upon a Case of Obses-
> sional Neurosis" (1909d: 181)

> One ought not to get into any discussions
> with the patient. If one does that one
> forces him into a fighting position to
> which, for inner reasons, he is only too in-
> clined; but if one omits them, then he
> will soon come forth by himself with
> confirmations.
>
> —Sandor Ferenczi to Freud, March 13,
> 1912 (Freud/Ferenczi 1993: 356)

The Wolf Man Meets Freud

The first of the Wolf Man's several gifts to Freud was reported in Freud's
first known comments on his new patient (Fig. 11). In a letter to his follower Sandor Ferenczi, written on February 8, 1910, apparently just days
after the Wolf Man had appeared for his initial consultation, Freud wrote:

> Every day after work I write on Leonardo [see Freud 1910c] and am al-
> ready on page 10. My writer's cramp is in full convalescence. As a con-
> sequence of your impressive exhortation to allow myself some rest, I
> have—taken on a new patient from Odessa, a very rich Russian with

Figure 11. Studio portrait
of Serge Pankejeff by
Pietzner, c. 1910 (Pankejeff
Papers, LC)

compulsive feelings, but I am more capable of accomplishment than ever.
(Freud/Ferenczi 1993: 133)

Although his interest was of long standing, Freud had begun actively
working on Leonardo da Vinci only in late October 1909 (ibid.: 85).
He lectured on the topic to the Vienna Psychoanalytic Society on December 1, 1909 (see Nunberg and Federn 1962–75: II, 338–52). But
obviously he felt that his progress had been slow. The letter to Ferenczi
suggests that part of his interest and energy in Leonardo was transferred to the Wolf Man's case. As we will see in more detail, the case
became an important part of a continuous project—also encompass-

ing the history of Judge Daniel Paul Schreber—in which Freud (with contributions from Ferenczi, Isidor Sadger, Karl Abraham, and others) struggled to understand the psychological origins and personal development of "homosexuality."

The very first consultation with Serge would have given Freud at least some evidence that the case could potentially contribute to this wider inquiry. A few days later, on February 13, 1910, Freud reported again on his new patient:

> On the whole I am only a machine for making money and have been working up a sweat in the last few weeks. A rich young Russian whom I have taken on because of compulsive tendencies admitted the following transferences to me after the first session: Jewish swindler, he would like to use me from behind and shit on my head. At the age of six years he experienced as his first symptom cursing against God: pig, dog, etc. When he saw three piles of feces on the street he became uncomfortable because [they reminded him] of the Holy Trinity and anxiously sought a fourth [pile] in order to destroy the association. (Freud/Ferenczi 1993: 138)[1]

Freud is being somewhat sardonic. The Wolf Man's "compulsive tendencies" often impelled him to follow women in the street and to search for the apartments of female prostitutes. Contracting gonorrhea from a servant girl had precipitated his neurotic crisis, beginning at age seventeen, which finally brought him to the psychiatrists. Launched a few months before he met Freud, his latest love affair—with Therese, a fellow patient in a sanatorium and the woman who later became his wife—manifested the same problem as all the earlier ones: although he fell for her "compulsively," he was utterly unable to make any further real decisions about the status and direction of the relationship (see Brunswick 1928: 272; Obholzer 1982: 26–29).

In 1909, the Wolf Man's mother had arranged for him to consult a physician in Odessa. At least some members of the medical establishment there had recently become interested in Freud's work; Moshe Wulff, an Odessa psychiatrist, had been in touch with Freud in December 1909, hoping to review Freud's books for a local newspaper (Freud/Ferenczi 1993: 112–13). The Russian psychiatrist Leonid Drosnes—he is called "Dr. D." in the *Memoirs*—eventually accompanied the Wolf Man to Vienna in January 1910, and a year later joined the Vienna Psychoanalytic Society himself (see Freud/Jung 1974: 306 n. 2; for the early history of psychoanalysis in Russia, see Carotenuto 1982: 196–205).

The Wolf Man's account of his treatment at the hands of Dr. Drosnes, starting in May and June 1909, shows that he must have already known something about psychoanalysis before he met Freud, in late January or early February 1910, for his first consultation:

> After Dr. D. had listened patiently to my complaints, he told me I had no reason to despair, for until now I had been going about treatment in the wrong way. He told me that emotional conflicts and suffering are cured neither by a long stay in a sanatorium nor by the physical therapy practiced there, such as baths, massages, and so forth. This was the first time I had ever heard such a thing from the mouth of a medical specialist, and it made a great impression on me because I, myself, through my own experience, had come to the same conclusion. It is, by the way, quite remarkable that I met this particular physician at the time, as he was probably the only person in Odessa who knew of the existence of Freud and psychoanalysis. [On this point, as we have seen, the Wolf Man was mistaken.] To be sure, Dr. D. spoke of Freud and Dubois [i.e., the positivist psychologist Emil DuBois-Reymond] in the same breath. He could not describe to me Dubois' psychotherapy. But he had read Freud's works, and was therefore able to give me some explanation of psychoanalysis. [. . .] Under these circumstances, then, it seemed to me that the only right thing to do would be to begin treatment according to Freud's method, as Dr. D. had briefly outlined it. Therefore I was very pleased when, without my requesting it, Dr. D. himself proposed this, and offered to come to our estate twice a week for this purpose. [. . .] Dr. D. did indeed know Freud's works, but he had absolutely no experience as a practicing analyst. I was the very first patient he attempted to analyze. So in my case the treatment was more a frank discussion between patient and doctor than a regular analysis in the Freudian sense. But even a discussion of this sort had a great deal of meaning for me, as I began again to hope that I could be helped. (Gardiner 1971: 79–80; cf. Obholzer 1982: 20)

In the light of his previous experience in "frank discussion" with Dr. Drosnes, the Wolf Man's initial "transference" to Freud—imperious and so overtly exemplifying primitive lusts and scatological language—might have been calculated simply to attract the analyst's attention. Freud may well have been skeptical of it. Nevertheless, the young man, Freud thought, was evidently helpless.

Traveling through Europe in search of a cure, the Wolf Man required constant attendance, moving his bowels only following enemas administered by a male helper, an unidentified "medical orderly" (Brunswick 1928: 267) or student who was accompanying Dr. Drosnes. (In the case history, this personage appears as the Wolf Man's "attendant" [74].) One of Freud's first steps in the treatment, apparently, was to put an end to these enemas: "When I was treated by Freud and told him about it," the Wolf Man told Obholzer, "he said—you know how psychoanalysts play around with subconscious homosexuality—well, that promotes subconscious homosexuality, and he [the attendant] could no longer give me enemas" (Obholzer 1982: 39).

The seriousness of the Wolf Man's condition, as Freud depicts it, cannot, of course, be taken for granted. In his *Memoirs* and interviews, the Wolf Man asserted that by the time he came to see Freud, he had been doing better. He was able to take part in many activities in Vienna appropriate to his wealth and leisured station in life (see Gardiner 1971: 82, 89; Obholzer 1982: 40). (Indeed, part of the problem in assessing the patient's circumstances revolves around the occupational and economic differences between analyst and patient: whereas Freud was up early and working late for little money, the Wolf Man rose late and stayed up late socializing, doing nothing to bring in an income.) He did not specifically deny Freud's portrayal of his overall apathy. But he tends to suggest that his malaise was worse when he was living at home in Russia. It is likely that Freud exaggerated the severity of the patient's disorder (in some ways simply a fashionable way to live) and downplayed the possibility that other advisors, or even the sheer escape provided by traveling far from home, had relieved some of his symptoms. As we will see, in describing his immediate problems to Freud, the Wolf Man himself may have been acting to some extent, performing a drama of his own, in this case literary. Freud was willing, for reasons of his own, to suspend disbelief on the point.

Freud makes a point of telling us that the psychoanalysis cleared up the patient's bowel problem and implies that the Wolf Man's difficulty had been entirely psychosomatic (e.g., 75–76). The Wolf Man told Obholzer, however, that his bowel troubles came from a veterinary medicine—apparently a purgative for horses—that had been mistakenly prescribed for him by a country doctor in southern Russia, and added that despite his psychoanalysis with Freud, his bowel troubles persisted throughout his life (Obholzer 1982: 47–48). Certainly Ruth Mack Brunswick's reanalysis of the Wolf Man (Brunswick 1928) indicated that the symptoms had survived Freud's treatment or had somehow returned. At this point, their specifically "homosexual" dimension—the Wolf Man's technique of relieving them by having his manservant administer an enema—had seemingly disappeared; more accurately, it had been transferred onto Freud himself and the Wolf Man's continuing dependence on psychoanalytic therapy. (In fact, in his memoirs the Wolf Man asserted that "the student who accompanied me and Dr. D. to Vienna was simply there to make a third at cards" [Gardiner 1971: 267], which contradicts what he later told Obholzer.) In general, we cannot fully believe either the Wolf Man's or Freud's depiction of the patient's history of bowel trouble, and especially of its "homosexual" significance.

Freud Awaits the Wolf Man

At the time the Wolf Man appeared, in the early months of 1910, Freud was strenuously promoting his long-standing emphasis on the preeminence of infantile sexuality. He felt he had to respond especially vigorously to the vacillations and doubts of several of his own followers, notably Alfred Adler (see Stepansky 1983; Handlbauer 1990).

Although Adler was elected president of the Vienna Psychoanalytic Society in October 1910, by this point his differences with Freud were irreconcilable. He resigned the position a short while later, in February 1911. In *On the History of the Psycho-Analytic Movement* (Freud 1914d) and elsewhere, Freud was severely critical of Adler's concept of "organ inferiority," later to be associated colloquially with the "inferiority complex" (see Adler 1907). For example, a few days after Freud briefly reported to Ferenczi on the beginning of the Wolf Man's treatment, he was complaining about Adler's lecture on "Psychical Hermaphroditism," given at the Vienna Psychoanalytic Society on February 23, 1910 (Nunberg and Federn 1962–75: II, 423–34; cf. Adler 1928). In this presentation, Adler urged that "psychical hermaphroditism"—a well-established term partly interchangeable with "contrary sexual instinct" (*konträre Sexualempfindung*), "inversion," and "homosexuality"—lies behind the neuroses: according to Adler's theory, as recounted by Freud, "the child suffers from its inferiority, which it takes to be feminine; from that there develops an uncertainty about its gender role, which is the original basis for all later doubt; it attempts a masculine defense, and when that fails, neurosis results—a bad speculation!" (Freud/Ferenczi 1993: 146 [February 25, 1910]). Despite Freud's negative remarks, in the case history of the Wolf Man, drafted four years later, he was heavily if somewhat surreptitiously dependent on the Adlerian idea of "masculine protest"—what Adler supposed must be a man's anxiety-ridden response to a feared inferiority or others' perception of "effeminacy" in his body and sexual organs, including (but not limited to) castration.[2]

Even Freud's most favored follower was turning out to be unreliable.

On March 31, 1910, Carl Gustav Jung was appointed the first president of the newly established International Association for Psycho-Analysis. But only a year later, he privately—but very strongly—criticized Freud's *Die Traumdeutung* (Freud 1900a) for the "insufficiently interpreted" dreams it reported and "for not revealing the deeper layer of interpretation" of Freud's own dreams (Freud/Jung 1974: 392 [February 14, 1911]). Jung played on an established worry of Freud's. In the book itself, Freud had already acknowledged that he had not included all of the material relevant to understanding his own dreams and noted that his anxiety about publishing the book had held back the printing of the manuscript for a year (Freud 1900a: 454, 477). During their trip to America in 1909, Jung had tried to extract personal information from Freud in order to interpret Freud's dreams; but, as happened on other such occasions, Freud was reluctant to reveal intimate material. According to Jung, at Jung's request for further associations to a dream, Freud exclaimed, "But I cannot risk my authority!" (Jung 1973: 158; see further Rosenzweig 1992: 64–65). Probably this experience simply reinforced Jung's impression of the many ellipses in *Die Traumdeutung*. By 1912, Jung took the incident to be a "symbol of everything to come" in the disintegration of their friendship (Freud/Jung 1974: 526 [December 13, 1912]). In response to Jung's doubts and objections, as early as March 1910 Freud seems to have accused Jung of "vacillating" in his commitment to Freud's thesis of the primacy of infantile sexuality in adult neurosis (see ibid.: 298–300 [March 2, 1910]). (For convenient summaries of the deterioration of relations between Freud and Jung from 1911 on, see Jones 1955: 137–51; Clark 1980: 316–38; Donn 1989; Schultz 1990; and Rosenzweig 1992: 213–19, the last three including new information from Jungian sources.)

Doubts about Freud's ideas were not, of course, restricted to his group of students and immediate followers. Freud's most vocal and influential critics, so he believed, were found among professional, nonpsychoanalytic psychiatrists. In the first session, the Wolf Man informed Freud that he had previously consulted some of these supposed detractors—for example, the combative and brilliant Emil Kraepelin (1856–1926), the most distinguished German psychiatrist of the day, professor of psychiatry in Munich since 1903, and founder of a world-famous clinic, whose monumental *Psychiatrie* was appearing in its eighth edition during the years Freud analyzed the Wolf Man. The Wolf Man saw Kraepelin twice, in March 1908 and in the autumn of 1908 (notes by Gardiner, Gardiner Papers).

In Freud's words, Kraepelin was the "Super-Pope" of psychiatry (Freud/

Jung 1974: 69 [July 1, 1907]), a dangerous enemy. Quite apart from his institutional influence, Kraepelin had proved himself to be a careful, discriminating, and subtle reader of Freud's works. In the sixth edition of his textbook, for example, he had properly understood but dismissed Freud's fundamentally unworkable hypothesis that the origin of a patient's neurosis could be found in early seductions (Kraepelin 1899: I, 511). In the seventh edition, he did seem to acknowledge the usefulness of the Freudian theory of psychic conversion (Kraepelin 1904: I, 709), and in the eighth edition he showed cautious interest in the "deep insights" provided by the "penetrating method" of psychoanalysis—but properly noted "that the physician exerts an uncommonly strong influence, wholly determined by his own preconceptions, and that to achieve the desired result requires an interpretative art commanded by very few" (Kraepelin 1909: I, 498–99; see further Decker 1977: 129–31). Although Kraepelin's influential psychiatric nosology was founded on an astounding range of case materials, he abstracted from these to generate what he called "clinical pictures" of psychiatric disease; he discouraged extended personal discussions with patients. From his point of view, Freudian psychoanalysis and its "case histories" must have seemed purely preliminary to—even a subjective distortion of—scientific psychiatry. One could easily overestimate his real interest in fighting Freudianism, for in his *Memoirs* (1987) there is no mention of Freud or psychoanalysis whatsoever.

In addition to Kraepelin, the Wolf Man had also visited Theodor Ziehen (1862–1950), professor of psychiatry in Berlin since 1904 and director of the famous Psychiatric and Neurological Clinic at the Charité. At times, Ziehen, like Kraepelin, expressed some sympathies toward aspects of psychoanalysis. But as time went on he became hostile; acting in his official capacity in Berlin, he supposedly attempted to suppress discussion of a paper by Freud's follower Karl Abraham, who was trying to set up a practice in Berlin (Freud/Abraham 1965: 84; see further Decker 1977: 160–63).

Both of these eminent specialists had failed to help the young Russian. Freud was delighted by an anecdote relayed by Abraham:

> A little satire from Ziehen's clinic: a demonstration of a case of obsessional neurosis. The patient suffers from the obsessional idea that he must put his hands under women's skirts in the street. [Note that the Wolf Man also followed women in the street; Freud was likewise to diagnose him as an obsessional neurotic.] Ziehen to the audience: "Gentlemen, we must carefully investigate whether we are dealing with a compulsive idea with sexual content. I shall ask the patient whether he also

feels this impulse with older women." The patient in answer to the question: "Alas, Professor, even with my own mother and sister." To which Ziehen says: "You see, gentlemen, that there is nothing sexual at work here." To his assistant: "Note in the case history—the patient suffers from a non-sexual but senseless obsessional idea." (Freud/Abraham 1965: 100 [February 11, 1911]; see also 101, 103)

Finally, it appears that the Wolf Man had also been briefly treated in the fall and winter of 1908 by Adolf Albrecht Friedländer (1870–1949) in his sanatorium near Frankfurt (see Gardiner 1971: 70–71). This "retarded guttersnipe"—a "liar, rogue, and ignoramus"—was a constant object of Freud's derision at this time (see Freud/Jung 1974: 253, 323; Freud/Ferenczi 1993: 177).

In the light of his struggles with Adler, Jung, Kraepelin, Ziehen, and Friedländer—all were suspicious of the Freudian hypothesis of infantile sexuality, though not necessarily of other aspects of Freud's system—the Wolf Man appeared, we can safely assume, as a possible living confirmation of Freud's most closely defended intellectual commitment, namely, the persistence of archaic, infantile sexualizations of the body in adult neurosis. Working from the initial "transference" and the patient's description of his present condition, and in the light of his wider preoccupations, Freud seems to have quickly constituted the Wolf Man as his "case" both of and for psychoanalytic interpretation itself.

The Dream of the Wolves

The second gift is harder to date. But it too came, as Freud says, "at a very early stage in the analysis" (*sehr frühzeitig*) (33)—according to the Wolf Man, "within a month or two after the start," that is, sometime in March or April 1910. The Wolf Man recalled for Freud a dream he had had at the age of four years.

> "I dreamt that it was night and that I was lying in my bed. (My bed stood with its foot towards the window; in front of the window there was a row of old walnut trees. I know it was winter time when I had the dream, and night-time.) Suddenly the window opened of its own accord, and I was terrified to see that some white wolves [*weisse Wölfen*] were sitting on the big walnut tree in front of the window. There were six or seven of them. The wolves were quite white, and looked more like foxes or sheep dogs, for they had big tails like foxes and they had their ears pricked like dogs when they are attending to something. In

great terror, evidently of being eaten up by the wolves, I screamed and woke up. My nurse hurried to my bed, to see what had happened to me. It took quite a long while before I was convinced it had only been a dream; I had had such a clear and life-like picture of the window opening and the wolves sitting on the tree. At last I grew quieter, felt as though I had escaped from some danger, and went to sleep again.

The only piece of action in the dream was the opening of the window; for the wolves sat quite still and without making any movement on the branches of the tree, to the right and left of the trunk, and looked at me. It seemed as though they had riveted their whole attention on me.— I think this was my first anxiety-dream. I was three, four, or at most five years old at the time. From then until my eleventh or twelfth year I was always afraid of seeing something terrible in my dreams." (29)

Later, replying to doubts that the dream had been dreamed in childhood at all, Ferenczi (1927) asserted that the report of the dream had been made to Freud in 1911, but he was almost certainly a full year off. In a letter to Freud of June 6, 1926, the Wolf Man confirmed that he had reported the dream early in the analysis (Lewin 1957: 449), that is, in 1910. As Freud notes in the case history, to the Wolf Man's verbal report of his childhood dream "he added a drawing of the tree with the wolves which confirmed his description" (*er gibt dann noch eine Zeichnung . . . die seine Beschreibung bestätigt*) (29) (Fig. 12). The whereabouts of the original drawing of the dream of the wolves is presently unknown. But Freud ensured that it was reproduced in all editions and translations of the case history published while he was alive.

There were many reasons, as we will see, for Freud's interest in the Wolf Man's drawing. His explicitly stated reason in the published case history— that supposedly the drawing "confirms" the verbal dream report—is important in itself. In the text, Freud has slowly led up to presenting the patient's dream; the report appears only in the fourth section of the study, subtitled "The Dream and the Primal Scene." At this point, because so much material and interpretation has been offered already, the reader cannot fail to understand the great significance of the reported dream for the entire account. Although it is clearly the centerpiece of the analysis, it is also, as it were, a confirmation of the preceding three sections in which Freud has been suggesting, without yet proving, the importance of infantile sexuality and childhood history in his patient's case.

We should note, however, that Freud's report of the patient's report of his childhood dream was itself taken from the essay, written a year earlier, in which Freud had first published it and briefly remarked on the dream's

Figure 12. Serge Pankejeff, drawing of the dream of the wolves, from Freud's *From the History of an Infantile Neurosis* (1918b)

associations with familiar fairy tales (Freud 1913d). Instead of merely re-using this text and instead of entirely rewriting it, in the case history of 1914 (as revised and published in 1918) Freud took the peculiar step of reproducing entire paragraphs of the earlier paper precisely as a *quotation* from himself—a report of his report of the patient's report of the dream. In part because the *verbal text* of the case history drifts so far away from the "reality" of the patient's dreaming—and, in turn, what that dream referred to—the *drawing* served as a "clear and life-like picture" (see 29) that seemingly reattaches Freud's representations to the reality to which they refer.

This point can be put slightly differently. Immediately after presenting the dream report itself, Freud goes on to describe the patient's associations to the dream, to add further material unearthed in the analysis, and to present his own interpretations. As Donald Spence has pointed out, this process of association and interpretation "would seem inevitably to erode the visual texture and the integrity of [an] original dream." Perhaps precisely because "there is no 'official version' of [a] dream image to which we can refer all disputes" (Spence 1982: 70), it becomes essential to Freud's account that the Wolf Man's crucial dream *image,* not just his verbal recounting of it, be presented in his study of it—for that study will engender numerous disputes about the reality to which the patient's representations supposedly refer. But if the drawing of the dream image ostensibly serves as one kind of "extratextual" guarantee that what Freud writes about the pictoriality of the dream can be believed, it is not immune to the very ambiguities it is supposed to circumvent.

The Primal Scene

In the principal historical interpretation offered in the case history, Freud deciphered the manifest elements of the Wolf Man's "wolf dream" as a hallucinated repetition of what he called the "primal scene." Specifically, he proposed, at the age of one and a half years, the Wolf Man had witnessed three episodes of *coitus a tergo* (intercourse from behind) between his parents, disheveled in their white underclothes, at about five in the afternoon in their bedroom on his father's estate, while the infant lay transfixed, and later irritated, in a crib nearby. We will return to the details of this reconstruction. At the most general level, Freud recognizes that his interpretation would seem to be highly implausible. The questions of the historical "reality" and analytic "confirmation" of the "primal scene"—about the status of Freud's psychoanalytic construction—preoccupy him throughout the manifest text of his historical narrative in the case history. As commentators have remarked almost ad nauseam, Freud cannot fully stabilize his construction of the patient's supposed primal scene. "There is no way of showing," Wittgenstein concluded, "that the whole result of [psycho]analysis may not be 'delusion.' [. . .] If you are led by psychoanalysis to say that really you thought so and so, or that really your motive was so and so, this is not a matter of discovery but of persuasion" (Wittgenstein 1966: 24, 27).[3]

The issue is not simply whether the "primal scene" actually took place as Freud reconstructed it. Freud's history rests principally on the consideration that no single actual or "real" event in the Wolf Man's childhood thinking—or in any psychic economy—should be regarded as fully the cause or as fully the effect of any other single event. Rather, any mental event or content gains significance through *Nachträglichkeit,* a "delayed" or "deferred" action or "retrospective reaction"—the most distinctive element of the Freudian concept of intentionality (see variously Ricoeur 1970; Derrida 1978, 1987; and Gardner 1990, 1993). In fact, the Wolf Man's primal scene at age one and a half, though not utterly unemotional, was relatively unimpressive to him. But in the historically forward or causal direction of his life (Fig. 13), between one and a half and four years of age the sexual meaning of the scene of intercourse, both terrible and desirable, was retrospectively created for the growing boy through his maturing sexual knowledge. In particular, his knowledge changed in response to the progressive sexualization of his body through the actions of others—for instance, an attempted "seduction" by his older sister at age three and a half (Fig. 14) and warnings about urination and display uttered by his beloved nursemaid, a foreign governess, and a maid in the household. (In Freud's narrative, these episodes are extremely tangled. "In reality," Mahony [1984: 21] points out, "Freud mentions four different seduction scenes and four different castration scenes." And like the "primal scene" itself, "seduction" or "castration threat" is difficult to locate historically and to confirm analytically. Indeed, like the primal scene, they may not actually happen; they are at least partly retrospective constructions that make sense of the past, produced from another, "future" vantage, including the time of the intersubjective psychoanalytic encounter itself.) By four years of age, the age of the wolf dream, the little Wolf Man supposedly *recollected* his "primal scene"—his dream was his interpretation of the scene—as a charged and impressive event of "feminine identification" with his mother and of desire for anal penetration by his father, cross-cut with a fear of castration and a narcissistic, "masculine" protest against it.[4] In sum, the fearful primality of the "primal scene"—its recollection in and as a neurosis—was established both prospectively and retrospectively only in its repetitions and revisions (see further Davis 1995a) (Fig. 13).

To use somewhat more vivid terms, the "primal scene"—an initial perceptual episode—constituted the first registration of a memory-to-be, a preliminary "breaching" of the system of the subject's consciousness. This trace progressively became a score, then a gouge, then a trench, a wound, a scar, a morgue, a crypt, a monument, a site, a citadel, and finally an entire territory within the subject—but always just to the extent that it merely

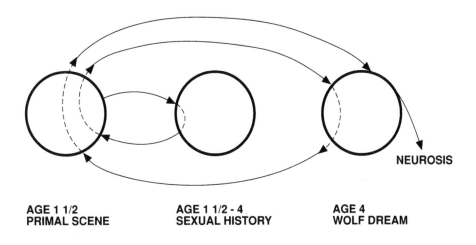

AGE 1 1/2
PRIMAL SCENE

AGE 1 1/2 - 4
SEXUAL HISTORY

AGE 4
WOLF DREAM

NEUROSIS

Figure 13. General structure of *Nachträglichkeit* in
the Wolf Man's childhood

repeated and reinscribed itself in a writing that necessarily reviewed itself
(see Abraham and Torok 1986; Derrida 1978, 1986).

Nachträglichkeit and Writing

The cycles of *Nachträglichkeit* that supposedly knot up the Wolf Man's
psychic history, his subjectivity, also constitute the very interpretive activity in which Freud comprehends that subjectivity and writes out its
history in the first place (Fig. 15). (For trenchant remarks on this feature
of the case, see Brooks 1984: 272–73 and Nägele 1987: 178.) The wolf
dream, the reader of the case history knows, was related by the Wolf Man
to Freud "at a very early stage in the analysis," that is, sometime in the
early spring of 1910. But Freud remarks that the "interpretation was a
task that dragged on over several years" (33). In fact, he says, "it was only
during the last months of analysis [that is, in the months before July 1914]
that it became possible to understand [the dream] completely" (33). Here
Freud is reminding the reader of a comment made in the introduction

Figure 14. Serge and
Anna Pankejeff holding
hands, family photo-
graph c. 1892–94 (Panke-
jeff Papers, LC)

to the entire study. The Wolf Man's resistance to analysis, Freud had remarked, remained intractable until Freud finally imposed a time limit on
their work. Under this constraint, "in a disproportionately short time the
analysis produced all the material which made it possible to clear up [the
patient's] inhibitions and remove his symptoms" (11). Even more important, "all the information" which enabled Freud to understand the patient's infantile neurosis—it was centered, the reader will discover in the
fourth section, in the wolf dream's recollection of the "primal scene"—
was "derived from this last period of the work" (11). Under the final pres-
sure, Freud says, the Wolf Man "gave an impression of lucidity which is

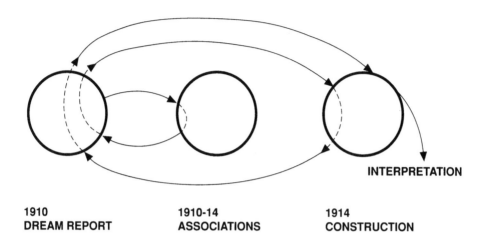

Figure 15. General structure of *Nachträglichkeit* in Freud's analysis of the Wolf Man

usually attainable only in hypnosis" (11). Indeed, at the very end of the analysis it was as if the Wolf Man reentered the dream world of the wolf dream, which had "left behind it" such a "lasting sense of reality" (*nachhaltige Wirklichkeitsgefühl*) (33), such a "life-like and clear picture" (*natürlich und deutlich Bild*) (29). We cannot date this technical breakthrough with complete precision; Freud does not provide the details. But it almost certainly occurred sometime late in the year 1913, for it apparently motivated Freud quickly to publish the wolf dream—now that the analysis was winding down and an interpretation was becoming clear—in his short paper "The Occurrence in Dreams of Materials from Fairy Tales" (Freud 1913d).

This essay, as we have already seen, was the text that Freud substantially quoted in the published case history of 1918. It stood closer, chronologically, to the report of the dream image (in 1910) than did the draft of the case history. Presumably Freud quoted it literally in 1914 partly in order to assure his readers that distortions had not crept into *his* report of the patient's report of the dream between the beginning of the analysis, in

1910, and the writing of the case history, in 1914—thus focusing our attention on the retrospective distortion that supposedly occurred between the dream itself, in late 1892 (when the Wolf Man was turning five), and the "primal scene" in mid-1888 (when the Wolf Man was one and a half). But the essay itself was written, of course, only when the dream image was *interpreted* (in late 1913); with the sole exception of the drawing of the dream, it actually stands closest of all, then, to the very moment of construction or interpretation within the analysis.

Immediately after Freud describes the wolf dream and its obvious connections with popular tales such as "Red Riding Hood," he outlines some of the patient's associations to the dream. These could be connections (that is, "associations" in the strict sense), interpretive opinions (probably determined partly by the patient's understanding of what Freud wanted to hear), or actual recollections. As an example of association, "one day" the patient interpreted the opening of the window in the dream: "It must mean 'my eyes suddenly open' " (34). As an example of recollection, on "another occasion" (*weiter Fortschritt*), the patient associated the tree in the dream with Christmas trees. Suddenly he remembered that he had dreamed the wolf dream on Christmas Eve, the night before his own birthday. In the text, Freud does not tell us when these "occasions" of association and recollection actually took place, but some of them almost certainly derive from the late period of the analysis. In particular, the connection between the opening window and the little boy's "eyes opening" suggests that the "primal scene"—the observation of the parents' intercourse—occurred after an awakening. Thus it is unlikely that the scene could have been constructed as Freud has it without the contribution of this detail. Because the overall construction dates to the end of the analysis, this association probably does too.

In the same paragraphs, moreover, we hear that "in the course of the treatment the first dream returned in innumerable variations and new editions, in connection with which the analysis produced the information that was required" (36)—just as "other dreams [. . .] followed [the wolf dream] soon afterwards" in the boy's childhood. Freud says nothing at all about these dreams that occurred during the analysis beyond noting the "return" of editions of the wolf dream (he does, however, give us several examples of the boy's other *childhood* dreams [e.g., 69, 85]). But the Wolf Man supposedly continued to dream "his wolf dream" in his reanalysis with Ruth Mack Brunswick. It is worth quoting two examples.

In a broad street [the Wolf Man dreams] is a wall containing a closed door. To the left of the door is a large, empty wardrobe with straight and crooked drawers. The patient stands before the wardrobe; his wife, a shadowy figure, is behind him. Close to the other end of the wall stands a large, heavy woman, looking as if she wanted to go around and behind the wall. But behind the wall is a pack of grey wolves, crowding toward the door and rushing up and down. Their eyes gleam, and it is evident that they want to rush at the patient, his wife, and the other woman. The patient is terrified, fearing that they will succeed in breaking through the wall. (Brunswick 1928: 288–89)

This "new edition" of the wolf dream was dreamed in 1926 or 1927. It is not, of course, an exact replication of the wolf dream, dreamed at the end of 1892 and related to Freud in 1910. It apparently shows the influence of a new transference, that is, of the new intersubjective relationship developed in the Wolf Man's new analysis, technically his third one: the "large, heavy woman" trying to go behind the "wall"— one of the three people the wolves want to attack—is presumably Brunswick herself.

More important, this "new edition" of the dream probably also reflects the Wolf Man's awareness of Freud's own interpretation of his history, published in 1918 and presented to him bearing Freud's autograph. Freud's interpretation—the 1918 case history—has, by 1926, become a subjective object for the Wolf Man, for he now dreams it, as his *own* subjectivity, for Brunswick. For instance, the "wall" with the wolves on one side and the analyst on the other appears to be a replication of the "veils" of memory that Freud, as we will see, "lifts" or "tears" in order to understand his patient—one of the most crucial metaphors in the text of the case history. In fact, the "grey" wolves in the new dream are no longer the patient's own, original wolves—the "white wolves" of the dream which "looked more like foxes or sheep dogs"—but instead are probably in part *Freud's* wolves, Freud's own personal construction of the Wolf Man's dream or even Freud himself: as the Wolf Man well knew after his years of analysis and acquaintance with Freud, Freud owned a favorite grey police dog. Such revisions seem to derive from the Wolf Man's continuing interest in Freud, unresolved upon the completion of the first analysis in 1914 and apparently in Freud's reanalysis of 1919 as well. But despite the changes, the basic elements of the original childhood "wolf dream" have been maintained. As before, the dream focuses on the "eyes" of the wolves and on their supposed desire to attack the patient, or at least his fear that they will do so. The most minimal transpositions of dreamwork intervene between the original wolf dream and this later example. The perfectly still wolves in the original dream, for example, are now "rushing up and down."

A second dream reported to Brunswick "was [as she wrote] in substance a clarified wolf dream":

> The patient stands looking out his window at a meadow, beyond which is a wood. The sun shines through the trees, dappling the grass; the stones in the meadow are of a curious mauve shade. The patient regards particularly the branches of a certain tree, admiring the way in which they are intertwined. He cannot understand why he has not yet painted this landscape. (Brunswick 1928: 291)

This version, like the other one, probably manifests the Wolf Man's awareness of Freud's published interpretation of his history and possibly of the various metaphors on which Freud's interpretation depended. In *Die Traumdeutung*, for example, Freud concerned himself with the "copious and intertwined associative links" among thoughts (Freud 1900a: 191) and, as we will see, returned again and again to the tree as the best model for or representation of the psychic system.

Like the first "new edition" of the wolf dream dreamed for Brunswick, this dream also seems to exhibit the Wolf Man's ongoing fantasy of and anxiety about not having been cured by Freud. Why, the dream apparently asks, has he not painted this landscape—no terrors appear in its daylight setting, and the "intertwining" tree, the parents' coupling, is something to admire—rather than the original wolf dream landscape, represented by the drawing in the case history itself (Fig. 11)? In fact, as a painter the Wolf Man almost exclusively depicted charming landscapes (Figs. 16–18)—without, however, including the touch of "mauve" stones, a detail perhaps derived from the *art nouveau* practices of his teacher "Painter G." His dream, then, recognizes the importance of his art both for Freud's understanding and for his own self-understanding; but it also suggests that Freud's "clear and life-like picture" of him in the case history and his *own* pictures of himself and his history have not been fully reconciled. Again, however, irrespective of the inevitable retrospective revision accomplished by the later dream, it too can be taken to exemplify the dreamwork of the ongoing wolf dream—one of Freud's "innumerable variations and new editions."

In sum, the Wolf Man's associations and other dreams in later periods of the analysis (from June 1910, after the wolf dream was reported, to

Figure 16. Serge Pankejeff (the Wolf Man), untitled landscape (Gardiner Papers, LC)

Figure 17. Serge Pankejeff (the Wolf Man), untitled landscape (Gardiner Papers, LC)

Figure 18. Serge Pankejeff (the Wolf Man), untitled landscape (Gardiner Papers, LC)

July 1914, the end of the analysis) retrospectively constituted the first wolf dream (recounted in April or May 1910) as exactly that which was so insistently repeated. For Freud, then, ostensibly the meaning of the patient's report of the dream as the disguised "primal scene" was only progressively revealed through retrospective connections (Fig. 15). Needless to say, such temporal relations in the creation and maintenance of meaning are the ordinary matter of a psychoanalysis. Whatever its "forward" drive, the analysis necessarily also includes a backward-looking, "anachronistic," "analeptic," or retrospective "historical" account, in which causes are recognized *to be* causes only after their effects have been felt—both in the patient's life after childhood and in the psychoanalysis itself. Strictly speaking, as Freud clearly recognized, this requirement should transform psychoanalysis into an infinite or "interminable" regress (see Freud 1937d), for an "effect" could be observed *as* an effect—producing an earlier "cause"—only by our being, in turn, beyond it.

From the vantage point of September and October 1914, when Freud was writing out the Wolf Man's case history, the highly complex *Nachträglichkeit* within the analysis (Fig. 15) could be smoothed over, or even somewhat obscured, in order for the *Nachträglichkeit* within the patient's life to be narrated (Fig. 13). But from the vantage point of February through May 1910, when the analysis had just begun and the wolf dream had just been reported, there was no such hindsight to be had. If hindsight occurred at all, it could not have involved Freud looking back over the Wolf Man's life or the material of the analysis, for at this point he hardly knew anything about either one; hindsight must have been of another order altogether. At the "very early stage of the analysis," there was no guarantee for Freud that the report of the wolf dream did or could have any special status for the hoped-for construction—for the "case" that the Wolf Man nonetheless had seemed, from the first consultation in early February 1910, to be offering him.

Freud's "Conviction"

In light of all this, Freud's expressly stated response to the report of the dream—retrospectively, he could see it as the "*early*" report of the dream—must especially interest us. Ordinarily, Freud recommended that an analyst should maintain an uncommitted, unprejudiced attitude toward a patient's representations, what he came to describe in a well-known formula as an "evenly suspended attention" (for example, Freud 1923a: 239). But with respect to the wolf dream, recounted at a "very early stage in the analysis," Freud formed his "conviction that the causes of [the Wolf Man's] infantile neurosis lay concealed behind it" (33). Freud's language is slightly ambiguous: "Der Patient hatte den Traum sehr frühzeitig mitgeteilt und sehr bald meine Überzeugung angenommen, dass hinter ihm die Verursachung seiner infantilen Neurose verborgen sei." If the patient, as the grammar of Freud's sentence has it, "very soon came to share" Freud's "conviction" about the dream, then, of course, Freud's attitude must have been established even *earlier*—namely, at the "very early stage" of the dream report itself, perhaps at the very moment (or at least in the very hour) it was related. Freud's "conviction" evidently had some specific content. He tells us, for example, that he worked out an "immediate interpretation" of the dream (33), presumably soon after hearing the report of the dream during those days or weeks when the patient was—"very soon"—coming to share Freud's *Überzeugung*. At this point, he settled, he says, on a preliminary "reconstruction" which included "some such fragments as these: a real occurrence—dating from a very early period—looking—immobility—sexual problems—castration—father—something terrible" (34).

But such an "immediate" interpretive effort was not absolutely necessary, and the tentative "reconstruction" (34) already goes well beyond what the report and drawing of the dream provide in themselves. In principle, Freud's "conviction" merely provided the forward push—the expectation of and commitment to a *future* interpretive construction using the particular materials of the wolf dream—animating the cycles of *Nachträglichkeit* within the analysis (Fig. 15) by which the history of the patient's *Nachträglichkeit* (Fig. 13) was to be knotted up. This energy was obviously quite intense. In the next few years it spilled outside the analysis itself. In the autumn of 1912, for example, Freud requested that his colleagues report to him any "dreams whose interpretation justifies the conclusion that the dreamers had been witnesses of sexual intercourse in their early years" (see Freud 1918b: 4). He was plainly seeking corroborating comparative evidence for his emerging picture of the "primal scene" interpretively constructed from and for the Wolf Man's dream—a quest for a "primal scene" of the psychoanalyst observing the patient's revelation of his "primal scene." He himself had just experienced this revelation, it seemed, but now he needed to "confirm" it. Indeed, in 1913, as we have seen, he published the dream itself (Freud 1913d). At the same time he

launched discussions on the "Oedipus complex" at the Vienna Psychoanalytic Society in order to preview his case (see Mahony 1984: 9).

Despite the strength of Freud's "conviction," and indeed because of it,
obvious dangers presented themselves. Within the psychoanalysis itself,
the push of "conviction" could very easily amount not to the corrobora-
tion but rather to the refutation of psychoanalytic interpretation. It could
return the analytic procedure to the very state from which Freud thought
he had liberated it—that is, to suggestion, a possibility to which he was
always especially sensitive (see further Borch-Jacobsen 1993). We have
already seen, for example, that Kraepelin had publicly implied that the
"insights" of psychoanalysis rested on the doctor's "interpretative art."
In the text of the case history itself, Freud attempts to stage-manage this
difficulty by formulating it as a worry about the "reality" of the primal
scene in the patient's own childhood experience: supposedly the question
is not what the doctor is suggesting to the patient (what *the doctor's* "convictions" are) but what the patient is suggesting to the doctor (what *the
patient's* "convictions" are).

Freud never directly says exactly how much of the perceptual material
of the primal scene was remembered by the Wolf Man, either before or
after Freud produced his reconstruction of it. The elderly Wolf Man later
asserted, "I have always thought the memory [of the primal scene] would
come, but it never did" (Obholzer 1982: 36). Assuming that he was telling
the truth, this statement has sometimes been taken decisively to refute
Freud's construction in the case history. There is no good theoretical reason, however, why the patient should have been able to *recall* the primal
scene as such—a particular perceptual event in his or her deepest childhood. As Freud insisted in his paper "Remembering, Repeating and Working-Through," drafted just after the completion of his work with the Wolf
Man in 1914, the "conviction which the patient obtains in the course of
his analysis [is] [. . .] quite independent of this kind of memory" (Freud
1914g: 149). Supposedly the significance of the primal scene—its sexualization and traumatization of the subject's psyche—is only retroactively
conferred upon it through the ongoing construction of the growing child's
sexuality and, more paradoxically, through its ongoing effect upon the
very psychic and social possibilities *for* that construction.

The "primal scene," then, cannot be regarded as a single, self-sufficient
event punctuating the patient's psychosexual or social development.
"Both traditionalist and revolutionary [thinkers] hold," Gardner (1990:
96) points out, "that the increments of the past exist in a determinate

present form, available as an object of judgment, whether that judgment characteristically consists in affirmation (for the traditionalist) or in revolutionary denial (for Sartre)." But any such "determinate" contemporary event-memory must itself be the complex intentional object—always under construction—of ongoing *Nachträglichkeit.* The oldest perceptual material feeding into this object need not be accessible to the subject's conscious recall: even though the initial perceptual impressions have long since faded away, the significance of the stimulus might have been registered or transcribed and retranscribed in later thinking. (We should not, of course, invoke "repression" to explain the fading of the initial impressions, for this would court tautology; fading is partly a consequence of other, probably ordinary perceptual and cognitive mechanisms, and perhaps of the more extraordinary events that Freud brilliantly characterized in his work *On Aphasia* [Freud 1891].) In her analysis with Freud, Princess Marie Bonaparte could not remember the "primal scene" that Freud constructed from and for her memories, fantasies, and symptoms, but its actuality—more exactly, the historical reality of the events which had supposedly provided the initial perceptual material for her ongoing *Nachträglichkeit*—was later confirmed by independent family sources (Bonaparte 1925). But whether or not the primal scene actually can or must be recalled, in the case history and in essays such as "Remembering, Repeating and Working-Through" or Bonaparte's note, it is always the *patient's* "conviction"—or lack thereof—that seems to be at issue, not the *analyst's.*

From the vantage point of autumn 1914, in writing out the case history, the evidence Freud had in mind for his "conviction" about the wolf dream would have been the numerous important associations, recollections, and symptoms—like the "new editions" of the dream—which the patient had gradually pitched in relation to it until the termination of the analysis in July 1914. But from the vantage point of that day in the early spring of 1910 when the dream was first reported and Freud's "conviction" was initially formed, this retrospective confirmation was not available. Whence, then, Freud's "conviction"?

III

THE DRAWING OF THE DREAM
OF THE WOLVES

> It seems that Freud stood to his patients'
> associations, dreams, symptoms, reminis-
> cences, and errors more as the painter to
> his pigments than as the sleuth to his
> traces of mud and cigar ash.
>
> —Frank Cioffi (1969: 205)

In 1910, when the wolf dream was reported, the Wolf Man did provide a "confirmation." Specifically, he offered a confirmation of his report of the dream, namely, the *drawing* of the dream (Fig. 12). At the same time as the Wolf Man presented a "confirmation" in relation to his report of the dream, Freud felt a "conviction" in relation to the status of the dream for the hoped-for case—a foreknowledge that the dream report did or could provide the forward energy animating the still-to-be-discovered connections (Fig. 15) of the upcoming necessary *Nachträglichkeit* of the patient's history (Fig. 13). The Wolf Man's particular "confirmation," then, *was* Freud's "conviction," at least in part. On these grounds we can say that from the moment of its introduction into the analysis, the drawing of the dream of the wolves was not fully distinguished from Freud's own self, desire, and knowledge. As a real artifact, it was an objective manifestation of the Wolf Man's subjectivity, deliberately used by Freud to reconstruct its history. But it was also, for Freud, Freud's own subjective object. This object was not identical with the Wolf Man's drawing but rather the grounds for its acceptance and interpretation by Freud. Before tackling the history of this object, however, we should notice the turmoil that signals its presence.

46

Textual Contradictions

Much of the contradictoriness of the text of the case history seems to be deliberately staged by Freud, though many commentators have taken it, too literally, as supposed evidence for the essential instability of Freud's narrative or for logical difficulties inherent in his reasoning—and, in turn, for underlying intellectual and other conflicts. But apparent contradictions which leave no loose ends by the end of the account are, of course, *faux* "contradictions"—textual effects set up from the beginning. One should not rush to assert, then, that textual "unclarities" or "indeterminacies"— the favored object of many contemporary literary-critical readings of the case history—exemplify a subjective object of Freud's or that they display unresolved conflict above and beyond his avowed subjectivity in the writing as such. Freud explicitly acknowledges his desire to produce a text designed to secure his readers' "conviction," and play with contradiction helps guarantee the realization of this ambition: one way to secure readers' final positive "conviction" about his interpretations is to suggest from the beginning, and throughout, that *their* doubts are also his own. Freud's text manages to suggest that the questions readers might raise, and which Freud appears to have missed, are answered as if Freud had not intended to answer them, even as if he continued to miss them until the very end— and thus, finally, as if they have been answered by the Wolf Man's real history itself rather than by Freud's merely tendentious narrative of it.

In relating the patient's report of his wolf dream, for example, Freud provides an ostensibly objective description of what the Wolf Man said to him in the analysis. He has the little Wolf Man wake up screaming from his terrifying dream with his beloved Nanya hurrying to his bed (29). Just a few paragraphs later, however, he has the little Wolf Man waking up and "flying for refuge to his nurse" (35). This doubt about the proximity and action of the nurse—and perhaps about where the dream was actually dreamed—helps provoke the reader's larger difficulties with the central claim of Freud's final construction. Could it really have been true that the one-and-a-half-year-old Wolf Man was sleeping in his parents' bedroom, the setting constructed as his "primal scene"? If the setting *of* the dreaming is unclear, can we believe the setting represented *in* the dream?

But wherever possible Freud will ultimately identify evidence allowing him to settle contradictions in a way that does not seem to reflect the strength of his own interpretive energy and its possible distortion of his report of the Wolf Man's own statements. Rather, remaining inconsistencies seem to derive from the *Wolf Man's* actual uncertainties about particular details and his delays, in analysis, in filling them in or establishing their relevance. Thus the text of the case history becomes, like the *Nachträglichkeit* of the analysis (Fig. 15) knotting up the *Nachträglichkeit* of the patient's history (Fig. 13), itself an instance of *Nachträglichkeit*—namely, the *Nachträglichkeit* of writing itself (Fig. 19).

To remain with the example noted a moment ago, though the reader might question whether the little Wolf Man actually could have seen his parents making love in their bedroom, Freud later uses material in the wolf dream to suggest that the little Wolf Man, suffering a malarial fever, had indeed been permitted to sleep in his parents' room when he was ill. (In fact, he produces "independent" testimony targeted at this possibility.) In addressing, if not directly answering, the reader's suspicion, the initial contradiction remains a contradiction only within the *Wolf Man's* narrative of his history—where did the dreaming of the wolf dream take place, and how did the nurse respond? It is not, seemingly, a contradiction infecting the larger, deeper interpretive construction Freud imposes on it— where did the "primal scene" take place and how did the Wolf Man respond? But though this latter question persists, of course, as a serious logical and historical difficulty, it is not outside Freud's direct textual management, control, and performance; it may be a local logical or historical contradiction, but it is not, for all that, necessarily a sign of the textual contradiction that would betray any fundamental doubt or unconscious conflict on Freud's part.

Indeed, the extremely precise management of a local contradiction is surely a sign that the writer is hardly in doubt at all: irrespective of wider logics or canons of historical "truth," he knows exactly what he wants to say and will evade any logical constraints in saying it. In the 1918 additions to the 1914 draft of the case history, Freud directly retracts his initial assertion that the primal scene actually took place precisely as his construction would have it. He resolves to leave the construction shadowy: "*non liquet*," he says, "it is not clear." Commentators have pointed to this statement as the most notable sign of essential instability in the text. But a definite resolution to leave the content of the construction indeterminate—"*non liquet*"—is not, of course, the same thing as an indeterminate resolution, a *non "non liquet,"* a *non anti-"non liquet,"* etc.

If we seized on such tremors in the text as evidence of the indeterminacy or failure of Freud's deep construction, as a number of commentators in-

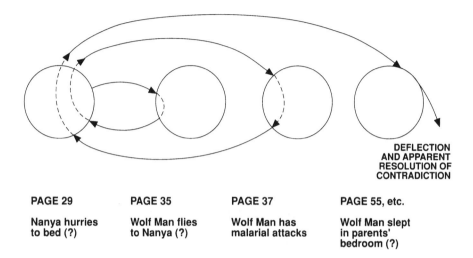

DEFLECTION
AND APPARENT
RESOLUTION OF
CONTRADICTION

PAGE 29

Nanya hurries
to bed (?)

PAGE 35

Wolf Man flies
to Nanya (?)

PAGE 37

Wolf Man has
malarial attacks

PAGE 55, etc.

Wolf Man slept
in parents'
bedroom (?)

Figure 19. Example of the structure of *Nach-träglichkeit* in the writing of Freud's case history of the Wolf Man

side and outside psychoanalysis have done, we would not really appreciate how Freud creates an energy of suspense in his readers. Like Freud himself in the course of the analysis, readers are allowed to feel certain skeptical "convictions" motivating their reading of the historical material and Freud's narrative of it. Freud needs this energy in order to secure our own final "confirmation" of his construction of the "contradictions" when, late in the text of the case history, contradictions that bear on the construction are supposedly resolved. From page to page of the case history, then, we confront contradictions. But in the final, retrospective construction developed from Freud's initial conviction, many of them are eliminated—a *Nachträglichkeit* for or in the reading (Fig. 20) which has been stage-managed in the *Nachträglichkeit* of Freud's writing (Fig. 19).

The Inconsistency of Dream Report and Dream Drawing

Having said this, however, we can readily see that certain peculiarities in the forward direction of writing out, and reading through, the text of the case history are not resolved by the end of the text, even if—as is

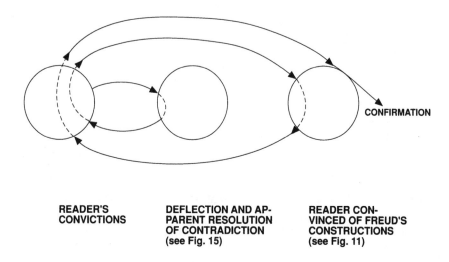

CONFIRMATION

READER'S
CONVICTIONS

DEFLECTION AND AP-
PARENT RESOLUTION
OF CONTRADICTION
(see Fig. 15)

READER CON-
VINCED OF FREUD'S
CONSTRUCTIONS
(see Fig. 11)

Figure 20. General structure of *Nachträglichkeit* in
reading Freud's case history of the Wolf Man

the case for some of the "contradictions"—this resolution would be no
more than an open acknowledgment of doubt. Most important for our
purposes here, the drawing "of the tree with the wolves" (29) (Fig. 12)
hardly "confirms" the reported dream. A great deal has been left out. The
dreamer dreamed, as he says, that it was night; he was lying in his bed
facing the window; the window opened of its own accord; the tree was
in front of the window; wolves were sitting in the tree looking at him;
he is frightened of being eaten up and—here the dream ends—he screams
and wakes up. The event of seeing that is the dream story might be partially implied in the drawing. The viewer of the drawing (Fig. 12) apparently occupies the position of the dreamer looking out his already opened
window, the sill or frame of which seems to cut off our view of the ground
itself and apparently any view of the upper trunk and branches of the tree
as well. But certainly in the drawing neither the bedroom nor the physical
presence of the window has been directly depicted.

In fact, at best the drawing depicts just one subordinate clause in the
entire dream report—namely, "some white wolves were sitting on the big
walnut tree." Even in this respect the drawing is vague. The wolves' *white-*

ness, twice noted in the dream report, can only be implied in a black-and-white drawing. And the fact that the tree is a walnut tree—usually distinguished by a tall, unbranching trunk and round, leafy crown—hardly seems to have been rendered by the Wolf Man's squat, truncated, leafless growth.

Some of this vagueness was resolved, but heavily reworked, in later oil paintings in which the Wolf Man depicted his wolf dream; some of these works were given or sold to psychoanalysts. Here, of course, the image is in color. In an example probably made in the 1950s (Fig. 21), the wolves are definitely white. Whereas the earlier drawing (Fig. 12) was ambiguous in its depiction of the tree trunk and treetop, the later painting roots the tree in a patch of actual ground and shows the tree top simply to be missing, as if blasted by lightning. Correlatively, the drawing's suggestion that the tree is so close to the window that the window frame cuts off our view of its bottom and top has now been replaced, in the painting, by the suggestion that the tree with wolves stands much farther back from the window, since we can now see the ground in which it is rooted. Finally, a recollection about the circumstance in which the wolf dream was dreamed—the patient recollected that he had his childhood nightmare "during winter time" (that is, he later remembered, on Christmas Eve)—has been transferred in the painting into the dream story itself. In the painting, it is obviously "winter time" outside the window.

Much of this reworking probably reflects the Wolf Man's retrospective awareness of Freud's interest in certain aspects of the dream, the dream report, and the dream drawing, and, like the "new editions" of the wolf dream dreamed for Freud and Ruth Mack Brunswick, probably embodies his ongoing desire partly to "confirm" and partly to challenge the final construction narrated in Freud's published case history. For example, how could the wolves in the painting succeed in "eating up" the dreamer, as he originally feared, if they are so far away from his window? The painting seems to recognize that Freud's final historical interpretation of the first dream was supposed to save the Wolf Man from the terror of the wolf-parents, who in the initial drawing are feared by the dreamer to be close enough to the open window to leap from the branches of the trees into the bedroom itself. (As we will see in more detail, the theme of the Wolf Man's *rescue* from the "wolves"—he is saved by Freud—is perhaps the most basic psychosexual and visual-textual component of the intersubjective dynamic of the entire case.) Because the painting was presented to psychoanalysts by a painter who was usually regarded by them as the possible

Figure 21. Serge Pankejeff (the Wolf Man), painting of the dream
of the wolves, c. 1950–60 (Gardiner Papers, LC)

living confirmation of Freud's interpretive technique, by the time he produced it—long after the analysis with Freud—perhaps his wolves were no
longer a real threat to him because it was so generally believed that Freud's
construction of their primal meaning had been correct. Be that as it may,
in the 1950s the painter has painted Freud's interpretation rather than—or
at least just as much as—his own childhood dream as first reported.

The Wolves and the Trees

Paintings of his wolf dream are certainly a special case in the Wolf
Man's pictorial production. But they should not be totally detached from
his history outside and before his psychoanalysis with Freud. The Wolf

Figure 22. Caspar David Friedrich, *Oak Tree in the Snow,* 1829 (courtesy National Gallery, Berlin)

Man's landscapes probably exhibit his educated-amateur understanding of pictorial tradition. Indeed, even the wolf-dream images themselves might have close pictorial associations with earlier works such as Caspar David Friedrich's *Oak Tree in the Snow* (1829) (Fig. 22), which similarly situated the viewer's subjectivity without depending on the Wolf Man's greater literalization—in the metaphor of the wolves—of Nature as an other, an unsettling presence attentively "looking" at us (see generally Koerner 1987). Another well-known work by Friedrich, *Solitary Tree* (*Der Einsame Baum*) of 1822 (Fig. 23), depicted an imposing but damaged oak tree sheltering a shepherd—a conventional pastoral allegory for the artist or perhaps a personification of Nature—and sheep, readily transformable into wolves through a tissue of proverbs, riddles, and folktales. In the anal-

Figure 23. Caspar David Friedrich, *Solitary Tree*, 1822 (courtesy National Gallery, Berlin)

ysis itself, the Wolf Man made several readily intelligible associations between wolves and sheep (see Sadovnikov 1986: 373–74 for traditional Russian sayings on the theme of wolves and sheep).

The sheep in Friedrich's painting might have been connected, for the Wolf Man along with many other viewers, to the Christian community (sheep = lambs) and to Christ himself (sheep = the shepherd, the Lamb of God). According to Freud, the patient's religious education and "religious obsession" were a major part of his childhood neurosis. Picking up the point, the psychoanalyst Albert J. Lubin has suggested that the tree in the Wolf Man's dream and drawing in part signified the cross on which Christ was crucified, especially as it is depicted in Russian Orthodox iconography; Lubin observes that the geometry of the tree in the wolf drawing permits

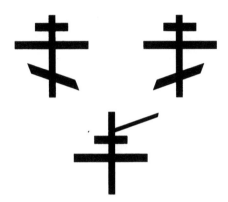

Figure 24. Diagram by Arnold J. Lubin comparing the Wolf Man's tree (Fig. 12) and the Russian Orthodox cross (after Lubin 1967)

one to see it as a somewhat distorted Russian Orthodox cross (Fig. 24) (Lubin 1967). (Lubin relayed this interpretation to Gardiner shortly after a visit with the Wolf Man in Vienna in 1961–62 [Gardiner Papers].) This somewhat strained explanation of the underlying formal similarity between the Wolf Man's tree and the wooden cross is probably unnecessary. Under the influence of St. Bonaventura's *Meditations on the Cross* (c. 1250) and the writings of other Christian mystics, in Christian iconography the Cross frequently approximates or takes the form of a natural tree (*arbor crucis*), with the leaves and flowers that bear fruit for Christians to eat (see Revelations 22). (Sometimes the tree has the form of a rosebush; it is also commonly related to the vine that symbolizes the coming Messianic age [Psalm 80] and the true Church [John 15] [see Bann 1991].) This tradition was replicated and transformed in the Romantic landscape painting which the Wolf Man seems to have favored—for example, in Friedrich's great *Tetschen Altar,* the *Cross in the Mountains* (*Kreuz im Gebirge*) of 1807–1808 (Fig. 25). The Wolf Man told Lubin that he wore his baptismal cross constantly until he was at least twenty years old; his "religious obsession" involved kissing icons, saying prayers, and crossing himself, probably in imitation, as he told Lubin, of the priests' actions at the iconostasis in Or-

Figure 25. Caspar David
Friedrich, *Cross in the Mountains* (the Tetschen Altar),
1807–1808 (courtesy State
Museum, Dresden)

thodox liturgy. Other material Freud reports in the case history tends to
support the theory that as a boy the Wolf Man saw himself as the wounded,
bleeding, crucified Christ and attempted to defend himself against the
various troubling implications of this association.

The idea that for the Wolf Man the tree with wolves partly signified
the crucified Christ is thus persuasive in context. But other iconographic
possibilities could also be explored. In Christian iconography, the tree
frequently appears as the Tree of Life (in turn, sometimes identified with
the Cross), the Tree of Knowledge, or the Tree of Jesse. (The tradition probably had an influence on scientific illustrations that Freud knew, to which

Figure 26. Caspar David Friedrich, *The Watzmann*, 1824–25
(courtesy National Gallery, Berlin)

we will turn shortly.) But despite the fact that the Wolf Man and Freud apparently "discussed painting" during the analysis (Obholzer 1982: 33), in the case history itself Freud does not really develop these possibilities—in part, perhaps, because he was not fully aware of the iconographic resonances of the Wolf Man's imagery that would have set him on the appropriate trail.

In his *Memoirs*, the Wolf Man remarks on his very early childhood interest in drawing trees, which he gave up when he found that his sister Anna could draw better ones. In addition, he attributed "the beginning of [his] activities as a landscape painter" to his visit to spectacular sites in the mountainous Caucasus, including the site of the death of the Russian poet Lermontov, whom he had heroized in his adolescence (see Gardi-

Figure 27. Carl Gustav Carus, *Eichen am Meer,* 1835 (courtesy State Museum, Dresden)

ner 1971: 9, 20–21, 28–34); it was precisely this kind of tremendous vista that Friedrich had favored (Fig. 26). We do not know whether the Wolf Man had ever seen Friedrich's work by the time he came to consult Freud in 1910. There were paintings and drawings by Friedrich in the Russian imperial collections, but until 1917 they remained in royal palaces (Asvarishch 1990: 19). Certainly, though, the Wolf Man had discussed landscape with his own painting teacher and probably would have seen paintings by Friedrich in the course of his travels in Germany, seeking a cure, in the years before his arrival in Vienna.

Many followers of Friedrich produced similar images. Prominent among them was the doctor, philosopher, and artist Carl Gustav Carus (1789– 1869). In works such as *Eichen am Meer: Motiv von der Insel Vilm, Ostsee* of 1835 (Fig. 27), Carus explored the dichotomy behind the wild trees of the north coasts of Europe and Great Britain, formed in interactions with the raw elements of wind and water, and the domesticated trees (*Parkbäume*) of the well-planned Central European towns (see Meffert 1986:

157, pl. 49, and, in general, Prause 1968)—the latter being the usual subject of the Wolf Man's typical landscape paintings (Figs. 16–18), also favored by traditionalist Russian landscapists of the mid-nineteenth century (see Sarab'ianov 1990: 66). This hackneyed contrast between the wild and the cultivated was a topic for both aesthetic and philosophical meditation throughout nineteenth-century letters—for example, in Carus's own essays on landscape (Carus 1831, 1841; cf. Brion 1988). All of the paintings by the Wolf Man that are currently accessible for study depict unpopulated, quiet landscapes and townscapes of parks, river valleys, or gardens, many, if not most, of them situated in and around Vienna. Quite a few of them include one prominent tree or just a few trees (see Gardiner 1971: 17, 20). It probably goes too far to say, as Lubin (1967: 161) does, that these "landscapes and trees in them were later editions of the childhood wolf dream."[1] In fact, quite the reverse: it is likely that the Wolf Man—who acknowledged the "romanticism" of his landscapes—at least partly intended to juxtapose the tree in his drawing of the dream of the wolves, a terrifying image of the wild, with the *Parkbäume* in his more usual pictures.

All these iconographical possibilities were probably quite unknown to Freud. They remind us, then, that from the vantage point of the Wolf Man, his wolf drawing was originally a somewhat different object from that subjectively constructed by Freud. Two iconographies, two hermeneutic possibilities, had to meet and mutually inflect one another when the Wolf Man drew a picture of his dream—*for* Freud but using *his own* pictorial resources. However we sort out this larger issue, the Wolf Man's painting of his dream (Fig. 21) suggests that the earlier drawing of it (Fig. 12) was quite an unstable object in the psychoanalytic encounter between Freud and his patient.

The Drawing as "Correction"

There is one dramatic discrepancy between the dream report and the dream drawing. The report tells us that there were "six or seven" wolves, but the drawing depicts only five. In writing out the case history in the autumn of 1914, Freud interpreted the numbers six and seven as residues of the influence of the story of "The Wolf and the Seven Little Goats" on the dreamer. In this fairy tale, he noted, "the wolf ate up only six of the little goats, while the seventh hid itself in the clock case" (31). Freud also expressly tells us, however, that the significance of this folktale became

evident only *later* in the analysis, after the dream report had been produced. At least for some time after the dream report had been made, then,
"there seemed to be no answer to the question" why there were six or
seven wolves in the dream (31).

Furthermore, a few pages later Freud directly interprets the *five* wolves
in the drawing: he has discovered that the little boy suffered from malarial
attacks as an infant and later from childhood depressions that "used to
come on in the afternoon and reached their height about five o'clock"
(37). (As we have already seen, this finding allowed Freud seemingly to
settle one troublesome point: "probably for the very reason of this illness,"
Freud reasons, the little Wolf Man was in his parents' bedroom rather
than the nursery [37].) But, of course, if we go back to the text of the
dream report, we find that the dreamer "dreamt that it was night," *not*
five in the afternoon (29). In order, therefore, to tie the dream to the
primal scene, in his final "comprehensive account of the relations between
the manifest content of the dream and the latent dream thoughts," Freud
takes the drawing illustrating five wolves as a "correction" of the dream's
distortion of the afternoon of the primal scene into its night of the wolves
(43 n. 2) ("In der zum Traum gefertigten Zeichnung hat der Träumer die
5 zum Ausdruck gebracht, die wahrscheinlich die Angabe: es war Nacht,
korrigiert").

Such "correction" is the exact opposite of a dream's usual process of
"secondary revision"—an "interpretation," located in the "manifest content" of the dream images, which the dream produces about itself and in
which it attempts to connect and render more coherent the otherwise
disparate, distorted dream thoughts (see Freud 1900a: 490). The supposed
"correction" does not actually revise the dream thoughts in the direction
of the greater, if more greatly distorted, clarity of the "manifest content."
Rather, it takes Freud closer to the unconscious, "latent" content. In other
words, far from being a "confirmation" of the manifest dream thoughts
or of the patient's "report" of the dream, the drawing takes Freud *beyond*
or *behind* them to the disguised content finally constructed as the Wolf
Man's "primal scene" (cf. Marinov 1991). Thus, to repeat, the drawing
is an interpretation of the primal scene not clearly distinguishable from
Freud's own interpretation of it. But because the "final comprehensive"
construction of the primal scene did not take place until the end of the
analysis, on what basis did the drawing—introduced so much earlier—
enable such a pre-interpretation or foreknowledge for Freud of the primal
scene in which it had supposedly been determined for the Wolf Man?

"Five," "Six," and "Seven" Wolves

In 1926, Freud's disaffected follower Otto Rank suggested—to broaden his conclusions slightly—that the Wolf Man's wolf dream had actually first been dreamed *in the years of the psychoanalysis,* that is, in 1910–14, a time when the patient, he argued, was clearly dominated by a strong transference to his analyst Freud. But the patient reported the dream, Rank continued, as a *childhood* dream, conforming to his obliging perception of the analyst's desires to discover childhood material (Rank 1926; see generally Rudnytsky 1991: 16–69). In current jargon, the patient, caught in a basic "personality disorder," conformed to his fundamentally narcissistic—alternately grandiose and masochistic—desire to constitute Freud's "most famous case." Specifically, Rank suggested, the Wolf Man took the "walnut tree" in his dream from the chestnut trees one could see through the window of Freud's consulting room. "My bed" was nothing other than Freud's couch. Finally, the "six or seven" wolves actually stood for Freud and his fellow analysts—for Rank recalled "a number of photographs of [Freud's] closest followers" that were hanging in the consulting room. "So far as I can remember," he wrote, "there were between five and seven of these photographs—a different number at different times—that is, precisely the numbers between which the patient oscillated in connection with the wolves" (that is, "five" in the dream drawing, "six or seven" in the dream report). The "closest followers" Rank had in mind were presumably the five initial members—not including Freud himself—of the "Secret Committee" of Freud's most trusted disciples, an organization proposed by Ernest Jones in June 1912, and formally recognized by Freud's presentation of special rings (bearing an image of Oedipus and the Sphinx) to the initial members on May 25, 1913.

Rank's publication caused a minor tempest among the Freudians. Freud himself wrote to the Wolf Man for clarification and reassurance. On June 6, 1926, the Wolf Man responded: "I have no reason to doubt the correctness of this memory [of the dream as 'confirmed' or 'corrected' by his drawing]. [. . .] My memory of this childhood dream never underwent any change" (Lewin 1957: 449). Freud provided this private statement to Sandor Ferenczi, to whom he had described the first appearance of the Wolf Man (Freud/Ferenczi 1993: 133, 138). To the Wolf Man's testimony he added his own assertion that when the analysis began, in 1910, there were "in all only two or three pictures hanging on the piece of wall in question." Ferenczi (1927) used the information to craft a lengthy and devastating review of Rank's book.

Writing to Ferenczi, Freud calculated that *in 1913 and 1914* the Wolf Man could have seen a total of five photographs in the consulting room (pictures of Karl Abraham, Hanns Sachs, Ernest Jones, and Rank and Ferenczi themselves). But the dream—whether it was a real childhood dream or an adult construction—was dreamed much earlier than 1913, that is, at a time when at best all that could be seen in the consulting room were the "two or three" photographs mentioned in Ferenczi's review. Ferenczi's review was apparently "written mainly at Freud's dictation" (Grosskurth 1991: 182)—so it must have been Freud who told Ferenczi that the dream "was produced in 1911," what Ferenczi wrote in his review in order to refute Rank's claim about the photographs. Freud's memory was mistaken here. Responding to Freud's query, the Wolf Man pointed out—as Freud's statements in the case history had clearly implied—that the dream was dreamed "near the beginning of [his] analysis, to the best of [his] recollection within a month or two after the start" (Lewin 1957), that is, in the spring of 1910.

Freud's little error, of course, did not affect his response to Rank. Whether the dream had been reported in 1910 or in 1911, in those years there were not, as Rank had claimed, "between five and seven" photographs of Freud's followers in the consulting room. From the strictest point of view, then, Rank stood refuted in his specific historical claim. Rank's *psychoanalytic* interpretation of the Wolf Man's drawing, however, was *not* refuted by Freud's testimony and further inquiries and by Ferenczi's review. Freud and Ferenczi did not acknowledge that at the time he made his dream report, the Wolf Man could have built *any* number of photographs hanging in Freud's consulting room into his description or drawing of the dream as an object to offer Freud. After all, the "five" wolves in the drawing, and the "six or seven" wolves in the dream report, were explicitly described by Freud as "distortions" or "corrections" of the underlying reality—namely, in his view, the *two* parents of the patient. If two parents, then why not "two or three" photographs?

Though potentially consistent with the published case history, Rank's interpretation—and what Ferenczi implied must be his faulty memory or outright deceit—nonetheless probably harbored his own subjective object. A famous photograph of Freud's "Secret Committee" of six followers, taken in 1922 (Fig. 28), showed the six analysts, including Rank himself in the upper left—seven analysts in all if we count Freud himself. The

Figure 28. Photograph of the "Secret Committee," 1922 (after Grosskurth 1991)

last member of the "Secret Committee," Max Eitingon, joined it in 1919, well after the Wolf Man's first analysis had ended. We might suppose that Rank was influenced by this photograph retrospectively to suppose that in 1910–14 there were "six or seven" photographs rather than the "two or three" (or at most five) actually present in Freud's consulting room. But especially in view of Freud's well-orchestrated attempt to muzzle him, the inadequacy of Rank's interpretation does not imply that Freud's preferred construction of the wolf drawing was any less free of subjectivity.[2]

Fairy Tales

Immediately following the paragraph introducing the evidence of the drawing (Fig. 12), Freud recounts the Wolf Man's first association to the dream. The patient connected the wolves, Freud says, with an image in a picture book he had possessed as a child. In this book, a "wolf was [illustrated] standing upright, striding out with one foot, with its claws stretched out and its ears pricked" (30). Questioned on the point by Freud, the Wolf Man thought the striding wolf with pricked ears came from the story of "Little Red Riding Hood." Freud himself, however, sought another association. "I raised a doubt," he says, "whether the picture that had frightened him could be connected with the [Red Riding Hood] story"—because, he goes on to claim, "this fairy tale only offers an opportunity for two illustrations [of the wolf]—Little Red Riding Hood's meeting with the wolf in the wood, and the scene in which the wolf lies in bed in the grandmother's nightcap" (31).

It is not at all obvious, however, why "Red Riding Hood" can be illustrated with only two wolf pictures. What about the wolf bundling Grandmother away—or the woodcutter bursting in to save Red Riding Hood by killing the wolf? Indeed, the most famous version of the fairy tale, presented in Charles Perrault's *Contes* (1697), was commonly illustrated with multiple wolves—as in the late-nineteenth century edition by Emile Guérin (Fig. 29), where we see the wolf making off for Grandmother's cottage while Red Riding Hood dawdles on the path (*bottom*), the wolf scratching at Grandmother's door (*middle*), and the wolf waiting for Red Riding Hood to join him in the bed (*top*) (see Zipes 1982: 27). Nonetheless, Freud sticks with the constraint he has purely imagined—justifying the further assertion that "there must therefore be *some other fairy tale* behind [the Wolf Man's] recollection of the picture" (31, my emphasis).

Sure enough, the obliging patient "soon discovered it" (31). During the analysis the Wolf Man searched the secondhand bookshops of Vienna "with tireless perseverance" until he found an old copy of the picture book itself. The wolf in question turned out to be the wolf of "The Wolf and the Seven Little Goats," depicted, as the patient remembered, with "one foot forward, with its claws stretched out and its ears pricked" (39). Under Freud's prodding, then, the Wolf Man confirmed his association to the dream in the same way that he had earlier confirmed his report of the dream—namely, by finding a picture both depicting and explaining the material he had reported. (Indeed, we might take this exchange as the fundamental form—commensurate with its fundamental theme or content—of the entire psychoanalysis for both the doctor and his patient.) But before the Wolf Man located the picture book, Freud could not have known that the wolf behind the patient's association was the wolf of "The

Wolf and the Seven Little Goats," for he had "raised a doubt" about "Red Riding Hood" on purely internal grounds. In fact, if he had thought he actually knew what the real fairy-tale connection was, he would not have needed to await what he describes as the *patient's* discovery of the correct illustration. Even beyond the story "The Wolf and the Seven Little Goats," then, there must have been "some other fairy tale" behind the Wolf Man's recollections in making associations to the dream report and his drawing.

Freud's Christmas Fairy Tale

On New Year's Day 1896, Freud, just forty years old, sent a long letter to his friend Wilhelm Fliess in Berlin. In it he described the latest elaborations in his developing theory of "nerve paths" and "neuronal motion" as the basis for a material psychology. Along with the letter, Freud included the draft of a short essay on psychopathology meant for Fliess's perusal. Closely linked to Freud's thinking in the past months, the draft (now known as "Draft K") contained the most lucid and thorough statement he had made to date of his hypothesis that hysteria, obsessional neurosis, and paranoia derive from a person's "repressing," in an act of psychic "defense," the unpleasurable memory of sexual feelings aroused before puberty, that is, the memory of what Freud believed had been the patient's sexual seduction in childhood (Freud 1985: 158–70 [January 1, 1896]). The essay both generalized and—by focusing on the "preconditions" of adult neurosis in "sexuality and infantilism"—radicalized Freud's and Josef Breuer's conclusions in *Ueber Hysterie*, published the preceding year (Freud and Breuer 1895d).

In proposing that neurotic sexuality "represses" a painful seduction, Freud encountered an empirical problem. Doctors and jurists commonly lacked direct contemporary evidence for a parent's, sibling's, or other person's seduction of a child, however compelling the *retrospective* evidence of the adolescent or adult patient's distorted sexuality, troubling memories, or debilitating neurosis might be. The lack of contemporary evidence, however, could always be due to faulty memories, the unwillingness of participants to address the facts, and the secrecy of the act of seduction itself. In principle, it was possible that empirical evidence of some kind—a surfacing memory, the testimony of witnesses—could be discovered, though whether it would hold up in court was another matter.

A logical problem with Freud's proposal was more troubling for the the-

Figure 29. Illustration to the story of Little Red Riding Hood from Emile Guérin's edition of Charles Perrault's *Contes,* c. 1880 (after Zipes 1982)

ory he had implicitly adopted. How could one account for the subjectively pleasurable sex life of a person whose previous sexual experiences, in the alleged childhood seductions, were supposedly painful? How could a frightening, disgusting, or dangerous early experience become the basis for the patient's erotic, albeit neurotic, fantasies and practices? In "Draft K" of 1896, Freud did not have a wholly complete or positive answer to this question. But he did recognize that "this [matter] should be explicable by a [general] theory of sexuality" in which it would be "a question in the first instance of a gap in the psyche." Some kind of jump or transformation occurs between the event of seduction itself—whatever its contemporary value as painful, pleasurable, or simply neutral—and later eroticism. To the extent that Freud at least recognized this "gap in the psyche," "Draft K" contained the germ of psychoanalytic psychopathology—a theory of fantasy and defense, quite distinct from the pure psychopathology of trauma embodied in the initial seduction theory. The draft essay sent to Fliess on New Year's Day was titled "The Neuroses of Defence (A Christmas Fairy Tale) [*Weihnachtsmärchen*]."

Freud quickly published substantial elements of his "Christmas Fairy Tale" in two essays finished in early February 1896, "Heredity and the Aetiology of the Neuroses" and "Further Remarks on the Neuro-Psychoses of Defence" (Freud 1896a, 1896b). And on April 21, 1896, he publicly presented the seduction theory of hysteria (even though it had already been questioned by the possibility of a "theory of sexuality" raised in his own "Draft K") as a lecture, "The Aetiology of Hysteria," presented to his Viennese neurological and psychiatric colleagues. Richard von Krafft-Ebing, the influential sexologist, chaired this formal occasion (see Freud 1896c for the lecture; Sulloway 1979: chaps. 4, 8, esp. 126–29, is an indispensable study of Freud's thought at this time). As the title of his public lecture implied, Freud asserted that actual childhood sexual experiences, or even "seductions," have a causal role in adult psychopathology. As in "Draft K," however, he registered his strong doubt that this proposal entirely exhausted the matter. He noted, for instance, that many *nonneurotic* adults recall supposed childhood "seductions." Even so, he dodged the need to decide how much weight should be given to the recollections of neurotics *or* nonneurotics: whether memories of childhood sexual experiences do or could become conscious at all is, he says, "a fresh problem we shall prudently avoid."

Perhaps because of Freud's irresolutions—or because the positive aetiological hypothesis he did offer was so dramatic, despite his stated reservations—Freud's listeners were, he believed, not at all impressed by his lecture. In a letter to Fliess after the meeting, Freud reported that his talk "was given an icy reception by the asses and a strange evaluation by Krafft-Ebing." Though Krafft-Ebing could not have known about the titling of the textual basis of Freud's lecture, the "Christmas Fairy Tale" sent privately to Fliess, his comment cut to the quick, dismissing Freud's work in a single sentence: "It sounds like a scientific fairy tale" [*Es klingt wie ein wissenschaftliches Märchen*], he pronounced caustically (Freud 1985: 184 [April 26, 1896]). A few months later, Freud read Konrad Rieger's description of his work as "a simply dreadful 'old wives' psychiatry.' " He embellished this in a letter to Fliess as "gruesome, horrible, old wives' psychiatry" (Freud 1985: 202 [November 2, 1896]; see Masson 1985: 203 n. 3). Much the same charge would be leveled against Freud in 1905 on the publication of the Dora case, written in 1901 (Freud 1905e; see Decker 1977: 164–65). But by this point, Freud could act as if he were merely "amused" by such opinions.

As Jeffrey Masson has noted, in 1896 Freud probably felt that Krafft-Ebing's response was "strange" because the older psychiatrist's own writings—such as the ninth edition of his *Psychopathia Sexualis* (1894), which Freud owned in a copy inscribed to him from the author—implied his familiarity with evidence for sexual seductions in childhood (Masson 1985: 218–19). Krafft-Ebing, then, must have objected less to Freud's empirical assertions about the incidence of seduction—he himself accepted them—than to Freud's claim for an aetiological link between childhood seduction and later pathology. But it is "strange," in turn, that Krafft-Ebing did not notice or appreciate Freud's own stated reservations about this link, first developed in "Draft K"; admittedly they were somewhat buried in the middle of the lecture.[3]

"Fairy tale," "old wives' psychiatry"—from 1886 through 1905 and beyond, Freud's hypotheses about the archaic stages of individual development had, he retrospectively imagined, been frequently equated with discredited folk theories about the mind. Indeed, though Freud made a show of shrugging off the parallel between his own and "old wives' " psychiatry, if the Wolf Man's Christmas fairy tale was a nightmare—"in great terror, evidently of being eaten up by the wolves, I screamed and woke up" (29)—by the time he came to write out the Wolf Man's case history in 1914, Freud's own "fairy tale" had become a nightmare too. In *On the History of the Psycho-Analytic Movement*, prepared in 1914 as the polemical counterpart to the case history, Freud recalled the "icy" reception he had received from his colleagues in 1896:

> I treated my discoveries as ordinary contributions to science and hoped they would be received in the same spirit. But the silence which my communications met with, the void which formed itself about me, the hints that were conveyed to me, gradually made me realize that assertions on the part played by sexuality in the aetiology of the neuroses cannot count upon meeting with the same treatment as other communications. I understood that from now onwards I was one of those who had "disturbed the sleep of the world," as Hebbel says. (Freud 1914d: 21)

In these sentences in the *History,* Freud conveniently forgot that he, too, had come to reject the assertions about sexuality sketched in the lecture of 1896; in 1896, by the term *Sexualität* he had meant actual childhood sexual experiences and seductions rather than the fantasies and defenses proposed in his later, more general *Sexualtheorie* or *"theory of* sexuality" (i.e., a causal analysis and explanation of "sexuality," not identical with the phenomenon itself). Moreover, it was part of Freud's story of his own work—part of the fairy tale, myth, or what Sulloway (1979), following Ellenberger (e.g., 1993), has called the "legend" of psychoanalysis—that he was isolated by his scientific contemporaries and professional competitors. There was indeed strong criticism of aspects of Freud's publications. But many works were favorably received in important journals, and he had influential defenders. In general, a systematic study of the pattern of reviewing of Freud's work does not support his extreme characterization (see Decker 1977). The hostile reception of the "fairy tale" of sexuality, then, was a "sexuality" of Freud's own—a fantasy about and defense against perceived threats and the frustration of desires.

In "Draft K" and his public lecture, Freud had already perceived a void in his existing account of sexuality. By maintaining but nonetheless mentioning a "prudent" silence about the mechanisms of the recall of sexual memories, he hinted at still *other* fairy tales somewhere behind or beyond the "Christmas Fairy Tale" of literal seduction, subsequent "repression," and resulting pathology. Even so, the Wolf Man's fairy-tale associations to the Christmas Eve dream could not have failed to remind Freud of his own "Christmas Fairy Tale." As we have seen, however, these associations were not yet available to Freud to underwrite his early "conviction" about the dream and his apparent acceptance of the drawing as its direct "confirmation." Rather, the drawing itself seemingly appeared to him as the fairy tale behind the fairy tales that the Wolf Man would shortly associate with the dream and the drawing—necessarily reminding Freud of his own "Christmas" and "scientific" fairy tales of 1896—which Freud would then investigate precisely for "some other fairy tale" behind them.

That *other* fairy tale—the fairy tale behind the tale of seduction, repression, and pathology—had emerged in Freud's work between 1896 and 1910 on the constitutive role of infantile and childhood sexual fantasy in the formation of neurosis. The drawing perhaps secured Freud's "conviction" about the dream because it was indeed the "correction" of the dream: for Freud, it may have directly visualized—it pictorially realized—the very structure of the repression of endogenous, infantile sexual drives and fantasies of which the dream itself was supposedly the manifestation and of which the entire analysis, from the first consultation onward, was becoming Freud's "case," his example and proof.

IV

PICTURES FOR REPRESSION

I am tormented by the problem of how it will be possible to give a two-dimensional picture of anything that is so much of a solid as our theory of hysteria.

—Freud to Josef Breuer, May 26, 1892
(Freud 1941a: 147)

I was therefore obliged to put [this history] together from even smaller fragments than are usually at one's disposal for the purposes of synthesis. This task, which is not difficult in other respects, finds a natural limit when it is a question of forcing a structure which is itself in many dimensions on to the two-dimensional descriptive plane.

—Freud, "From the History of an Infantile Neurosis" (1918b: 72)

So it was that his mental life impressed one in much the same way as the religion of Ancient Egypt, which is so unintelligible to us because it preserves the earlier stages of its development side by side with the end-products, retains the most ancient gods and their attributes along with the most modern ones, and thus, as it were, spreads out upon a two-dimensional surface what other instances of evolution show us in the solid.

—Freud, "From the History of an Infantile Neurosis" (1918b: 119)

Now listen to this. During an industrious night last week, when I was suffering from that degree of pain which brings about the optimal condition for my mental activities, the barriers suddenly lifted,

> the veils dropped, and everything became transparent—from the details of the neuroses to the determinants of consciousness.
>
> —Freud to Wilhelm Fliess (Freud 1985: 146 [October 20, 1895])

In 1910, when the Wolf Man appeared for his first consultation, Freud depended on the models of the psychic apparatus which he had most fully expounded in the seventh chapter of *Die Traumdeutung,* published in November 1899 with the date of 1900 (Freud 1900a). There he provided literally "the most general schematic picture of the psychic apparatus" (Fig. 30) (Freud 1900a: 537). Freud's diagram depicts the temporal sequence and the direction of nervous "excitation," anchored in perceptual stimuli (W = *Wahrnehmungen*), passing through the system from perception at one end to motor activities at the other. As the overall structure of the diagram implies, "reflex processes remain the model of every psychic function" (ibid.: 538).

Freud supposed that the psychic apparatus will retain traces of "the perceptions which impinge on it" (ibid.)—what he calls memory traces (*Erinnerungsspuren*) (Fig. 31). Because one system cannot simultaneously admit modification through perception *and* preserve modifications in memory—a basic rule of Freud's entire psychology—a *second* system must transform the momentary excitations of perception into the more permanent traces. The basic rule that one and the same psychic system cannot perform two functions applies here too. Perceptions occurring simultaneously in time are linked together in one memory trace; temporally disjunct perceptions linked by similarity and "other kinds of coincidence" are preserved in other memory traces (ibid.: 539). In his diagram, Freud represents three such *Erinnerungsspuren*. Implicitly there could be an indefinitely large series of them. Because perceptual excitation passing through the psychic apparatus cannot be transmitted and preserved by one and the same system, the system of memory traces must be nonconscious in relation to the terminus at which we are "conscious" of discharge—when we are aware of the motor, speech, or other acts devolving from the stimulations we have received. This nonconscious system is rep-

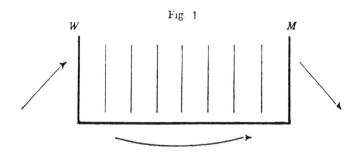

Figure 30. Freud, *Die Traumdeutung,* Fig. 1 (1900a)

resented in Freud's diagram as a set of lines branching off the main route of the arrow of excitation and discharge.

Having set up his general "schematic picture" of the psychic apparatus, Freud integrated his specific hypotheses concerning dreams, developed earlier in *Die Traumdeutung* in the chapter on the dreamwork (Fig. 32). In dreams, it seems, "two psychical agencies [exist], one of which sub-

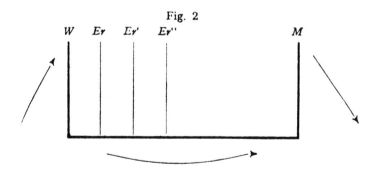

Figure 31. Freud, *Die Traumdeutung,* Fig. 2 (1900a)

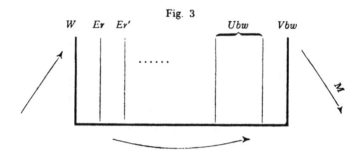

Figure 32. Freud, *Die Traumdeutung,* Fig. 3 (1900a)

mit[s] the activity of the other to a criticism which involve[s] its exclusion from consciousness" (ibid.: 540). In our daily waking life, Freud suggested, some perceptual stimulations reach consciousness and voluntary movement without any deviations. This energy is routed through the psychic system which is closest to the terminus of discharge—or, to put the same point in terms of the general "schematic picture" (Fig. 31), the system which is least affected by the branching or siphoning off of psychic energy into permanent memory traces. This system for the temporary holding of the energy derived from stimulation and its routing toward an ultimate discharge is called the "preconscious" (*Vorbewusstsein*). Only that energy routed from the main arrow toward discharge into permanent traces, branching off the main arrow, actually constitutes the "unconscious" (*Unbewusstsein*).

In this light (Figs. 31, 32), we can define the "unconscious" as the system branching off the route toward the ultimate discharge. It is the system of branched- or siphoned-off—and to that extent pooled or stored-up—psychic energy. Since the only outlet for the branched-off, pooled-up energy of the "unconscious" lies through the system closest to the terminus, the "preconscious," the preconscious—just because not all energy can be discharged all at once—can be said to exert a "criticism" of and control upon the unconscious.[1]

In turn, the dreamwork becomes a special instance of these relations. In sleep, stimulations received during the preceding day are working their way, as it were, toward discharge; they are preconscious thoughts close to the main route of discharge in the preconscious system. Nearby unconscious thoughts might be attached to them, presumably through similarity or "other kinds of coincidence" (ibid.: 542); therefore they too tend toward discharge. But because motor or speech activity (as Freud incorrectly believed) is impossible during sleep, discharge of the preconscious and unconscious thoughts can supposedly involve only a vivid sensory hallucination. In other words, in dreams excitation is "moving backwards" in the psychic apparatus, or "regressing" (ibid.), *from* the motor terminus *to* the perceptual terminus; in sleep, the perceptual terminus has supposedly become the only available terminus of discharge. To that extent the dreamwork retraces the sequence in which permanent memory traces branched off from the main route of discharge. In the process of discharging the dream-thoughts, it follows, more permanent and earlier memory traces will be attached to, or transcribed into, them; the dreamwriting as it were picks up and carries with it material already written on the medium. Therefore the resulting dream, Freud could say, manifests "unconscious" material.[2]

The "Schemas" and the "Architecture" of Sexuality

In 1910, and certainly in 1899, as the explanations in *Die Traumdeutung* suggest, Freud conceived his diagrammatic pictures as schemas for the organization of the psyche—with its "copious and intertwined associative links" (Freud 1900a: 191)—as a branching network of mental contents and associations. In the most significant precursor to the "Christmas Fairy Tale," for example, the untitled manuscript of September and October 1895 now known as the *Project for a Scientific Psychology,* Freud considered the case of a patient, "Emma," who came to therapy suffering from an inability to shop for clothes by herself (Fig. 33) (Freud 1950: 353–56; a superb and detailed discussion of Freud's sources and procedures in this kind of analysis, rooted in germ theory, has been presented by Carter 1980 and especially by Macmillan 1990, 1992). Freud connects her present fear with two memory systems. One is a more recent memory of Emma, at the age of twelve, being mocked on account of her clothes by two shop assistants, one of whom attracts her. The other is a complex of earlier, more disturbing memories: at the age of eight, Emma's genitals were fondled through her clothes by a shopkeeper, but despite this unpleasant experience, she returned to his shop a second time.

Freud pictured the entire set of relations as a set of interconnected nodes

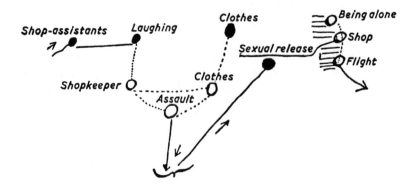

Figure 33. Freud, diagram of the structure of Emma's "hysterical repression" (1895)

(see Freud and Breuer 1895d: 298–90). Left and right in the diagram indicate the begining and end of a transmission of psychic energy (see Figs.
30–32), while up and down indicate the relative antiquity of the memory
traces. Although Freud was "tormented by the problem of how it will be
possible to give a two-dimensional picture of anything that is so much
of a solid as our theory of hysteria" (Freud 1941a: 147), his graphic schema
conjoins established conventions for diagramming transmissions, waves,
or reflexes in psychics, mechanics, and psychophysics (left to right is always the start to finish of a process) and conventions for diagramming
stratigraphy in archaeology or an architectural elevation (the lowest level
is always the first to be deposited). Needless to say, however, when the
two temporalities—on the one hand, the ongoing *discharge* of an excitation, and on the other, the ongoing *deposition* of a system of memories—
have been superimposed in a single visualization, it is difficult to say exactly what and where the particular traumatic cause of Emma's phobia
might be. Indeed, we should probably say that Emma is ill in, or as, her
Nachträglichkeit as such, the delayed impact of her memories, *as a whole*—
not in or at any particular node along the way (see further Laplanche
1976: 41–42; Møller 1991: 70–73).

Freud's diagram of Emma's case (Fig. 33) clearly depended on widely
known graphic conventions. But it also assumed his own earlier *Sexualschema* or "schematic diagram" for sexuality (Figs. 34, 35), a visualization
apparently formulated in early January of 1895.[3] This diagram maps the
entire reflex arc from a sexually appealing perception, entering the system

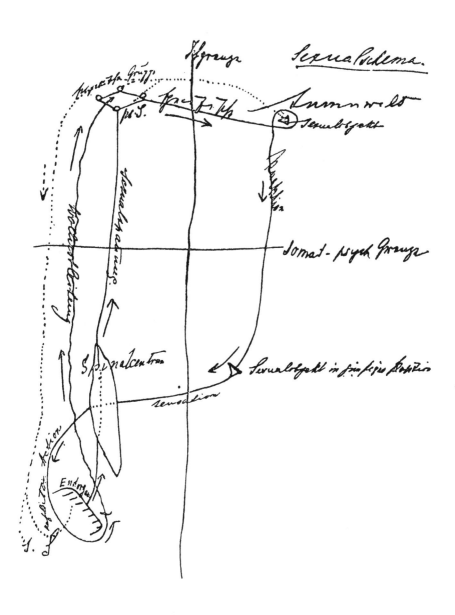

Figure 34. Freud's *Sexualschema* (1895)

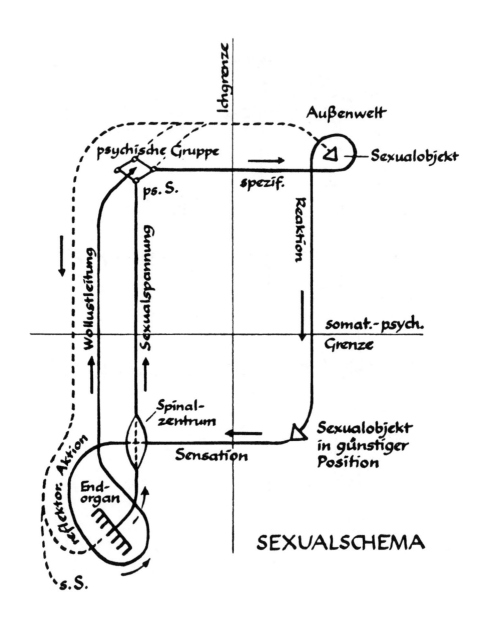

Figure 35. Transcription of Freud's *Sexual-schema* by Gerhard Fichtner (Freud 1986)

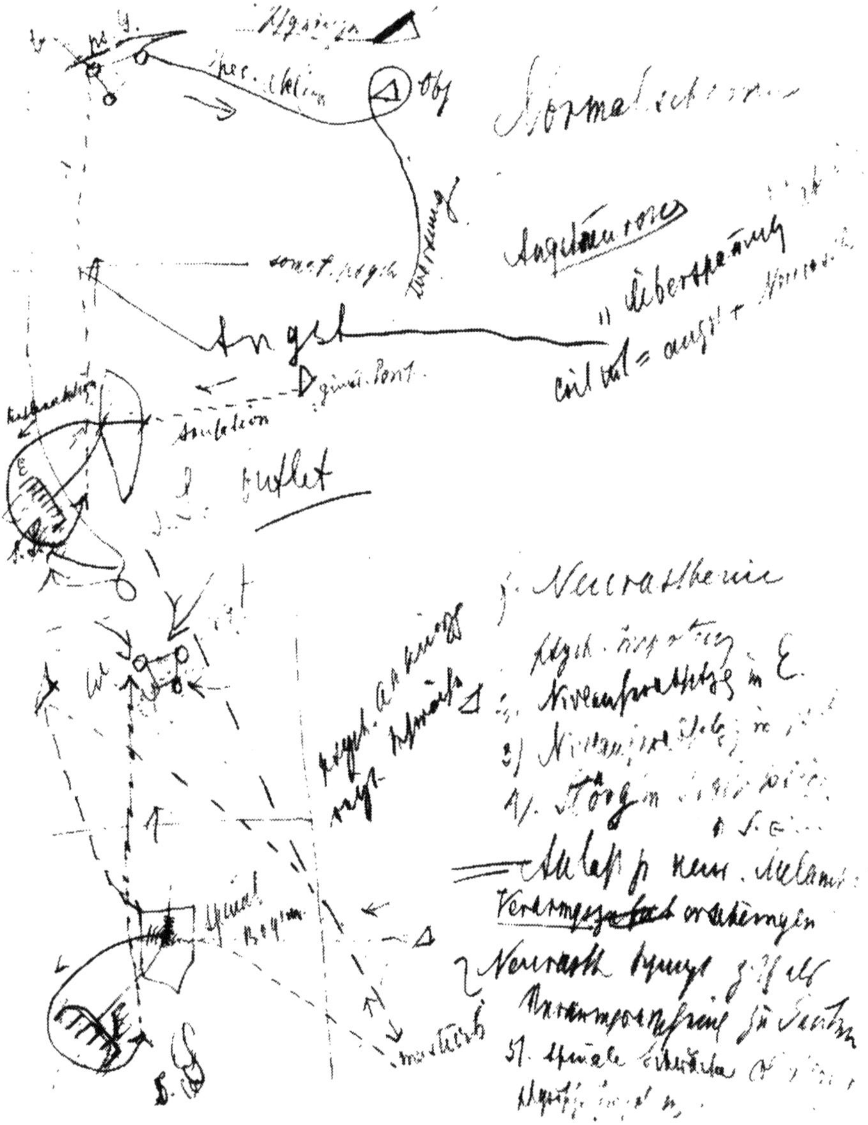

Figure 36. Freud's *Normalschema für Hysterie und Neurasthenie* (1895)

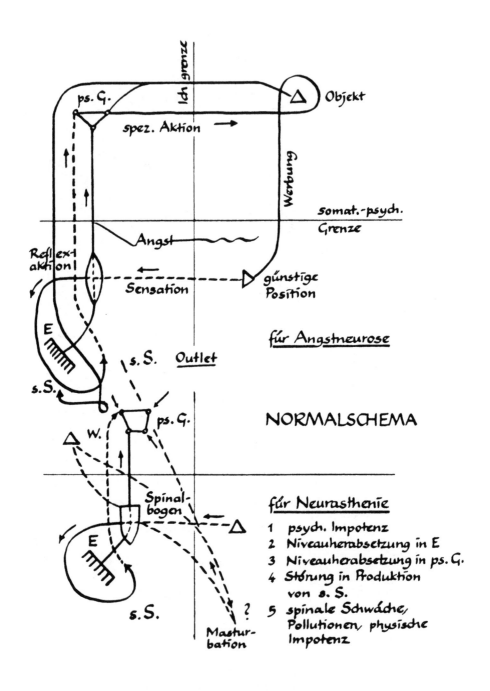

Figure 37. Transcription of Freud's *Normal-schema* by Gerhard Fichtner (Freud 1986)

on the left, to the ultimate partial discharge of these perceptions on the right. Emma's problem would seem to be the dislocation and disturbance of the *Sexualschema*. In her hysterical repression, the arrow of discharge has been skewed by one branching-off too many—an example of the general possibility Freud visualized in a more complex and as it were "theoretical" diagram accompanying the *Sexualschema* which he labeled the *Normalschema* for "anxiety neurosis" and "neurasthenia" (Figs. 36–37).[4]

If the diagram of Emma's repression and the *Sexualschema* and *Normalschema* are any guides (Figs. 33–37), hysteria must be like a building falling down as fast as it is being erected, though it must also have some constant (the earlier) bricks (Figs. 30–32) (cf. Laplanche 1989: 60–61). Freud schematically generalized this "Architecture of Hysteria" in a letter to Fliess written on May 25, 1897, containing a short essay with this title (Fig. 38) (Freud 1985: 245–48; also Freud 1950: 250–53). In his diagram, Freud depicted the variously older and younger memory traces in the network as they have become attached to a patient's present-day symptoms, represented by little triangles like flowers or turrets. William McGrath (1986: 191–94) has suggested that the diagram replicated the architecture of medieval German towns as Freud might have known them or had seen them illustrated in early modern prints. Equally likely, the diagram simply assumed the psychophysical and archaeo-architectural conventions mentioned already—but certainly the visual implication of a fortresslike structure, if McGrath is right, was consistent with Freud's emphasis on the "neuro-psychoses of defence" (Freud 1894a, 1896a).

The diagram represents the analyst's work by broken lines making "repeated loops through the background thoughts of the same symptoms." In the eighth such loop, the analyst and patient—joint historians of the patient's memory—are supposed to be connecting the deepest, oldest thoughts to the most recent symptom. Like an archaeologist descending the strata of an excavation, or a restoration worker descending the facade of a building from above, they climb down the memory system and climb out again—the up-and-down movement represented in the diagram.

But there are really *two* left/right movements here. In its own properly temporal development, the memory system was laid down, from left to right, as stimulations impinging on proprioception; these were selected, delayed, and diffused by the systems of consciousness; ultimately they will be either "repressed" or "discharged." (In this respect, the diagram is identical to, but more general than, the case pictured in Freud's diagram of Emma's hysterical repression [Fig. 33].) In their review of this history, however, the analyst and patient move *from* the right (the present position of contemporary repressions and discharge) *to* the left (the past history of stimulations and delay). In view of Freud's long-standing, but often buried, identification of psychoanalysis and Talmudic or cabbalistic interpretation, it is perhaps significant that in the diagram the writing supposedly produced or guided by the analyst has (like Hebrew) to be read from right to left (see further Bakan 1958). But this particular point of reference is not absolutely necessary: Freud also knew, for example, that Egyptian hieroglyphs should be read from the direction toward which the ideogrammatic figures are facing (he was interested in learning about hieroglyphs at least as early as the late 1890s, when he probably acquired two books on Egyptian by E. A. Wallis Budge [1895, 1896]) and that a left-handed engraver cuts the plate working from the edge that his hand does not cover, that is, from the right.

In the same year that he drafted the "Architecture of Hysteria," in fact, Freud expressed interest in the "bimanuality" of Leonardo da Vinci—that left-handedness or ambidextrousness often thought to have helped him produce his extraordinary mirror writing (Freud 1985 [October 9, 1898]). This was actually a way of calling attention to the artist's ambiguous sexuality. At this time, both Fliess and Freud were intrigued by the possibility that bimanuality was the somatic correlate of psychosexual "bisexuality." Leonardo's writing was literally preposterous, putting before or in front what should come after or behind. In medieval semiotics, Renaissance rhetoric, and eighteenth-century comments on morals and manners, preposterousness was the most general condition—both physical and "grammatical"—of all supposed sodomies in sex, dress, or comportment; for an eighteenth-century British traditionalist, for example, the sight of men kissing other men was appalling because "under this Pretext vile Catamites make their preposterous Addresses, even in the very streets" (Anonymous 1740: 12). We must return to the potentially troubling implications, possibly embedded in Freud's diagram, of identifying the analyst's investigations—his "writing"—with the sodomite's activities; we have already seen that the Wolf Man himself would dramatically raise the issue: in the first consultation, he wanted "to use [Freud] from behind."

In mapping the present history of analysis (from right to left) onto or over the past history of repression (from left to right), Freud's diagram suggests that psychoanalytic interpretation can literally or materially *recover* what the patient's history contains. Its image of a counterwriting—the red, broken lines traveling back over the path of the black, solid lines— leaves little room for the possibility that the present work of psychoanaly-

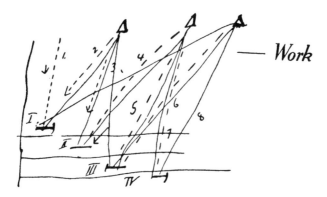

Figure 38. Freud's diagram of the "Architecture of Hysteria" (1897)

sis, from "right" to "left," must have its *own* history of stimulation, selection, delay, diffusion, repression, and discharge from "left" to "right."
The diagram does not show that what would seem to be the *review* of
repression—a reading from right to left of what was written left to right—
is in itself actually a *repetition* of repression, a writing that is *always going
only from left to right,* from initial stimulation to ultimate discharge.

To put the point another way, the diagram does not complete its own
implicit argument. The "deepest, oldest" thoughts of the patient, to be
recovered by the analyst, have been positioned by Freud in the lower left
corner of the diagram. The "deepest, oldest" thoughts of the analyst, then,
must be positioned in the *upper right* corner—that is, in the lower left
corner if and when the page is turned upside down. Regarded this way,
the diagram of the "architecture of hysteria" potentially represents *two*
separate diagrams of "hysterical" repression—one mapping the patient's
thoughts and symptoms and the other mapping the analyst's thoughts and
symptoms—turned upside down in relation to one another and superimposed. Freud seems to have partially recognized this meaning: he did distinguish two writings within the diagram, with the black, solid lines used
to represent the patient's history and the red, broken lines used to represent the history of the analytic interpretation itself. But in 1897 he had not
yet developed a comprehensive theory to describe and explain the relations between the two. The schema, precisely because it is a schema, substantially preceded the theory of transference and countertransference.

Despite its ambiguity, Freud's schema does strongly suggest that there is some kind of systematic relationship between the two separate diagrams, turned upside down in relation to one another and superimposed—or between the two writings, the patient's and the analyst's. Visually the red and the black writings seem literally to thread through one another. The very fact of graphic superimposition, in other words, suggests that a *third,* independently meaningful writing emerges from the overgridding of the two underlying writings; black and red together constitute the specifically psychoanalytic or intersubjective "work"—a black-and-red writing, as it were. But graphically the superimposition of the two underlying writings can occur only when the two separate diagrams are inscribed on wholly transparent pages; for, again in wholly graphic terms, if one diagram (oriented upside down in relation to the other) were merely placed on top of the other, rather than allowing the other still to show through, it might actually block the other out.

Freud's graphic schema handles this problem by implying that the analyst's (red) writing reviews the patient's (black) writing by being, in two dimensions, *beside* and, in three dimensions, *behind* or *on top of* it. The two sets of lines running parallel with one another are evidently intended to suggest (following established graphic conventions in the pictorial representation of functions on the x/y axes) that they are somehow regularly related, that the one actually *transcribes* or *translates* the other rather than *merely* parallels it. But Freud cannot have his cake and eat it too. If the two writings are superimposed (and thus potentially blocking each other out), they cannot be beside each other, and if they are beside each other (and thus potentially translating each other), they cannot be superimposed: in the psychoanalytic "work" or joint historical investigation of patient and analyst, one has either complete repetition in which meaningful review cannot occur, or complete review in which meaningful repetition cannot occur.

It is not surprising, then, that Freud's diagram avoids filling in the complete picture of the analyst's position in relation to the patient's. To do so fully would visually indicate the disjunctive connection—the loss or gap between the two writings—that would belie Freud's explicit claim, in explaining the diagram, that the patient and analyst working together "make *repeated* loops through the *background* thoughts of the *same* symptoms" (my emphasis). Freud clearly means his viewer to understand the red lines simultaneously repeating and reviewing the black lines to be marks which merely clarify, correct, and improve them. According to graphic convention, the analyst's writings are *editorial* comments, as it were, on the patient's writing, even though they must also be wholly transparent to or translations of it. (They are, after all, *broken* lines. According to graphic convention, they are not dominant or independent functions but subordinate and attendant ones. But if the analyst's writing is merely dependent and partial, how does it succeed in reviewing or reading the patient's writing? How does the editor help without *rewriting*?) Because the editorial comments are supposedly repetitions and reviews without repression, there is no need to represent the position from which they are derived— namely, the analyst's deep or old memory system (in a lower left corner) and its contemporary manifestation of symptoms (in an upper right corner), turned upside down and superimposed on the position, the patient's, that we are actually shown. The analyst's red writing is, as it were, evenly hovering right beside, behind, or on top of the patient's black writing, as if it is nothing but a free-floating attention to it—an editing without a rewriting, a redrawing without an erasing, a "work" without origins or symptoms of its own. If we accept the physical and psychophysical concept of *Werk*, it is a wholly forceless force; if we accept the cultural concept, it is a wholly nonauthoritative, authorless representation.

A schema such as Freud's tendentious visualization of the "architecture of hysteria" and the "work" of psychoanalysis succeeds partly because a viewer does not quite know which established graphic conventions to apply to it. Presumably, in fact, it has been composed creatively in the diagrammer's unique combination or superimposition of conventions. We end up applying several potentially incompatible codes—the conventions of physics and mechanics; of archaeology and architecture; of the orthography of Latin or German and the orthography of Hebrew or Egyptian; of geometry and optics; of the representation of solids and the representation of surfaces; of drawing opacity and drawing transparency; of palimpsest and pentimento; of mapping and surveying; or of handwriting and rewriting or reading and proofreading themselves. In fact, no single set of such conventions enables us to grasp Freud's schema. Taken too far or in isolation, each set is inconsistent with the logic or argument Freud hopes to achieve; each must be applied in a partial way.

The Disanalogies

Later on, Freud related two physical models to the psychic apparatus and its psychoanalysis—the telephone (Freud 1912b) and the so-called mystic writing-pad (Freud 1925a). These models were explicitly developed by Freud as analogies for psychic phenomena he was attempting to describe; they were not organizing schemas, like the diagrams we have just surveyed, which Freud simply assumed—and may or may not have expected his viewer-readers to recognize—from various fields of graphic production in science and the arts. Freud partly selected his explicit analogies for the psyche and its psychoanalysis—such as the telephone, "mystic writing-pad," or archaeological excavation—in order for his readers to derive information from the obvious *disanalogy* in each case, which he carefully indicates.

For example, Freud's well-known—and much overdone—analogy between the history of the mind and the history of the city of Rome, developed most extensively in *Civilization and Its Discontents* (Freud 1930a: 60–63), was based on his own long-standing acquaintance with the city (see Grigg 1973) and familiarity with the excavated layout of Pompeii (see Tögel 1989). But in pointing to these sites, Freud wanted principally to show that the history of the mind has a property that the archaeology of Rome, as it is conventionally or could practically be mapped, drawn, or described, does *not* have. (Indeed, as his footnote indicates, Freud had a particular description of Rome in mind, namely, Hugh Last's [1928] famous analysis of "The Founding of Rome," the reconstructions in which were only partly "archaeological"—for Last also extensively used textual sources precisely because the archaeology was so partial and discontinuous.) In the mind, supposedly all of the traces of the past are simultaneously present at once, without disappearance or loss, though they must be distributed at different points or nodes in a differentiated structure. Though archaeologists sometimes represent two or more temporal phases of a construction on the same plan, it is impossible, as Freud recognizes, to be complete: at some point, the later features, as the draftsman draws them, must dislocate, occlude, or even obliterate the earlier—just that deletion Freud claims does *not* characterize the mind. Indeed, when the archaeologist digs a site, the stratigraphic levels must progressively be destroyed, removed to be preserved in a museum, or represented in photographic, written, or other form of documentation. The archaeological analogy for psychoanalysis, in other words, only "shows us how far we are from mastering the characteristics of mental life by representing them in pictorial terms" (Freud 1930a: 62).

Various commentators notwithstanding, Freud's "archaeological" metaphor asks us to imagine psychoanalysis as an archaeology that does not actually exist. (The best treatments are by Anzieu 1986: 182–212; Bowie

1987: 14–44; and Møller 1991: 31–56.) Indeed, psychoanalysis is an imaginary archaeology which could make sense only on the model of still *other* practices which Freud does not describe but simply takes up from earlier investigations and inventions such as the "Architecture of Hysteria" (Fig. 38)—for example, the mapping that keeps track of the excavation, the collecting that preserves the remains, the restoration that returns them to their "original" condition, and the written description that collects together what must remain physically discrete. None of these practices is inherent in any archaeology as such, but at least some of them must be its enabling conditions.

Despite claims to the contrary, the archaeological metaphor, then, does not really organize Freud's picture of psychoanalysis. (In my view, this also holds for Freud's analogy of the "mystic writing-pad" [Freud 1925a], though here the disanalogy with the mind is somewhat less pronounced. The analogy of the telephone approaches the condition of the schemas—it embodies Freud's basic assumptions and relays his own image and fantasy of his endeavor—but it is not especially prominent in the explicit text of Freud's metapsychology.) Rather, Freud's metaphors for psychoanalysis—founded in part on more basic schemas he does not deliberately or explicitly identify in his theoretical writing—organize his picture of archaeology. Explicit analogies are, to use Freud's own words, limited and superficial—an "idle game" (Freud 1930a: 62); they are just as subject to the truly organizing schemas as the rest of his text. Here I am interested in these organizing schemas: they render Freud's text intelligible or unintelligible, as the case may be, in the first place.

Association and Neuronal Structure

In the ambiguous visualization and tendentious explication of relations among mental contents, Freud's work of the late 1880s and earlier 1890s was decisive. During these years he completed two detailed monographs on the pathological organization of perception, thought, and motor activity in aphasia (Freud 1891; cf. 1990a) and cerebral palsy (Freud 1897a). These works made his neurological reputation. Two samples of his model building must suffice here.

Following Carl Wernicke (Wernicke 1967: 40–42), Freud schematized the principal aphasias as the two "center aphasias," namely, a sensory aphasia afflicting the perceptual nerve pathways and a motor aphasia afflicting the motor nerve pathways (Fig. 39). By contrast, the "conduction

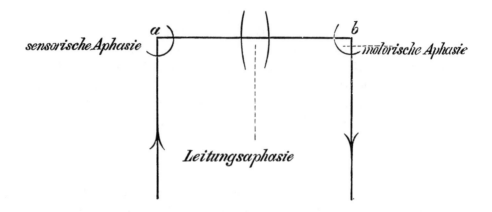

Figure 39. Freud, diagram of the organization of aphasia (1891)

aphasias" (*Leitungsaphasie*)—"confusion of words and uncertainty in their
use"—afflict a central, interior area of the mind (Freud 1891b: 5). The
similarity to the later diagrams in *Die Traumdeutung* (Figs. 30–32) should
be obvious.

Later in the monograph on aphasia, Freud schematized the analysis of
words as "complicated concept[s]" (Fig. 40) (Freud 1891b: 47). The schema
underlies what he would later say in *Die Traumdeutung* about association
in the primary process. The word concept consists, he supposed, of two
complexes of mental images. The first, the sound-image of the word, consists of the associations with the word as it can be felt when it is spoken
aloud (a kinesthetic image), as it can be printed, and as it can be scripted.
The second, the complex of object associations, associates the sound-image with perceptual images of the object, with visual images of it pre-
dominating. The sound-image is relatively closed and stable, represented
in the diagram by the closed loop. But the largely visual object associations
are depicted in the diagram as branching out open-endedly as new perceptual impressions are added and associations continually forged.

The very structure of Freud's schemas for mental concepts ("word concepts") (Fig. 40), hysterical repression and distortion (Figs. 33–38), and
for the psychic apparatus (Figs. 30–32) all imply that Freud considered
psychological relations to have a neurological basis and reality. Ultimately
the branching network of concepts should be explicable as the neuronal
network itself.[5]

Nerve processes had been studied and drawn by Freud himself all

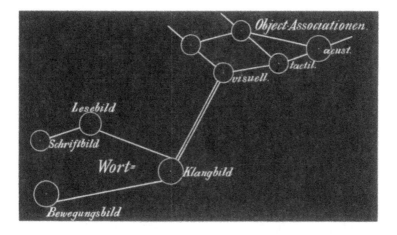

Figure 40. Freud, diagram of the "word
concept" in aphasia (1891)

through his twenties, from 1876 to 1886, though his bad drawings were
mocked by his friends (Anzieu 1986: 285). (The subjective object considered in this study is clearly connected at various points to Freud's many
anxieties and rivalries; in the "Botanical Monograph" dream, the monograph recalled to Freud the drawings he had made [Freud 1900a: 172].)
For example, in one of his first scientific publications, of 1878, originally
a presentation (probably illustrated) at Brücke's Physiological Institute in
Vienna on July 18, 1878, Freud made a "complete survey of the spinal gan-
glia of *Petromyzon,*" a species of suckfish. He depicted what he described
as the "T-shaped branching of the [nerve] fibres"—so-called "fibres of passage" and "subsidiary fibres" and other complex neuronal ramifications
(Fig. 41) (Freud 1878; see Freud 1897b: 228–30 for summaries of his other
papers on "The Structure of the Elements of the Nervous System," as he
titled a lecture at the Psychiatric Society in 1882). We can readily compare
Die Traumdeutung's "discharge" through the "preconscious" and the "permanent memory traces" (Figs. 30–32) with this representation. The results of the *Petromyzon* research established an important biological analogy invoked in Freud's later considerations of other psychic processes (see
Freud 1916x: 340).

To take a second example, in one of his last histological publications,
written in Paris while working with Jean-Martin Charcot, Freud concerned himself—as his graphic schema indicates—with the *Verbindungen,*
or "binding up," of the nerve bodies and fibers of the medulla oblongata

Figure 41. Freud, drawing of section of the spinal ganglion of *Petromyzon ammocoetes* (1878)

(Fig. 42) (Freud and Darkschewitsch 1886). As the diagram shows, supposedly nerves are materially "bound up" with one another.

As a *psychological* notion, however, *Verbindung* (or *Bindung*) and its cor-
relates—the flow, linkage, and discharge of psychic energy—presented many
logical difficulties. These were built into psychoanalytic psychology to
the extent that it always preserved Freud's underlying neurological imagery. Jacques Derrida (1978: 206) has succinctly identified the general
form of Freud's problem: the Freudian account of psychic defense requires,
or constructs, a psychic apparatus that is apparently nothing but a "weave
of pure traces." In Derrida's view, this model is the strength as much as
the drawback of the Freudian account of mental processes; for Derrida, it
offers a perspicuous image for both consciousness and textuality as such.
But one should not lose sight of the inherent paradox. What, or who, could
weave the "weave of pure traces" but yet another "trace"?

In his own way Freud was alert to this problem. The *Project* of September
and October 1895 exemplified the most central theoretical difficulty and
in some measure addressed it. What Freud here calls the "quantity" of
psychic energy impinging upon the psychic system must vary, as basic
psychophysics required, with the strength of the stimulus. In a purely
mechanical and energetic model of the mind, Freud deals with this varia-

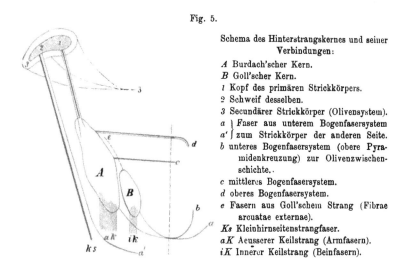

Fig. 5.

Schema des Hinterstrangskernes und seiner
Verbindungen:

A Burdach'scher Kern.
B Goll'scher Kern.
1 Kopf des primären Strickkörpers.
2 Schweif desselben.
3 Secundärer Strickkörper (Olivensystem).
a) Faser aus unterem Bogenfasersystem
a') zum Strickkörper der anderen Seite.
b unteres Bogenfasersystem (obere Pyra-
midenkreuzung) zur Olivenzwischen-
schichte.
c mittleres Bogenfasersystem.
d oberes Bogenfasersystem.
e Fasern aus Goll'schem Strang (Fibrae
arcuatae externae).
Ks Kleinhirnseitenstrangfaser.
aK Aeusserer Keilstrang (Armfasern).
iK Innerer Keilstrang (Beinfasern).

Figure 42. Freud, diagram for the "binding" of nerve fields in the medulla oblongata (1886)

tion by supposing not only that neurones "ramify" but also that they are differentially constructed: they possess what he calls "thicker or thinner" branches or paths (Freud 1950: 314). He devised a basic branching diagram to express this concept (Fig. 43). Here, one quantity of energy (1Q) entering the neurone will be completely transmitted on pathway I to the terminus of the system, the connection with another neurone (at alpha). Pathways II and III remain inert. A quantity of energy twice as great as the first (2Q) will transfer along pathways I and II to both alpha and beta. And a quantity three times as great (3Q) will transfer along all three pathways, I, II, and III, to discharge at alpha, beta, and gamma. The principle is the same as that operating at a highway toll booth: more lanes open up to handle more incoming cars at the same rate of flow achieved with fewer lanes and fewer cars.

One must also, however, consider the "quality" of psychic energy on a scale from relatively pleasurable to relatively unpleasurable (Fig. 44); one of Freud's fundamental aims in the *Project* was to integrate the quantitative and qualitative perspectives, helping to push his psychophysics toward a "psychology." According to Freud's second diagram, a pleasurable sensation discharges itself in direct, full fashion, passing from neurone a to b

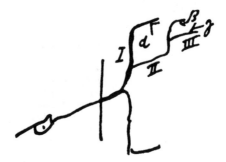

Figure 43. Freud, diagram
of the "contact barrier" and
the binding of psychic
"quantity" (1895)

and so on. By contrast, direct and full discharge of an *un*pleasurable sensation would supposedly do damage to the organism. Unpleasurable sen-
sations, then, are diffused by being partly siphoned off along alternate
pathways—represented in the diagram by the loop of neurones alpha-beta-
gamma-delta.

Freud's technical term for this movement was "lateral binding" (translated in the *Standard Edition* as "cathexis"). It assumes "statically charged
(cathected) neurones branching off from the main channel, which are
thus in a state of enhanced readiness for the transmission of current"
(Holt 1989: 80). Such "laterally-bound" loops supposedly become locali-

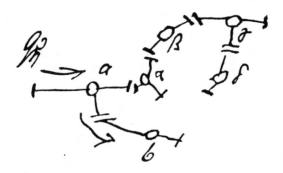

Figure 44. Freud, diagram of the "contact barrier" and the "lateral binding"
of psychic "quality" (1895)

ties of siphoned-off or reserved unpleasure which "defend" the psychic apparatus from the damaging unpleasurable discharge. And apparently this system, once it has been established, exerts an inhibiting effect on discharge—and guards against excessive unpleasurable discharge—simply by "surrounding" other neurones and partly absorbing their (unpleasurable) transmissions. As Robert L. Holt has observed, Freud's notion seems to imply that "perhaps *all* the ego neurones are lateral to one another after all, which would be topologically *possible,* granted sufficient arborization of dendrites" (Holt 1989: 83, my emphasis). In other words, Freud's "theoretical" model of physical-psychological process generalized far beyond the actual phenomena of neuronal *Verbindung* that could be observed in anatomical and histological studies (Figs. 41, 42)—for one of the very aims of the contemporary anatomical and histological study of the nervous system was, of course, to *disentangle* nerve processes and establish their many and separable if interacting routes in and through the spinal cord, lower brain, and cortex. (Freud himself had provided an exemplary and innovative account of neuronal distinction and ramification in the cortical masses in his anonymously published article "The Brain" [Freud 1990b].) The most innovative neurology of the day—John Hughlings Jackson's (1884) neuroevolutionary hypothesis, to which Freud was intellectually responsive despite his training under the more conventional Theodore Meynert (Andersson 1962: 70)—required strict attention to the different rates and periods at which the interacting components of the nervous system developed. Again, one could grasp the apparently total nervous *Verbindung* only as a specific stratigraphy of individual, separable, evolving *Verbindungen* and, equally important, gaps between or fissures in developmentally emergent masses of functionally coherent *Verbindung*.

A total "arborization of the dendrites" would seem, in fact, to be inconsistent with the very concept of *Verbindung*. But paradoxically, Freud's concept of a total—or at least a comparatively extensive—*Verbindung* requires what Holt (1989: 83) delicately calls a "sufficient" arborization of the dendrites. From Freud in "The Brain" (1990b), "The Neuro-Psychoses of Defence" (1894a), *The Project for a Scientific Psychology* ([1895] 1950), and *Die Traumdeutung* (1900a) to Jean Laplanche in *Life and Death in Psychoanalysis* (1976) and Gilles Deleuze and Felix Guattari in *A Thousand Plateaus* (1987), the question of the "arborization" of the nervous/psychic system—its relative interramification and "totalization" in *Verbindung,* of a topography of "lateralization" versus intrinsic dispersal—has been the most fundamental and most troubling theoretical (we might say architectural) image in Freudian metapsychology.

One problem first appeared to Freud as a straightforward bioanatomical question, to be resolved by the careful histological techniques Freud himself helped to pioneer (Freud 1884a, 1884b, 1990b: 52–55). But it was never, of course, really such: the entirely theoretical Cartesian concept of the reflex (Descartes 1649) applied to the raw material of the more or less coherent brain mass required one to ask how the nervous mass could be differentiated *such that* reflex (or "reflex-arcs") could exist at all. Even disposing of the psychophysical reflexology and macroscopic neuro-anatomy altogether, as some contemporary psychoanalysts would hope to do (e.g., Laplanche 1989), the question—precisely because it is and always was a philosophical one—must persist as a purely psychological or even "linguistic" one about cognitive structure and history, about what Jacques Lacan, for example, calls the "sliding [*glissage*] of the signifier." Thus Freud's own visualizations of the structure of repression have been replicated in neo-Freudian cognitive inquiries such as Stanley Palombo's (1973) essay "The Associative Memory Tree." Because arborization, as Holt (1989: 106) notes, is a "quantitative, not an all-or-none, concept," finally one cannot avoid questions about the depth and origins of the roots, about the height and extensions of the branches, and about the coherence and differentiation of the neuronal/cognitive growth (see especially Weber 1982)—however easy, and misleading, it has been to speak of these processes merely as if they were indefinite, indeterminate, or interminable, that is, lacking a material structure and hence a "biology." Freud never lost sight of this stricture: the arborization of mental contents, as such or as a "total" theoretical possibility, is of virtually no interest to us, living, as we do, in some *specific* treehouse where one false step might be a fatal plunge.[6]

Agency and Biology

In keeping with their Cartesian origins, Freud's basic schemas for "lateral binding" (Figs. 43, 44) raise the fundamental question of homuncular or human agency—what, in "The Brain," he had called the "volition" and the "ethical considerations" which supposedly "complicate" (that is, materially ramify and differentiate) and perhaps even guide autonomic and unconscious reflex (Freud 1990b: 62–64). At the neuronal "contact barrier" itself—at the supposed point of contact between neurone a and neurone b (Fig. 43) or between neurone a and neurone alpha (Fig. 44)—the system must somehow know in advance whether the incoming quantity of energy, transmitted by neurone a, is pleasurable or unpleasurable. If the "contact barrier" exists somewhere deep *inside* the psychic apparatus, far removed from the initial impingement of stimuli, there seems to be no way for it to acquire this "knowledge": by the terms of the model itself, any unpleasurable sensation would not have been transferred to it, or "discharged," from a more forward neurone. The neurone might be placed at the integumental or proprioceptive *surface,* the "perceptual terminus" of *Die Traumdeutung,* including "inside" surfaces of the body such as the back of the mouth or the sensitive membrane and musculature of the rectum and sphincter; Freud's labeling system in the diagram (Fig. 44) does seem to denote the neurone closest to impinging stimulation. But here it would have to be equipped with antennae capable of detecting the "quality" of the stimulus approaching but not quite impinging on it; it must have a way to detect whether a pathway (such as I) should be opened up for direct transfer and full discharge of a pleasurable quality or an alternate pathway (such as II or III) provided to "defend" later neurones from an unpleasurable quality. (Phrased in terms of psychological rather than metapsychological categories, the embodied mind *asks* itself "to shit or not to shit?" "to suck or not to suck?" and so on, and *advises* itself of its answer—then discharged. These questions are asked and answered in or under—we could even say *by*—"repression," qua psychic agency, at least when a system of lateral *Verbindungen* has been developed from the "contact barriers." But the issue here is the very possibility of that agency.) It is not simply as if the highway tollgate has various lanes periodically opening up depending on the number of incoming vehicles. It is also as if all of these lanes are equipped in advance with sensors to distinguish among and control the relay of different types of vehicles. But whence this preternatural awareness—literally, this preposterous consciousness?

In 1895, Freud asserted that "it is easy to imagine how, with the help of a mechanism which draws the ego's attention to the imminent fresh cathexis of the hostile mnemic image, the ego can succeed in inhibiting the passage [of quantity] from a mnemic image to a release of unpleasure by a copious side-cathexis [lateral binding] which can be strengthened according to need" (Freud 1950: 324). Obviously, however, this phrasing just describes the phenomenon in question; it does not explain it. Whence this "attention"—this observing homunculus which detects or knows what it perceives and what to do about it—in a purely mechanical, energetic model of the mind?[7]

One possible answer struck Freud as feasible even at the time he was drafting the *Project.* But to develop it fully would require him to compro-

mise his mechanical, energetic model of an autonomous, indefinitely mo-
bile psychic energy. He would not definitively state it, in fact, until *Totem
and Taboo,* published in 1912, and the Wolf Man case history, drafted in
1914—probably because those texts reevoked the original notations and
visualizations (Figs. 43, 44) in a new interpretive context, emphasizing
less the problems of anatomy and structure and more the problems of
evolution and history. In the last surviving section of the *Project* of 1895
(a final part, possibly explaining the earlier models, is lost), Freud asked
how the "indications of quality"—as pleasurable or unpleasurable—"interest the psychic system in the [impinging] perception."

> [This interest *(Interesse)*] would seem to be the mechanism of psychical
> attention. I find it hard to give a mechanical (automatic) explanation of
> its origin. For that reason I believe that it is biologically determined—
> that is, that it has been left over in the course of psychical evolution
> because any other behavior by the psychic system has been excluded
> owing to the generation of unpleasure. (Freud 1950: 360)

In other words, a species that permitted the full, immediate discharge
of unpleasure could not survive—for at the same time as it experiences
total unpleasure, it is presumably being totally annihilated. "Attention
[i.e., the distinction of quality]," Freud concludes, "is biologically justi-
fied" (ibid.).

Despite the elegance of this solution, Freud was dissatisfied with it. He
must have seen how it compromised his seduction theory—and, later, any
purely ontogenetic history of subjectivity—by apparently locating the origins of pleasure and unpleasure, and, more important, the truly decisive
discrimination between them, in the history of the species. (In a highly
sophisticated study of the "division of attention," Teresa Brennan [1992:
83–124] notes that Freud assumed that the "energy" of attention must
derive from *within* the subject, that is, that he failed to entertain the ways
in which it could be *inter*subjectively produced. It is not possible to take
up this stimulating observation here beyond noting that although it may
help solve the "economic," it does not really address the "historical" problem.) Freud's enthusiasm for the biological explanation waxed and waned
through several letters to Fliess. But in "Draft K" of January 1, 1896, the
"Christmas Fairy Tale," he put phylogeny aside—as well as the rest of the
material inquiry initiated by the *Project,* drafted three months earlier—in
order to pursue the purely autonomous vicissitudes of ontogenetic "sexuality." But despite this psychological or "psychoanalytic" turn—psychoanalysis has carefully preserved it from contamination by the greater part

of Freud's work for the first half of his life—the biological explanation haunts the account, especially as it was embodied and continually relayed through Freud's thought in graphic, schematic form.

The Memory Tree of Repression

For the moment, we can propose that the first element in Freud's subjective object in or as the Wolf Man's drawing of his dream was simply the associative memory tree of repression as Freud himself had schematized it. Whether conceived materially as neuronal *Verbindungen* or psychologically as associations among mental contents, Freud envisaged the psyche as a system or network of branching interconnections. He depended on this image throughout his mature psychoanalytic writings. In the case history of the Wolf Man, for example, he considered the several meanings of feces for the patient—and, implicitly, for himself—as they "branch off" (*abzweigen*) from one another (82). Innumerable instances of such figures of speech could be cited.[8]

This visual metaphor, or close analogs, had not been invented by Freud himself. In 1861, for example, the polymathic Carus illustrated one of his major philosophical works, *Natur und Idee,* with a flowering plant depicting the human psyche (Fig. 45) (Carus 1861: 459–61). The diagram visualized a thesis Carus had stated in the opening sentence of *Psyche,* an earlier, better-known book: "The key to the knowledge of the nature of the soul's conscious life lies in the realm of the unconscious" (Carus 1846: 1). In the diagram, then, the soul's "conscious life"—Carus divides it into "admiration" (and the "idea of the beautiful"), reason (and the "idea of reality"), and "freedom of the will" (and the "idea of love")—is ultimately rooted in dream life and what he called "the unconscious."

By the 1920s, Freud certainly knew Carus as a "precursor of psychoanalysis"; he published an essay on the subject in his journal of applied psychoanalysis (Graber 1926). But we do not know how much he knew about Carus when his psychological and psychoanalytic ideas were being developed. He may have owned two works by Carus (1846; 1853), although the pages of one book are uncut; the provenance of the copies in question is uncertain. In a more general way, Freud may have been quite indebted to Romantic medicine and philosophy, especially if it was mediated through his friendship with Fliess, more learned in the tradition than Freud himself (see Galdston 1956; cf. Sulloway 1979: 146–47). But Carus's terms for the unconscious, *Unterbewusste* (or *relative Unbewusste*)

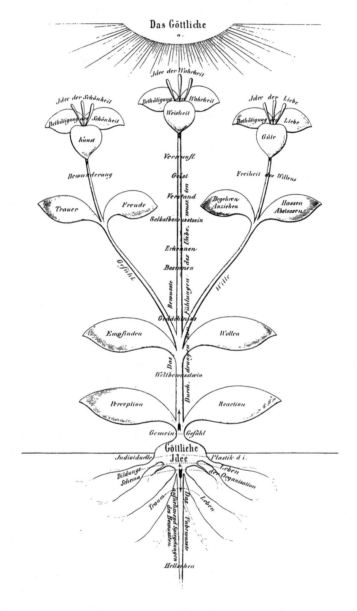

Figure 45. Carl Gustav Carus, *Natur und Idee,* Fig. 1 (1861)

and *absolute Unbewusste,* can be mapped only very roughly onto Freud's terms "preconscious" and "unconscious" respectively (see Abeln 1970: 28 nn. 126, 131). If anything, then, Freud might have been struck by the intellectual clarity, the metaphorical power, or merely the graphic suggestiveness of a schema such as Carus's (Fig. 45) without knowing the precise meaning Carus had given to it.

Often Freud's own views on art seem to have been fashioned after specifically Romantic aesthetic ideas, common enough in his social circles; his favorite painter, the Swiss artist Arnold Böcklin, a long-time resident of Austria, fashioned "symbolic" literalizations of many Romantic themes. Carus was a notable exponent of Romantic art and aesthetic theory and had even argued that pictorial art stems in part from "unconscious" forces (Carus 1857: 235–45). Moreover, Carus was a friend of and later a commentator on Caspar David Friedrich (Carus 1847), whose own work—apparently influential, in turn, on the pictorial practice of the Wolf Man—manifests some interest in Carus's science and philosophy (see Dobrzecki 1982: 34–41; Meffert 1986: 137–74). We cannot say, however, if Freud and the Wolf Man considered this possible common precursor—the peculiar convergence of some of their apparently independent interests—when they "discussed painting." Because it is not possible to establish whether Freud knew precursors such as Carus's schema, it is preferable to rely on the iconography of Freud's own metaphorical visualizations.

The Patient's Veils

As Freud's 1897 diagram of the "architecture of hysteria" had already indicated (Fig. 38), although the analyst might objectively identify the particular psychic structure of the memory tree of repression, the patient himself or herself is not, of course, subjectively aware of it. It must be progressively revealed within the *Nachträglichkeit* of analysis by "looping" down into the unconscious and hooking up, analytically, the memories, associations, and symptoms that have been "bound up" there. But from the perspective of an observer positioned *within* the little turrets in the "architecture of hysteria"—that is, inhabiting or experiencing his or her hysteria or neurosis—the branching structure of the psychic system has another visual, architectural, or material aspect altogether. As Freud explained to Fliess in the letter accompanying an earlier version of "The Architecture of Hysteria":

> Everything goes back to the reproduction of scenes. Some can be obtained directly, others always by way of fantasies set up in front of them. The fantasies stem from things that have been heard but understood subsequently, and all their material is of course genuine. They are protective structures, sublimations of the facts, embellishments of them, and at the same time serve for self-relief. [. . .] In this I see a great advance in insight. (Freud 1985: 239 [May 2, 1897])

Or, as he would often say more succinctly, the deepest memories—in the late 1890s he judged them to be traumatic events, but he later understood them to include intrinsic desires and fantasied scenes as well—are "veiled." In *Die Traumdeutung,* for example, primitive wishes are said to be the very "center of our being" (Freud 1900a: 36, cf. 86, 168). But they are "veiled behind an indeterminateness" (Freud 1909d: 163), an "obscurity" created by the "disguise" and "lies" of defensive repressions (Freud 1905c: 155; 1910a: 35, 41) or—to use the term most commonly employed in Freud's writings—the "amnesia" of the psychic apparatus about itself (Freud 1905d: 191; 1916x: 204, 312; 1925e: 221; 1933a: 28).

In the first sentences of the case history of the Wolf Man, Freud tells us—probably exaggerating somewhat—that the patient, recovering after a mental breakdown that occurred in his eighteenth year, "was entirely incapacitated and completely dependent upon other people when he began his psychoanalytic treatment" (7). He does not proceed, however, to a detailed description of the adult Wolf Man's complaints. Instead, he turns back to the patient's childhood neurosis. In the second section of the case history, he summarized the facts of the Wolf Man's childhood, using information the Wolf Man had evidently recounted at the beginning of the analysis and supplementing it with material which he had discovered or reconstructed by the end of the analysis. In the third through sixth sections, he introduced and reviewed the supposed evidence for his conclusions about the patient's childhood—the "primal scene," seductions and threats, the wolf dream, the childhood phobia and obsessional ritual—in staggeringly close detail. In fact, it was only in the *seventh* section of the case history, well after constructing the principal childhood scenes, that he returned to the actual condition or complaint that had brought the young man to his consulting room in early February 1910.

> When he came under my treatment he had become accustomed to enemas, which were given him by an attendant; spontaneous evacuations did not occur for months at a time, unless a sudden excitement from some definite direction intervened, as a result of which normal activity

of the bowels might set in for a few days. His principal subject of complaint was that for him the world was hidden in a veil, or that he was cut off from the world by a veil. [*Seine Hauptklage war, dass die Welt für ihn in einen Schleier gehüllt sei, oder er durch einen Schleier von der Welt getrennt sei.*]

This veil was torn [*zerrissen*] only at one moment—when, after an enema, the contents of the bowel left the intestinal canal; and he then felt well and normal [*gesund und normal*] again. (74–75)

Or, again, even later in the text:

The analysis would be unsatisfactory if it failed to explain the phrase used by the patient for summing up the troubles of which he complained. The world, he said, was hidden from him by a veil; and our psychoanalytic training forbids our assuming that these words can have been without significance or have been chosen at haphazard. The veil was torn, strange to say, in one situation only; and that was at the moment when, as a result of an enema, he passed a motion through his anus. He then felt well again [*Dann fühlte er sich wieder wohl*], and for a very short while he saw the world clearly [*und sah die Welt für eine ganz kurze Weile klar*]. (99)

The Wolf Man probably phrased his "complaint" in something like the words Freud attributes to him, most likely in the very first consultation or in the first few sessions of the analysis. Despite being described well after Freud has reconstructed the forgotten scenes of the Wolf Man's childhood, the complaint which motivated his search for a cure may have helped, along with the initial "transference," to establish Freud's "conviction" that his patient could become the best case of the "veil of amnesia" he had so often invoked before.

Freud himself had suffered from occasionally severe bowel problems— chiefly a mysterious but chronic constipation—since the 1890s. In the fall of 1909, on his trip to the United States, in addition to an attack of appendicitis, Freud was chagrined at having to put aside his air of authority: he had difficulty finding bathrooms, to which he had to be taken, and also, it seems, contemplated enemas or a proctological inspection of his prostate. According to Jung's later report, while touring New York City, Freud even urinated in his trousers at one point. Jung offered to analyze Freud's fears of public embarrassment over this problem—he was soon to go on stage at Clark University in Worcester to deliver his lectures on psychoanalysis (Freud 1910a)—but Freud, as noted earlier, prevented him from pursuing intimate associations to one particular dream on the grounds that he could not risk his "authority" (see Jones 1955: 59–60; Gay 1988: 567; Rosenzweig 1992: 64–70). After his return from the U.S., toward the end of 1909 Freud sought relief for his continuing discomfort during a three-week sojourn at the spa at Karlsbad, where he had regularly been taking a "cure." Though the rest might have done him good, apparently he had no better luck than the Wolf Man had had the year before for his similar problem at Friedländer's sanatorium outside Frankfurt; though he was not opposed to spa treatments as such, Freud had viciously mocked this institution for the bad psychological medicine Friedländer provided in addition to the usual baths, massages, and mild food.

Presumably Freud immediately connected the Wolf Man's initial "transference"—the patient would like to "use" Freud "from behind" and "shit on [his] head"—to the patient's complaint about his ostensibly organic bowel difficulties. Most likely, in fact, the "transference" Freud reported to Ferenczi actually arose in the context of the patient's description of his problems with evacuation. (In this "transference," then, the Wolf Man did not necessarily mean that he wanted to *sodomize* Freud, though Freud obviously took him to be saying so, at least in part: he may have meant, at least in part, that he wanted to use Freud—or the psychoanalysis—as a toilet into which he could finally shit. As we will see in more detail, Freud's "homosexuality" went out to meet the patient as much as the patient directed his "homosexuality" at Freud.) But the patient would, Freud obviously hoped, find relief in the psychoanalysis. It would lift the "veil" that prevented him—especially his bowels—from functioning. At the same time, it would answer Freud's critics, who complained that he had never presented a fully analyzed case and had failed even to clarify his own dreams completely, drawing a veil over the most intimate material. If the Wolf Man was truly going to shit on Freud's head, the possible "case" which such "transference" anticipated would enable Freud to shit on his critics—producing the fully detailed and complete psychoanalytic interpretation that they claimed he had, in Jung's words, "not revealed." The psychoanalysis would make possible what the bathroom and the bathhouse could not—though despite the Wolf Man's "transference" it would not be Freud whose "veil" would be lifted or penetrated.

These preliminary exchanges obviously implied that Freud's psychoanalytic interpretation—the case produced from the Wolf Man shitting on Freud—must itself be "shit." As it was finally written out, the text of the case history defended against this interpretation. Most notably, though it gradually revealed the Wolf Man's general complaint about his bowel problems, it never explicitly described the Wolf Man's initial "transference" to Freud; this information was reserved for Freud's privileged correspondent Ferenczi. Thus the case history denies the reader an essential clue in reconstructing Freud's position in preparing and writing it. By not revealing that the Wolf Man wants to "use [Freud] from behind," for example, the case history avoids any suggestion that the case history, or the Wolf Man himself, administers an enema to Freud, who has "not revealed" a full interpretation of a case: instead, it celebrates the apparent fact that Freud administered the final, and only fully successful, enema to the patient (for a somewhat parallel but wholly internal reading, see Fish 1989).

For the Wolf Man himself, the "veil" was not merely a metaphor for screened or censored memories. He literally felt himself to be veiled; the world was hidden from him (cf. Martin 1960; Brivic 1991). Therefore this "veil," and the complementary tearing of the veil, required Freud's explicit interpretation. In a *tour de force* of interpretation in the seventh section of the case history, "Anal Erotism and the Castration Complex," Freud linked the tearing of the veil—during enemas, the Wolf Man could once more "see the world clearly"—to the opening of the window in the wolf dream and in turn to the opening of the little boy's eyes in the primal scene, which, Freud maintains in this chapter, caused the excited observer to pass a stool. Working in the forward temporal direction of the Wolf Man's history, then, Freud follows the Wolf Man's "most intimate expression of his homosexuality" (101), from his infantile wish to be born of his father and to satisfy him sexually, to his adult dependence on enemas given to him by his attendant, and at last to the final "lucidity" gained in the psychoanalysis (even though the reconstructed primal scene itself might not be fully clear).

Whatever Freud's ambitions and immediate associations, he may well have begun the analysis with no view about exactly where the Wolf Man's "veil" might be found. A few weeks later, however, the drawing seemed literally to produce it, presenting or depicting a barrier "cutting off" the world, in the place of the opening window in the dream report. In turn, the connection ultimately enabled a complete construction to confirm Freud's initial conviction about the case, namely, tearing veil = opening window = opening eyes or adult neurosis = childhood neurosis = infantile sexuality.

In his drawing of the dream report (Fig. 12), however, the Wolf Man had not directly depicted the way in which "suddenly the window opened of its own accord" (29). Instead, his drawing appears to illustrate a later clause in the dream report—namely, "some white wolves were sitting on the big walnut tree," standing "in front of the window" (29). Regarded in this way, the drawing, as we have already seen, does not objectively "confirm" the dream report by fully illustrating this element of the dream story. Nevertheless, because Freud probably sought to interpret the patient's "veil" from the very beginning of the analysis, and because the drawing replicates the branching tree of repressed associations revealed whenever the "veil of infantile amnesia" is lifted, Freud could immediately regard the drawing as showing the tree trunk and the treetop occluded from the dreamer's (and the viewer's) sight by the window frame (= the veil). In paintings of the wolf dream produced after reading Freud's published case history (for example, Fig. 21), the Wolf Man painted the top of the tree, its whole trunk, and the ground itself. The "window" that veils one's view retreated, then, to the picture frame itself, an obliging "confirmation" of Freud's own interpretation of the Wolf Man's initial complaint.

"The interpretation of dreams," Freud noted in an "introductory lecture" of 1916–17, "is like a window through which we can glimpse the interior of [. . .] the mental apparatus" (Freud 1916x: 447). At the end of the analysis, in a burst of "lucidity" the Wolf Man provided associations enabling Freud to retrace the branchings of the patient's repressions. For both Freud and the Wolf Man, the veil was torn and the world could be seen clearly: as Freud had put it to Fliess, "the veils dropped, and everything became transparent—from the details of the neuroses to the determinants of consciousness" (Freud 1985: 146 [October 20, 1895]). The dream report and the drawing had already provided the impetus for and intimation of this success: the dream itself was supposedly experienced by the dreamer as a natural and intelligible picture (natürlich und deutlich Bild) (30). But from the Wolf Man's point of view, the window as a veil was not directly drawn by or in the drawing when it was produced in the analysis, whatever Freud's later construction: the dream and drawing precisely offered a "clear picture" and not a "veil." We can conclude, then, that Freud tracked the ambiguously available association between window and veil—clarified by the Wolf Man in later paintings—in part on the basis of his own long-standing metaphorical association between the "branches of memory" and the "veil of amnesia." "By picturing our wishes as fulfilled," Freud had written in the last sentences of Die Traumdeutung, "dreams are of course leading us into the future. But this future, which the dreamer takes as the present, has been moulded by his indestructible wish into a perfect likeness [Ebenbild] of the past" (Freud 1900a: 621).

V

THE HOMOSEXUAL ROOTS
OF REPRESSION

> After all, the best of what you know may
> not be told to the boys.
>
> —Goethe, *Faust*, Pt. 1, Scene 4, often
> quoted by Freud (Freud 1985: 285 [De-
> cember 3, 1897], 299 [February 8,
> 1898]; Freud 1900a: 142, 453)

From 1895 to 1899, when Freud completed *Die Traumdeutung*, his research on the structure of repression—the network of laterally bound
mental contents veiled by time and censorship—was not confined to
neurology, hysteria, or the general schema for the psychic apparatus. As
the best confirmation of his developing psychology, he scrutinized his
own repressions.

Divided Roots

In the mid-1890s, in his public presentations Freud depicted repression
as the siphoning off of unpleasurable memories of objectively traumatic
events—such as Emma's veiled memories of the shopkeepers (Fig. 33). Repression, then, could supposedly be tracked to a single point of origin:
the network of associations springs from a single historical root. The very
construction of the relevant schemata—from the "branching T-shaped
fibres" of the earliest histology to the "most general schematic picture of
the psychical apparatus" (Figs. 30–44)—encouraged and sustained this investigation.

But in his own self-analysis, from 1895 to 1899 and beyond, Freud could not always recall the origins of repression. Instead he believed he had found an indefinitely ramifying network of memories of pleasant and unpleasant events and fantasies. Whether or not an objectively traumatic event establishes an unpleasurable memory, he concluded, conflict between or among the subject's thoughts must be *inherently* unpleasurable. Repression apparently organizes conflicting thoughts in order to reduce the quantity of the unpleasure at any psychic locality. On this view, it cannot be tracked to a single point of origin. The root of repression is divided; it is not, or not only, a single trunk, but instead a system of roots. Like the branching structure of the resulting network—or dissemination—of repressed memories, the *causes* of repression are branching, distributed in many different events and fantasies in the subject's life history that may eventually come into conflict with one another.

On the night of April 27–28, 1897, Freud dreamed about his friend Fliess. He reported the dream to him in a letter the following day (Freud 1985: 236–38 [April 28, 1897]; there is a partial facsimile in Grinstein 1990: fig. 2). In the dream, he received a telegraph message from Fliess reporting his whereabouts. "Printed in blue on the telegraph form," the last word in the message, "Secerno," was clearly readable, but the word before it, prefaced by the word "Venice," was obscure. In the dream Freud felt it was "Via" or "Villa," or possibly "Casa." *Die Traumdeutung* introduced this dream as an example of the way in which dreams manage to represent a conflict in the dreamer's thoughts that would be logically irresolvable—an unsurmountable "either/or" (Freud 1900a: 317). Freud's letter to Fliess reports more intimate material; since it depended on specific knowledge shared by the two men, Freud did not recount all of it in the published version. (See further Anzieu 1986: 218–22 and Grinstein 1990: 91–118; neither presents some of the background materials for the dream noted here.)

In the Via/Villa Secerno dream, two and possibly more words seem to the dreamer to be simultaneously present—they are somehow superimposed or juxtaposed—as he struggles to read the vague printing. (Considering Freud's general visual-graphic model of repression and its analysis in "The Architecture of Hysteria" [Fig. 38], it is not surprising that an instance of superimposed writings—in this case, both inscriptions were produced by the dreamer/analyst himself—serves as a paradigm.) As Freud remarks, "each of the three alternatives for the first word turned out on analysis to be an independent and equally valid starting-point for a chain of thoughts," a structure that he diagrammed in his letter to Fliess (Fig. 46).

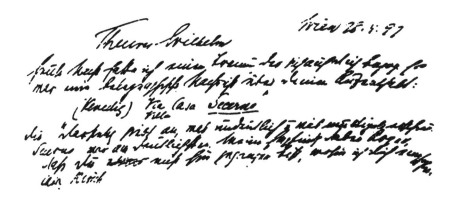

Figure 46. Freud, diagram of the visual presentation of words in the "Via Secerno" dream (1897)

The inherent conflict among the thoughts, Freud explains, holds between an annoyance with Fliess and a desire to be together with him—perhaps best embodied in the word "Secerno" (cf. Latin "to separate," "to reject"), a detail not explicated in *Die Traumdeutung*. Freud had recommended a hotel to Fliess—the first part of its name was "Casa"—but Fliess had not gone there; "Via" and "Villa," other alternatives, were associated with Fliess's "promise of a congress [a rendezvous] on Italian soil."

In fact, each of the two points of origin in Freud's desire to be with Fliess is itself divided or multiple (see Fig. 47). The association to "Via," Freud says in his letter, is to the "streets of Pompeii, which I am studying" (see Tögel 1989: 68–102). He has no particular Via in mind but only the many streets of the city. The association to "Villa," he tells Fliess, is to "Böcklin's Roman villa." Because he does not specify the title of the painting in the letter, presumably it was one that both he and Fliess already knew. In fact, Böcklin painted six closely related works with the title *Villa by the Sea*. Two of them (Figs. 48, 49), dated 1864 and 1865, were hanging in a gallery in Munich (Andree 1977: nos. 173, 174), where Freud and Fliess met for several intense "congresses."

Both William McGrath (1986: 187) and Alexander Grinstein (1990: 132) have remarked on the paintings' general air of melancholy and imagine, for unstated reasons, that Freud somehow identified with the woman

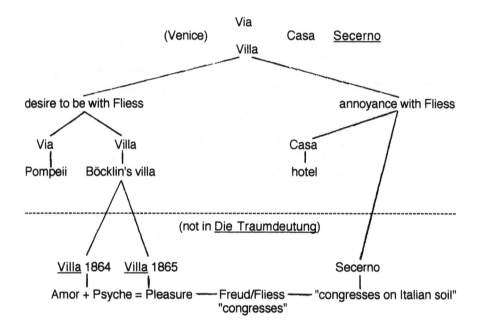

Figure 47. Diagram of the structure of repression in the "Via Secerno" dream

in the depicted scene. But they do not notice the particular iconography of the paintings, which can be traced back through works by Claude and the Caracci that Freud might have known. Böcklin depicted Psyche—the contemplative, perhaps weeping, woman standing by the sea—transported to the kingdom of Amor. According to the myth, the daughter of Psyche and Amor, finally united after much doubt, struggle, and loss, was Pleasure. Freud's association, then, is to the *two* men looking at *two* paintings of the origin of pleasure from her *two* parents (Fig. 47). But this highly sexualized scenario—especially its homosocial or homoerotic dimension—is not rendered in Freud's account in *Die Traumdeutung* even though it may have been quite palpable to Freud's immediate correspondent Fliess. It was such elisions that led Jung and others to complain. "I miss," Jung wrote, "a specific reference to the fact that the essential (personal) meaning of the dream[s] [. . .] has not been given" (Freud/Jung 1974: 392 [14 February 1911]). But for Freud "the best of what you know may not be told to the boys."

Figure 48. Arnold Böcklin, *Villa by the Sea*, 1864 (courtesy Bayerische Staatsgemäldesammlungen, Munich)

The Specimen Parapraxis

The most telling instance of the dividedness of the origins of repression became the so-called specimen parapraxis of psychoanalysis itself. In a letter to Fliess in late September 1898, Freud reported a slip of the tongue that had taken place the previous week (Freud 1985: 326–27 [September 22, 1898]). During a short train ride with a "lawyer from Berlin"—an obvious association to Fliess, who lived in Berlin—Freud "got to talking about pictures," as he and Fliess had done about Böcklin's and many others. "I could not find," he says, "the name of the renowned painter who did the Last Judgement in Orvieto, the greatest I have seen so far" (Fig. 50). (Freud had been in Orvieto the previous summer with his brother Alexander and a student and patient, Felix Gattel [see Tögel 1989: 94–96].) He goes on briefly to explain the slip. He must have considered the example very in-

Figure 49. Arnold Böcklin, *Villa by the Sea*, 1865 (courtesy Bayerische
Staatsgemäldesammlungen, Munich)

teresting, for less than a week later the slip had been written up as a short
essay, "The Psychical Mechanism of Forgetfulness" (Freud 1898b), reused
in turn in 1901 as the beginning of his second major psychoanalytic book,
The Psychopathology of Everyday Life (Freud 1901b: 2–7; for detailed considerations, see Anzieu 1986: 359–62; Schimek 1974).

As Freud's diagram of forgetting the name of Signorelli shows (Fig. 51),
the repression served as a fine instance of lateral binding. In Freud's essay
and diagram, the repressed thoughts which he represents in their *Verbindung* concerned, as he says somewhat vaguely, "death and sexuality." One
underlying thought was a joke he had heard about one's sexual activities
coming to an end—that is, "death." The other source was the news of the
suicide of a patient he was treating for a sexual disease. The repression
derived, then, from two memories connected with an inherently conflicted subject, "death-and-sexuality," that were themselves conflicting,
one making light of the subject and the other deadly serious.

Again, however, "the best of what you know may not be told to the

Figure 50. Luca Signorelli, *Teaching of the Antichrist* (with portraits of Signorelli and Fra Angelico), from *Last Judgment* cycle, Orvieto (photo Northwestern University Library)

boys." The lateral binding that supposedly organized the forgetting of the name of Signorelli (Fig. 51) continued to organize Freud's own explication of it in his essay and diagram. During the parapraxis he could not recall Signorelli's name. But he "was able," he says, "to conjure up [Signorelli's] pictures with greater sensory vividness than is usual with me." He could visualize the artist's self-portrait in the fresco (Fig. 50). "With serious face and folded hands," the artist stands looking out at the viewer. Freud also

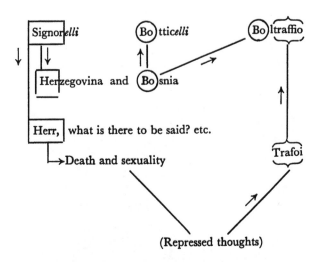

Figure 51. Freud, diagram of the structure of
repression in the forgetting of the name of
Signorelli (1901)

recalled, he says, how the self-portrait was "put in a corner of one of the
pictures [i.e., one of the frescoes in the cycle], next to the portrait of [Sig-
norelli's] predecessor in the work, Fra Angelico da Fiesole." (In Freud's
day, following Vasari's biography [1991: 268–73], Signorelli was generally
understood to have been commissioned in 1499 to finish work on frescoes
thought to have been begun by Fra Angelico and Gozzoli fifty years earlier.) But despite the way in which the forgotten name of Signorelli was
being disturbed by the image of Fra Angelico—Freud recalls his full name
and historical relation to the frescoes—this detail is *not* included in the
diagram of the structure of the repression (Fig. 51).

It seems likely that the association to "Fra Angelico da Fiesole" was to
Fliess himself. Initially suppressed by Freud in writing up the Signorelli
slip itself, it reappeared dramatically at the end of his short essay on forgetfulness. "In connection with the tendentious nature of our remembering and forgetting," Freud (1898b) here appended an account of a *second*
slip, practically an afterthought to the main presentation. In this slip, he
had forgotten the address of someone he was supposed to visit in Berlin,
where, he says, "he would rather be devoted entirely to his friend" (i.e.,
Fliess). The duty to call on this unnamed person would "interfere with

[Freud and Fliess] being together," like Signorelli and Fra Angelico in the fresco. Therefore the address (like the name in the first slip) gets forgotten.

Freud's self-analysis was completed by 1901, and *Die Traumdeutung*, its partial representation, had been published (Freud 1900a). By this point and perhaps partly as a consequence of writing about it, Freud's attachment to Fliess had begun to fade. At the same time, Freud became increasingly clearheaded about its nature. As he wrote to Fliess:

> There is no concealing the fact that the two of us have drawn apart to some extent. [. . .] You take sides against me and tell me that "the reader of thoughts merely reads his own thoughts into other people," which renders all my efforts valueless. If that is what you think of me, just throw my "Everyday Life" [*The Psychopathology of Everyday Life* appeared that year] unread into the wastepaper basket. (Freud 1985: 447 [August 7, 1901])

Despite their growing separation, however, Freud did announce his plan to adopt one of Fliess's central scientific ideas—namely, the theory of the "root" of repression in conflict deriving from the inherent biological and psychic possibility that a person can make both homosexual and heterosexual choices of erotic object, what Fliess and others called "bipolarity." The "chief insight," Freud recognizes, is "that repression, my core problem, is only possible through reaction between [these] two sexual currents. [. . .] The idea itself is yours [. . .]—and I see that you are right" (ibid.).

Freud's earlier letters to Fliess show that it had actually taken him some time to accept Fliess's idea. In *The Psychopathology of Everday Life*, written in 1901, Freud was willing to acknowledge his borrowing. But even here, Freud's account—it is actually the story of a slip of the tongue—expresses his conflict. According to the book, in the summer of 1901 he had told Fliess that the problem of neurosis could be solved by assuming "the original bisexuality of the individual." But then Fliess reminded him, he says, that the idea had actually been recounted by Fliess to Freud two and a half years earlier (i.e., in 1898) at a meeting in Breslau (Freud 1901b: 144). Here Freud was probably forgetting—or pretending—that Fliess had not been in possession of the idea as long as he had: the friends had apparently discussed bisexuality even earlier, possibly as early as 1896, in meetings at Nuremberg and elsewhere (see Freud 1985: 212 [December 6, 1896], 292 [January 4, 1898], 465 [July 26, 1904]).

By 1904, Freud felt himself to be the actual inventor of the idea of psychic bisexuality. If Fliess was his "predecessor in the work," in his own mind he was, without question, the real artist. (In the late 1890s, as "The

Architecture of Hysteria" [Fig. 38] and other documents show, "work" was one of Freud's favorite terms for the activity of psychoanalysis.) The two men finally fell out completely over this matter. A book by Hermann Swoboda—"of which I am in more than one respect the intellectual originator," Freud asserted to Fliess (Freud 1985: 461 [April 16, 1904])—and a later one by Otto Weininger promulgated ideas about biological and psychic bisexuality that Fliess felt to be his own, stolen and circulated by Freud as his creation. The matter ended in court (for the tangled story, see further Roazen 1975: 84–85).

Problems of originality and borrowing are at the heart of Vasari's biography of Signorelli, the text lying behind Freud's description of his slip. The slip is not merely about Freud's dependence on Fliess in completing his scientific work, paralleling Signorelli's completion of the frescoes begun by Fra Angelico. It is also about Michelangelo's later "imitation" of Signorelli's "inventions." For Vasari, Michelangelo's "kind borrowings" from Signorelli were a way of praising him; his work became more significant through the retrospective attention of a far greater artist (see Vasari 1991: 271). Freud's identification with the painters probably oscillates among Fra Angelico (= Fliess as the predecessor in the work and = Freud as the real beginner), Signorelli (= Freud and = Fliess as the source for the greater Freud's borrowings), and Michelangelo (= Freud, who "kindly borrows" from an earlier thinker to make something much greater). This added complexity to the slip, the further doubling of its already acknowledged doubleness, accounts for Freud's repression of essential elements in its explanation—for again, like the direct association to Fliess himself (Berlin address slip) and the indirect association to Fliess (Fra Angelico), the association to Michelangelo was not included or explicated in Freud's diagram (Fig. 51).

Later Freud could articulate—and perhaps even discharge—some elements of his intense relationship with Fliess. It had provided a good deal of the material for but also much of the disturbance in *Die Traumdeutung* and related writing. Fliess was Freud's "predecessor in the work" in many ways. The erotic and competitive dynamics of their friendship were, he knew, repeated with later friends, students, and rivals such as Adler, Jung, Wilhelm Stekel, and even Ferenczi, though in this last case the two men's eroticism and rivalry was muted enough for them directly to describe its "homosexual components" to one another (Freud/Ferenczi 1993: 214, 217–18 [September 28 and October 3, 1910]). As Freud straightforwardly confessed to Ernest Jones in 1912, midway through his work with the Wolf Man, in his ongoing memory of Fliess "there is some piece of unruly homosexual feeling at the root of the matter." In this statement Freud was referring specifically to his thoughts about Munich, where, among other things, he and Fliess had evidently been to the gallery together.[1]

Before his falling out with Jung, in his extensive correspondence with him Freud remarked in various ways on the "wounds of the Fliess affair" (Freud/Jung 1974: 382 [December 22, 1910]). At one point, for example, he led Jung to believe that it had been Fliess who had abandoned his affection for Freud; Fliess had supposedly developed a case of "paranoia" about Freud (and psychoanalysis) which Freud now detected in others as well (ibid.: 121 [February 17, 1908], 376 [December 3, 1910]). But at the same time Freud also held Fliess ultimately responsible for his own ongoing anxiety about any "dwindling correspondence" from friends and followers (ibid.: 209 [March 9, 1909]). The inconsistency of such sentiments did not escape him; they were the latter-day branches of the "unruly homosexual feeling at the root of the matter."

Homosexualität

None of Freud's comments implies that he had ever had an overt homosexual—that is, a sexual—relationship with Fliess. But we should not ignore Freud's choice of specific words by supposing, as some historians have done, that he was describing only an emotional or romantic male friendship (*Freundschaft*) of the kind almost expected to occur among German-speaking intellectuals. Epistolary and other records of these romances—for example, between J. J. Winckelmann and his friends Berendis, Usteri, and von Berg (Winckelmann 1778, 1784), or between Johannes von Muller and his friend C. V. von Bonstetten (Müller 1802)— had been published since the end of the eighteenth century. (Some of the records were more troublesome than others. The diary of the poet August von Platen-Hallermünde was not fully published until 1896– 1900, and the writings of both Lenau and Grillparzer were grist for the mill of Isidor Sadger's [1908, 1909a, 1909b, 1910] early psychopathographies of historical homosexualities, crude but surprisingly influential studies which Freud both encouraged and criticized.) In the light of what was known about, and thus could be expected in, the strongest—even the most romantic—male friendships, Freud was pointing to specifically "homosexual" qualities in friendships that *need not* but in a few particular cases do possess them.

Freud's sexological lexicon in the year 1910 was an extension of the concepts he had deployed with stunning and controversial effect in the first edition of *Three Essays on the Theory of Sexuality* (1905d), further extended in papers such as "Analysis of a Phobia in a Five-Year-Old Boy" ("Little Hans") (Freud 1909b) and "On the Sexual Theories of Children" (Freud 1908c) (despite their dates of publication, the former was written before the latter). For Freud, "homosexuality" is rooted in—indeed, it is the same thing as—unconscious "homosexual" or same-sex-directed fantasies and fears. Freud's concept puts the emphasis on truly *unconscious* (as opposed to conscious) thought and on *psychological* (as opposed to somatic) conditions; moreover, it does not necessarily refer to any actual sexual or erotic *practice*. In all of these respects it should be carefully distinguished from established sexological descriptions of congenital or acquired "inversion," "contrary sexual instinct" (*konträre Geschlechtsgefühl*), "contrary sexual feeling" (*konträre Sexualempfindung*), and even "homosexuality" (*Homosexualität*) in the sense initially intended by Karl Maria Kertbeny (see Herzer 1985) and Karl Heinrich Ulrichs (Kennedy 1988). All of these terms had somewhat different meanings or connotations, at least by the time Freud came to write the *Three Essays,* and though Freud did not always completely disentangle his usage from them—for example, the established sense of *Empfindung,* as we will see momentarily, continued strongly to shape the Freudian concept—it is clear that he worked explicitly in relation to and often in reaction against them.

Ulrichs had rejected the notion that "contrary sexual feeling" was acquired by a man through "vicious" practices—chiefly onanism (see especially Kaan 1844)—or through an early seduction. Committed above all to legal reform and social emancipation, originally trained as a jurist, and writing principally for legal and medical readers, Ulrichs asserted that *Homosexualität* was a congenital condition. (Ulrichs's thought was probably known to later readers—we do not know whether Freud was among them—mostly through Magnus Hirschfeld's somewhat truncated one-volume edition [1898] of the twelve pamphlets of *Researches on the Riddle of Male-Male Love* that Ulrichs produced between 1864 and 1879, though some lawyers and psychiatrists, we know, did read some of the originals; one unfortunate consequence of the Hirschfeld omnibus edition was its tendency to suggest a unity to Ulrichs's project when in fact he very carefully distinguished between different descriptive, explanatory, and forensic dimensions or implications of his general topic.) A man could not be held morally or legally responsible for his erotic interest in and sexual relations with other men—so long as he did not attempt to have sex with minors or violate other laws which Ulrichs did not challenge in themselves. To some extent, then, *Homosexualität* in Ulrichs's sense performed a double conceptual function. At one level, it distinguished specifically social sexual and erotic relations from a more general "sodomy," which traditionally included not only masturbation and heterosexual anal or oral copulation but also sexual relations with animals and demons (see especially Sinistrari d'Ameno 1883). Though Ulrichs's own views are unclear, such practices and relations could still be condemned as unhealthy, unnatural, or immoral not only because they supposedly remain within the reach of a person's will but also because they supposedly do not embody the other-directedness, the fundamental sociality and especially the procreativeness, of eroticism and can be seen, then, only as a kind of personal or solipsistic gratification.

At another level, however, *within* the domain of intersubjective eroticism and sexual relations "homosexuality" designated one's relative lack of moral responsibility for his interests and actions. In Ulrichs's scheme and especially in his juridical arguments, the "homosexual" supposedly cannot be responsible for his interest in other men; it is entirely innate in or natural to him. But a "pederast"—as Ulrichs's willingness to turn him over to the law implies—supposedly is responsible for *his* interests and actions and can thus properly be punished, for whether or not he is a "homosexual," he supposedly takes a *further* and morally specific step in deliberately setting out to seduce underage males, whether or not they are "homosexual." Thus "pederasty" remained somewhat outside the definition or, more properly, the conceptual ambition of Ulrichs's new category. Indeed, in Ulrichs's scheme and its descendants, it is not really clear whether the "pederast" is a "homosexual" at all—whether, for example, his taste derives from another, independent source, such as an essential "pedophilia," sadism, or fetishism, or alternatively, as the classical Greek concept had it, from an essentially aesthetic and ethical position, a pedagogical *eros,* that does not, in itself, require sexual expression.

Ulrichs's legal-juridical conceptualization was highly strategic. Pederasty had traditionally aroused the greatest moral and legal disquiet, ranging from amusing satires on the boy-loving proclivities of priests or educators to heavily punitive prosecutions of men caught "seducing" younger men or boys. (Apparently, no systematic study has been made, but it is striking how many reports of sodomy trials from the fifteenth through the mid-nineteenth centuries involve substantial age differences, often up to a full generation, between the two males involved. Conversely, it is perhaps significant that legally tolerated sodomitical networks—such as some of the sex parks and clubs of eighteenth- and nineteenth-century Europe—were imagined as institutions for participants in *non*pederastic relations, whatever the actual ages of the boys and men involved.) Though no absolutely clear separation between the homosexual and the pederastic could be made, Ulrichs's new concept of homosexuality at least partly preserved same-sex eroticism from contamination by the pederastic—and thus, in turn, tried to create room for greater moral acceptance, legal tolerance, and social understanding. In this his scheme was ultimately at least partly successful. Even among self-identified "homosexuals," and almost by definition, pederasty has continued to be rejected as vicious or seen as an independently rooted moral perversion of homosexual instinct or feeling. Certainly the modern *opponents* of "homosexuality"—implicitly recognizing the moral and legal field within which the concept was devised to intervene—continue to try, as far as possible, to tie it to or even define it as "pederasty" or pedophilia.

Ulrichs's preferred *explanation* of congenital *Homosexualität*—we should stress, again, that in itself it simply *described* a specific juridical-legal possibility within the wide and confused field of moral responsibility in sexual and broadly sodomitical relations—was a more narrow matter. Referring to embryological researches, he believed homosexuality to be the psychic equivalent of certain prenatal anatomical mix-ups, resulting in a man's having a "woman's soul" (and vice versa in the case of homosexual women). But his writings—in particular the way he divided up his inquiries from 1864 to 1879 (see Ulrichs 1898, although the edition is partial)—clearly show that he distinguished between the general hypothesis, which underwrote his political and legal arguments (as in *Vindex* [1864] and *Vindicta* [1865]), and his etiological speculations (as in *Gladius furens* [1868] and *Memnon* [1868]), which he recognized were dependent on a partial and contentious (though he believed scientific) literature as well as by-then-outdated traditions of Romantic soul-psychology.

Ulrichs's general hypothesis was not fully accepted by Krafft-Ebing, the most prominent sexologist of the 1890s and early 1900s. But Krafft-Ebing's interest in homosexualities seems to have been stimulated, even inaugurated, by reading Ulrichs, as he confessed to Ulrichs himself in 1879 (Kennedy 1988: 70–71). After some hesitation, he did come to agree that certain "contrary sexual feelings" could be innate; in editions of his *Psychopathia Sexualis* published in the later 1890s and early 1900s, he increasingly replaced this term with *Homosexualität*. By the turn of the century, only a few fairly well-defined groups of certain reformers, sexologists, and scientists saw homosexuality entirely as a fact or feature of postnatal development. Not surprisingly, they were chiefly identified with the developing "psychotherapeutic" industries of the 1890s; academic psychiatry, such as Kraepelin's, frequently connected with the state asylums and university hospitals, often disagreed with and sometimes disparaged them. The psychotherapists sought their patients among middle- and up-per-class paying customers. Basically they claimed to be able to "cure" a man's "acquired" vice by helping him *de*acquire it—for example, by hyp-notically implanting the suggestion in an "impotent" man troubled by homosexual feelings that he should go home and have sexual relations with his wife (e.g., Schrenck-Notzing 1895; Berillon 1908–1909).

Though the whole matter was never fully clarified at the time, by about 1900 a writer's choice of terms tended to locate him specifically on this spectrum of innatism versus acquisitionalism or developmentalism, and thus, in turn, to identify him in the professional and political fields—as research psychiatrist, for example, versus psychotherapist, or as law re-former versus state prosecutor. Whereas *Homosexualität* and to a lesser extent "inversion" suggested a congenital condition, possibly an embry-onic abnormality, "contrary sexual feeling" was an attitude and—in most usages of the term—a disorder of the moral instinct, a social vice or "per-verted" volition. (The relation between reflex and volition was, of course, a matter of intense theoretical interest among contemporary neurolo-gists and psychophysicists; in his essay "The Brain," Freud himself urged that in certain if unspecified circumstances, volitional "ethical considera-tions" could interact with or regulate reflex [Freud 1990b: 62–64]. The debate about *Homosexualität* was organized, in part, along these lines.) Terms such as "similisexualism" and certain attempts at purist scientific etymologies never caught on, partly because they did not clearly operate in this lexical and conceptual field. There were many variations in these usages; sometimes they were quite incoherent. But a polemical or minority viewpoint could readily be recognized as such precisely in its choice and handling of terms. For example, a homoerotic emancipationist such as Benedict Friedlaender (1904) deliberately distinguished himself from *ho-mosexualist* emancipationists by insisting that "same-sex sexual love" (*gleichgeschlechtliche Liebe*)—Elisar von Kupffer's (1899) "chivalric love of comrades" (*Lieblingsminne*)—was not a question of congenital nature *or* developmental vice. Rather, for him same-sex sexual love is a mature, self-conscious aesthetic, political, and moral interest, associated particularly with the traditions of aristocratic militarism (though Friedlaender him-self did not belong to the high-placed homoeroticist circles of Alfred Krupp or Prince Eulenburg). Pitched equally against reformers such as Ulrichs, therapists such as Schrenck-Notzing, and medical scientists such as Hirschfeld, this approach was a calculated reanimation of the homo-

eroticist understanding in the German-speaking traditions of Winckelmann and Frederick I of Prussia and, more recently, in some of the English
writings of Walt Whitman (e.g., 1882–83) and John Addington Symonds.

The case of Symonds is complex but instructive for our purposes here.
He would almost certainly have been known to Freud for his *Renaissance
in Italy* (1875–86), though his sexology was not: his privately printed *A
Problem in Greek Ethics*, drafted in the early 1870s, was printed in only
ten copies for friends in 1883. As Symonds's personal copy (now in the
British Library) suggests, this text was later revised—probably in the early
or mid-1890s for his collaboration with Havelock Ellis, ultimately published as *Sexual Inversion* (Ellis and Symonds 1896, 1897). *Greek Ethics* was
a historical examination of Dorian (e.g., Cretan and Spartan) pederasty
(paiderastia) and Athenian (specifically Socratic) homoeroticism founded
on Symonds's own reading of the classical texts (in writing it he did not
know about comparatively complete studies written earlier in the century).

Symonds's inquiry was undertaken under the shadow of the question inherited by the nineteenth-century homoeroticist tradition from Winckelmann: in the modern world, could the erotic practices—even the institutions—of ancient Greek pederastic and Socratic love be revived (see Davis
1995b)? As his posthumously published autobiographical memoir shows,
Symonds (1984) experienced what he interpreted as personal versions of
"Greek" feeling, typically though not necessarily associated with peda-
gogic situations—strong emotional attractions to and sexual yearnings
for much younger men, such as the lads in his Greek literature classes at
Clifton College in Bristol. The model for his self-understanding here was
the history of Socrates and Charmides or of Lysias and Autolycus (narrated by Xenophon). At the same time, however, Symonds had strong "romantic" feelings—his generally frank autobiography does not indicate
that these were expressed sexually in any substantial way—for his social
equals, men his own age or a few years younger (certainly not boys), of
his own class, education, and intellectual preoccupations, such as his great
friend Henry Graham Dakyns. Here the models, within his own immediate social milieu, were equally obvious and generally accepted, even if
Tennyson's "In Memoriam" had raised a few eyebrows in the clubs.

Reading Whitman, however, astounded Symonds. Whitman apparently
cross-fertilized what would have seemed to Symonds to be the distinct domains of Dorian pederasty and Victorian friendship, pulled together under Whitman's rubrics of "comradeship" and "adhesiveness." Whitman's
British and European middle- and upper-class readers, erotically less ad-

venturous and socially more constrained than the poet, had no real way to classify him, though they vigorously debated the evidence (well after his death, for instance, a controversy broke out in the pages of the *Mercure de France* concerning, among other things, the supposed homosexual orgies that had taken place at Whitman's funeral). Symonds felt that he needed to know something more about the poet—namely, whether the erotic abandon and ethical-political fellowship figuratively depicted in Whitman's poetry and identified in his essays translated into actual homosexual sex. With this information, Whitman could be pinned down as a Dorian *or* a Victorian. But of course the point—the puzzle—was the irreducible synthesis Whitman had effected, in part, it seemed, because of his American origins and originality. Gradually Symonds came to believe, however, that Whitman probably embodied *Homosexualität.* In the mid- and late 1880s, Symonds had begun to encounter this new category in European psychiatric and sexological writing, which he summarized with great clarity in his second privately printed tract, *A Problem in Modern Ethics* (probably 1891). His late book on Whitman (1893) ventured his conclusions very delicately without really appearing to go beyond the usual references to Whitman's capacious eroticism and solicitous interest in comrades.

Approximately at the time he began reading European sexology, Symonds began writing his autobiographical memoir (1984). It was partly conceived as a potential (though he knew unpublishable) contribution to the accumulating representation of homoeroticism in print in Europe. Symonds was now able to organize his life's experiences—both "Dorian" (homosexual-pederastic) *and* "Victorian" (homoerotic-romantic)—under a single umbrella. He learned about *Homosexualität* not only through Ulrichs, whose general hypothesis and emancipationist perspective he embraced in *Modern Ethics.* He also studied German psychiatry and its case histories—beginning with J. L. Casper's *klinische Novellen* (1863; cf. 1881), precursors of the "clinical pictures" produced by Kraepelin—of *konträre Sexualempfindung.*

It is not irrelevant that Symonds's father had been one of the contributors to the mid-nineteenth-century concept of "moral insanity," which its chief English-language exponent, James Cowles Prichard, had noted must include "moral phenomena of an anomalous and unusual kind, [. . .] certain perversions of natural inclination which excite the greatest disgust and abhorrence" (Prichard 1835: 24; cf. Symonds 1871: 135–39; see also Tuke 1891). Probably partly for this reason, the younger Symonds tended to understand his own congenital condition to be "morbid"—a subject *for* medicine and psychiatry and, for many years, submission to his father's advice. He thought that he had good introspective confirmation for his view. He had long been sickly and at least partly interpreted certain problems—such as his extraordinary difficulties with his eyesight—to sexual sources. In the latter part of his life, then, a second contradiction replaced the first: if he had found it difficult at one time to reconcile Dorian pederasty and Victorian friendship, he now found it difficult to reconcile joyful Whitmanian "adhesiveness" and morbid *Homosexualität*.

His collaboration with Havelock Ellis promised to help resolve this quandary. Their book on same-sex sex, love, and friendship was first published in German in 1896, after Symonds's death in 1895, in a translation by the sexologist Hans Kurella, then in a quickly suppressed English edition of 1897, and finally (deferring to Symonds's friends and heirs) in a much-reorganized and revised 1897 edition under Ellis's name only. (This last appeared as volume I of Ellis's announced *Studies in the Psychology of Sex;* later, it was much reprinted—for example, in the editions of 1901 and 1906—as volume II of the influential *Studies,* a major source for Freud [1905d], among others, possibly because Ellis disliked the fact that he had begun his series with a study of "abnormal" sexuality.) Symonds contributed a good deal of material—including a revised version of *A Problem in Greek Ethics,* part of the literature survey contained in *A Problem in Modern Ethics,* case histories gathered among friends as well as his own, some revealing personal correspondence, and at least two interesting independent essays, later dropped by Ellis, on *Soldatenliebe* (the nonpederastic love of soldiers) and on the Roman *concubinus* (the homosexual consort of Roman gentlemen).

Ellis was not a medical man and belonged to freethinking circles familiar with British brands of Whitmanianism and with Ulrichs-style emancipationism. As their correspondence shows, he tried to get Symonds to reduce his emphasis on the supposed morbidity of *Homosexualität*.[2] Though "homosexuality" was the term they most commonly used between them, by 1897 Ellis seems to have thought that it was hopelessly associated with pathology. Ellis's view generally won out. In the English editions of their work in 1897 and on, he used "sexual inversion" for his title and more or less throughout the text, replacing Kurella's German *konträre Geschlechtsfühl* (Ellis and Symonds 1896), a phrase which emphasized perceptual-physical *sensation* or reflex over any specific conscious *emotion,* and possibly suggesting that Symonds and Ellis—following Albert Moll (1893), whom they had both read—had originally written "contrary sexual instinct."

Terms such as "homosexuality" and *konträre Geschlechtsfühl* indicated the deep-seated, long-term biopsychological dimensions, probably congenital, of the male-male eroticisms described in the volume—in accord with the perspective that Symonds had reasoned toward so painfully in his own self-analysis. In dropping them, Ellis forfeited some power in his own analysis, compromised the thrust of some of the materials gathered by Symonds, and left considerable room—against the grain of his own antiauthoritarian leanings—for therapeuticist etiologies such as the suggestion therapists' and Freud's. The volume ended up being more superficially descriptive—less decisive and penetrating at an explanatory level—than either author had probably intended. Most troubling, its vocabulary for "inversion" did not permit a rigorous distinction between "inversion" of the subject's sexual object-choice and "inversions" of other dimensions of male and male/male (or female and female/female) eroticism—such as "inversions" of sexual accoutrements, in "fetishism," or of erotic self-presentation, in "transvestism." Freud regarded this supposed conflation (despite what we might now see as its partial but innovative recognition of "gender" difference) as a serious theoretical and discursive flaw, which he also identified in the work of German-speaking homosexualist sexologists such as the emancipationist and activist Magnus Hirschfeld (e.g., 1991). He made his complaint into a centerpiece of his discussion of "inversion" and "deviations in respect of the sexual object" in the *Three Essays on the Theory of Sexuality* (1905d).[3]

Inversion, Instinct, and Feeling

The section on "inversion" in Freud's *Three Essays* (1905d) was based almost entirely on what, for him, were secondary sources. (Recently this text has been read very productively by Arnold Davidson [1987], Jonathan Dollimore [1991: 169–204], and Teresa de Lauretis [1994], all of whom are especially interested in the Freudian concept of "perversion" and perverse object-choice. All recognize that "homosexuality remained a problem for Freud"; "try as he might he never accounted for it" [Dollimore 1991: 204]. Most likely many elements of the Freudian "account" have not yet been identified.) Through Krafft-Ebing's *Psychopathia Sexualis* (1894), Freud could reach back to the cases and interpretations presented by Casper (1863) and other German medical observers (useful English abstracts were published by Shaw and Ferris [1883]). Through Symonds and Ellis (which he knew as Ellis 1897, 1901), he could gather a good deal of historical, literary, and other information, though he combined it with his own extensive knowledge of the history of civilization and, of course, with his previous explorations of "sexuality." We will consider some of his other sources momentarily.

In these famous pages, as well as in scattered remarks in other parts of the *Three Essays,* Freud tended to write *Inversion* where he meant to designate the probably congenital but in his opinion *non*pathological condition described by Ulrichs (1898) and by Ellis and Symonds (1896, 1897). By contrast, he would generally write *konträre Geschlechtsfühl* (or *konträre Sexualempfindung*) where he meant to designate a man's actual erotic and moral attitudes and sexual practices, whether or not he is an "invert" and whether or not these attitudes and practices are seen as a "perversion." The term *Homosexualität* covers *both* of these cases and for that reason easily confused unwary readers. Indeed, Freud applied *Homosexualität* to cases where there is neither *Inversion* nor *Empfindung;* as we will see momentarily, this seemingly terminological or classificatory fact embeds a crucial theoretical insight.

In the next few years, the conceptual and perhaps actual slippage between "inversion" and "contrary sexual feeling"—disguised by the increasingly universal application of the term "homosexuality"—would become a matter for Freud's intense scrutiny: the complex historical, psychological, and biological analyses offered in the Leonardo, Schreber, and Wolf Man cases (Freud 1910c, 1911c, 1918b) all explicitly contained substantial "theoretical" contributions to this problem. Immediately after the *Three Essays,* Freud's investigations were more preliminary. But his terminological and interpretive decisions established the framework for his later thinking on the subject.

For instance, in the narrative of "An Analysis of a Phobia in a Five-Year-Old Boy," "Little Hans" (Freud 1909b), the little boy's *Homosexualität* appears qua *Inversion* in Hans's alleged overemphasis on, or excessive attention to, the penis—not only his own but also his sister's (which was apparently missing) and a zoo animal's (which was apparently enormous). Hans's "inverted" interest here, if that is what it is, would ultimately seem to require an account of a primary or primal homosexual repression in the sense required by the *Project* of 1895 and *Die Traumdeutung* (1900a). For good reasons, however, Freud does not offer it in the paper: he had not actually psychoanalyzed Hans but had simply recounted and interpreted the little boy's father's observations. In "On the Sexual Theories of Children" (1908c), written shortly after "Little Hans" and clearly as an attempt to address its gaps, and in *Leonardo da Vinci and a Memory of His*

Childhood (1910c), Freud makes the little boy's early interest in the phallus—and, when he is *overly* interested, his inability to give it up—the centerpiece of the etiology of *Homosexualität:* attachment to the penis is, as it were, the most primary of the secondary repressions. In perhaps the most important species of *Nachträglichkeit* identified by Freud, this early attachment is supposedly both recalled and reorganized in the growing boy's experience of "castration threats" and resulting "castration anxiety." But the *explanation for* this *Interesse*—the account of the primary repression itself—remains vague, though *Leonardo* offered a new theoretical category, "narcissism," to handle it. In fact, the only structural and historical account of a primary homosexual repression conforming adequately to the terms of Freud's own psychology—*Empfindung* somehow already knows, originally, that its *Interesse* should be in preserving and valuing the penis at all costs and despite all mature and rational evidence for its relative unimportance, which amounts, for all intents and purposes, to a "congenital" *Inversion*—would be presented in the Wolf Man case history. But there, oddly enough, as we have already seen in part, the site of the primary repression—the construction of the primary *Interessen* determining secondary repression—is not the penis at all but the anus. This was so, we can now begin to see, because the intersubjective determination of "homosexuality" in the case of the Wolf Man concerned the two men's attitude to the anus which each was presenting for (the penis of) the other; throughout Freud's exploration, in fact, "homosexuality" is less a matter of the essential "narcissistic" relation of a man to his penis and its ongoing projection onto other men's bodies—as *Leonardo* (Freud 1910c) and a few other texts tended to suggest—and more broadly an issue of the recognition of his penis, of his body and general personal identity, by others with and toward whom he takes up both a psychological and a social relation as master or as slave.

Importantly, despite Little Hans's overattention to the penis, he is not necessarily an invert or *Homosexual*. In fact, despite his possible inaugural *Inversion,* his "homosexuality" appears chiefly qua *Empfindung* in his expression of affectionate homosexual sentiments, echoing those of traditional homoerotic romance; embracing a slightly older male cousin, he exclaimed, "I *am* so fond of you!" Freud's analytic burden throughout the paper is rhetorical or narratological: he must somehow establish a plausible continuity between the several roots and manifestations of Hans's *Homosexualität*—for to show how ordinary or slightly extraordinary *Empfindungen* (presumably all little boys enjoy seeing the little boys who enjoy seeing them) somehow depend on or devolve from a peculiar *Interesse,* the possible *Inversion,* of the subject would be, of course, to justify depth-psychological method and the specifically psychoanalytic quest for structures of primary and secondary "repression." But the reader of "Little Hans" will note that the supposed causal connection between Hans's "interest" in the penis and his "affection" for his male cousin has been imposed quite arbitrarily by Freud; though temporally sequential, their inner or essential relation, their intrapsychic connection in *Nachträglichkeit,* remains purely hypothetical.

The *Three Essays,* "Little Hans," and related papers were very carefully crafted conceptually. But throughout them the operative term *Homosexualität* risked becoming merely one of the most useful devices for papering over the gaps, empirical and theoretical, between instincts, interests, and feelings. *Homosexualität* finds homoeroticism in all these phases, faculties, or registers of the subject and *as* temporally and causally interconnected phases or registers. For precisely this reason, application of the term in this sense, quite different from Kertbeny's and Ulrichs's, was vigorously resisted at the time by those determined to maintain distinctions or what we might now call "difference"—for example, by the circle of Friedlaender, when any account would extend *Homosexualität* from feelings to instincts, and by the circle of Hirschfeld, when any account would extend *Homosexualität* from instincts to feelings. Among all contemporary inquiries, psychoanalysis—both theory and therapy—was by far the most committed to such strong "lateral" or archaeological and teleological movements through the supposed whole arborized structure of the psyche right down to the bottom of its roots.[4]

In addition to distinguishing *Inversion* and *konträre Geschlechtsfühl,* the *Three Essays* clearly recognized that sheer *Homosexualität,* the brute fact of "contingent" male-male sexual relations between men on shipboard, in prisons, and elsewhere, does not say anything one way or another about whether the sex was a consequence of either *Interesse* or *Empfindung* in the senses intended. The invert is irresponsible because he cannot help it; a man suffering "contrary sexual feeling" is responsible because he *can* help it; but the casual or temporary homosexual is irresponsible because he also cannot help it, though for different reasons than the invert. The difference between invert and casual homosexual, then, is the measure and quality of their *Empfindung,* for while the invert cannot help feeling lust or love for his partner, the casual homosexual cannot help *not* feeling for him. The complex permutations that could be engendered from this basis cannot be explored here. They would include, for example, the experience of a "homosexual" among sailors, prisoners, or other male societies—for example, as represented in Pierre Loti's influential novel *Mon Frère Yves* (1887), which impressed Symonds greatly, or, later, some of Genet's narratives—and of "men of feeling" in relation to "homosexuals" who love them, as in certain novels by Louis Couperus (e.g., 1891) and several German writers of the Wilhelmine era (for the latter, see Jones 1990).

Though none of these points were novel in themselves or considered separately, Freud's way of interrelating the terms led him, probably partly unaware, to a very distinctive perspective. Whether or not a man is a congenital invert (at points Freud would need to excavate the psyche to the "bedrock" of a person's heritage or biology), what must interest us are the specifically psychological vicissitudes of his feeling (*Empfindung*), affect (*Affekt*), and interest (*Interesse*)—for which the model of repression, developed in the period 1897–1901, already provided a rich descriptive and flexible explanatory approach. More specifically, the invert's "feeling" is, as it were, *more* irresponsible than a man's moral constitution when he displays "contrary sexual feeling," for which—the law said—he was thoroughly responsible. Nonetheless he is more *responsible* than that creature, ruled by his congenital nature, who had been imagined by the emancipationist homosexualists, for the Freudian "homosexual" does manifest a feeling, although, and most crucially, it is not *he himself* who is wholly responsible for it: the invert, or what Freud newly dubbed the "amphigenic" homosexual—the absolute opposite of the "contingent" homosexual—cannot help feeling for another man *when that man (he thinks) feels for him.* The Freudian homosexual is an uneasy, puzzling synthesis of the congenital homosexual, practicing contingently or not, and general *Empfindung* between men, inverted or not. In "Little Hans," for example, the "first sign" of the boy's "homosexuality"—"though," Freud says, "it will not be the last" (1909b: 9)—was his response to his cousin's visit: when the other boy arrives at Hans's house, Hans must be taking his appearance as a sign of the other's special interest or favor—or else worries that the other is *not* interested—for him to cry out, while embracing the other, "I *am* so fond of you!"

Homosexuality and Intersubjectivity

Little Hans's behavior can be taken as an exemplary case. But in more general terms, for a man to be "homosexual" in Freud's lexicon from 1905 to 1910 is for him to be "passive," "receptive," "dependent," or even "seductive" in relation to the desires of other men *for him*—their desires to befriend him, to accompany and admire him, to share with him, to compete with him, to challenge or attack him. In turn, pathologies of this formation could easily be identified; the basic approach would even predict them. Ordinary neurosis presumably remains fundamentally moral, responsible, and other-directed (as the early Freudian approach to the legal responsibility of neurotics suggests). But in the processes Freud had already tracked in his "economic" models of libidinal transformation, ordinary neurosis can become an excessively irrational neurosis or a psychosis, increasingly amoral, irresponsible, and inward-looking, such as the homosexual "paranoia" supposed to result from the projection of *frustrated* seductiveness—originally encouraged, in turn, by the other's original, if perhaps erotically unfeeling, attention—back on to the other, now reimagined as a dangerous pursuer. Not surprisingly, such excrescences constituted the actual cases of Freudian homosexuality *in analysis* or, at least, in the clinical situations the Freudians observed at second hand—the "impotence" or "paranoia" of "repressed" homosexuals, the manias or obsessions of "sublimated" homosexuals, the "phobias" of "latent" homosexuals. But they should not be confused with the general metapsychology of Freudian homosexuality as such.

The Freudian concept of "homosexuality," then, decisively emphasizes—in fact, absolutely requires—an actualized intersubjective situation. Indeed, Freudian "homosexuality" is just (and only) a property of particular intersubjective male-male and female-female relations: it is the property which marks, in ways and for reasons to be defined, the slight overestimation, the marked excess, or, perhaps, the tremendous deflection and distortion of that affectionate, morally responsible *Empfindung* which should properly characterize such relations in self-regulating, self-defending, and self-perpetuating "civilized" society. Of course, the slide from slight overestimation, as in Hans's affectionate response to his cousin, to baroque distortion, such as Judge Schreber's paranoia, requires a good deal of precise thought—but here, as I have already noted, nothing more than a flexible, imaginative application of the economic principles of libido will be required. The fundamental problem lies at the *beginning* of the slide: what launches the subject into the peculiar management, the perverse economy, of its intersubjectively created, and socially justifiable, "homosexuality," possibly creating, in the end, formations of "homosexuality" which are neither intersubjectively feasible nor socially desirable?

The full measure of the difference between Freud's approach and the rival conceptualizations already sketched was not really taken at the time, even by psychoanalysts. All of the conceptualizations, of course, had a political dimension, for they translated into, or had been initially designed to make, direct recommendations about law and social policy. In this regard, they remained continuous with well-established canonical and secular discussions of sodomy and of "hermaphroditism," to which they often bear close conceptual or logical similarity—for example, to discussions about whether adult sodomites' sex partners, such as dumb animals, could be punished, or whether "hermaphrodites" could be permitted to marry or to bear witness to a legal instrument.

What has been said so far implies that Freud's approach was aligned with the liberalism but not necessarily with the *libertarianism* of the emancipationists. On the one hand, he never regarded homosexuality as such as a threat to the social order, unless an individual homosexual's unhappiness—largely caused by his failure to be recognized *by* others in the way he found himself desiring their interest—leads to a potentially sociopathic transformation of his behavior. On the other hand, homosexuality as such cannot be permitted to flourish unchecked—for it has been understood to begin *in* a transformation of the truly social or moral subject, that is, in a slight economic perversion—its causes remain unspecified—of his intersubjective moral centering. Hence a fully libertarian response to the "biological" existence of "homosexuality" would ultimately conflict with the liberal commitment to the maintenance of a social order protecting individuals from the pathic interferences of others. It is not a contradiction to notice that Freud spoke out publicly in support of certain homosexual defendants at the same time as Freudians—or influential jurists influenced by early psychoanalysis—testified against homosexual "criminals."

The political and legal questions which were originally at stake in Freud's formulation of an intersubjective approach to homosexuality deserve further research. But clearly Freud's approach has been enormously influential ever since. For example, a present-day debate about so-called essentialist versus so-called constructionist concepts of homosexuality embeds the more fundamental distinction between—the genuinely philosophical debate about—a basically non-Freudian and monadic as opposed to a basically Freudian and dyadic account of "homosexuality" as a species of personhood. The principal rival conceptions had all focused on a man's wholly individual, independent, and, in fact, generally solipsistic subjective experience of emotional yearning and sometimes sexual desire for another man. This *Empfindung* is supposedly never wholly recognized and erotically reciprocated by that other, and its natural *or* social origins in some special *Instinkt* or *Gefühl* remained mysterious (for example, in terms of the theory of natural selection) precisely because of the basic atomism of the approach.

By contrast, as I have been urging, Freud saw homosexuality as that which is solicited in and drawn out of a man *by* another: a man's "homosexuality" is the psychic complement—more exactly, the psychosocial product—of the homosexuality *directed at* him by another. Not all of the Freudians managed to grasp this point, which we might fairly call the basic psychoanalytic one; Isidor Sadger, for example, tended to reproduce the image of a homosexual as an isolated being—a kind of psychological "sport of nature"—longing for connection with others who are not and cannot be like him (Sadger 1908, 1909a, 1909b). Whence the "homosexuality" of the other derives is, of course, a crucial problem; a logical regress seems to be embedded in the Freudian view, partly motivating, for example, its apparently unnecessary interest in the psychosexual or sociopsychic events of deep prehistory as well as Freud's own obsessive interest in "group" dynamics, especially in his own male network. (For sheer bulk of pages, Freud probably wrote more about this last topic, broadly conceived, than about anything else; see especially Freud 1985; Freud/ Jung 1974; Freud/Abraham 1965; Freud/Ferenczi 1993; Freud/Jones 1993.) Most important, this other, whatever the source of *his* "homosexual" desire, is conceived *as* a subject, as having desires, knowledge, and aims of his own which constitutively affect the subject in question, the subject of self- or psychoanalysis, in an intersubjective connection. The rival conceptions, rooted in the traditions of pederastic and homoeroticist representation in European art and literature, tended to conceive the other as the pure *object* of the subject's peculiar (and necessarily unrequited) desire; when intersubjective expression or liaison, the interpersonal complement of *intrapsychic* intersubjectivity, had been socially barred, the eighteenth- or nineteenth-century homoeroticist could imagine himself only to be utterly alone, communing with subjects like himself only in nostalgic and utopian fantasy (see further Davis 1994, 1995b, n.d.).

At the deepest level, a fundamental shift in the imagination of gender distinguishes the pre-Freudian and the Freudian lexicon. In pederastic and homoeroticist representations, the masculine "homosexual" subject's homoerotic object—a beautiful boy, a romantically disposed friend—was conceived to be like a woman, that is, to occupy the feminine position in psychosexual relations. This object is the target, at least, of "male" desire, imagination, pursuit, and control, however frustrated. In the Freudian representation, however, the masculine homosexual subject *himself* occupies the feminine position—for he is the erotic object of another man's desires, evoking in him his "homosexual" feeling. In his actual use of the term in case descriptions or the analysis of a "total" psychic structure, typically Freud considers a man's *Homosexualität,* his current of "homosexual" fantasy, to involve the wish—it might or might not be acted out in the overt dynamics of the relationship—to occupy a "feminine," a passive and receptive, position in relation to other men (see Freud/Jung 1974: 353 [September 24, 1910]).

Adding to the conceptual complexity of all this, of course, was the more superficial fact that "effeminacy" had long been partly identified with the pederast or homoeroticist, and more recently with the "invert" or "homosexual." Here, like certain homosexualists of the day, Freud asserted the potential "masculinity" of the homosexual position—the fact that the man who might be psychologically "feminized," homosexualized, by other men's desires for him need not appear or act as if he were female. (Indeed, he might well have attracted the others' desire precisely because of his successful erotic and social embodiment of the purest "masculine" possibility—for example, in athletic prowess or intellectual charisma.) As a male child matures, he necessarily becomes anxious about the inherent conflict between this "homosexual" feeling and his supposed adoption of a masculine, heterosexual status. The ordinary man's problem is not so much his "homosexuality" as such—it can well be the sign (literally the symptom) of his masculine intersubjective success—but its possible "femininity," its potential to deprive him imaginarily or actually of the very basis of his masculine attractiveness to other men in the first place, namely, his male (usually specifically phallic) beauty and prowess. In turn, a man's comparatively mature resistance to maintaining the purest and earliest form of his "homosexuality" ordinarily results in a reaction-formation, typically a (homo)phobia. Masculinity is thus restored—though "homosexuality" is continuous—in the psychic activity of fending off femininity.

In sum, Freudian "homosexuality" is the psychic registration of the way a man has and has not been able to get on with other men; it is the record, ultimately, of their (non)desire for him. This intersubjective history will vary from one institution to another in society (for example, in marriage, games, travel, and public politics) and according to a man's occupational or economic situation and other factors (such as his ethnicity or race) which Freud himself did not really investigate. But, as the case history of the Wolf Man shows, Freud did concern himself closely with what he believed must be the irreducible psychic formations brought to any and all such interpersonal connections—namely, the dispositions of personal temperament and the habit- or feeling-systems, chiefly Oedipal, laid down in the earliest family experience.

The Homosexual Preconscious

Within this broad field, of course, a considerable differentiation of homosexual types—and an account of the several pathologies derivable from or parasitic upon mundane homosexuality—can and must be put together. The Freudians' interest in homosexuality seems to have increased substantially in the years 1908 and 1909. Four years earlier, the *Three Essays on the Theory of Sexuality* (1905d) had offered a description of homosexuality in terms of "bisexuality." This account was based almost exclusively on Freud's surveys of the medical, psychiatric, and sexological literature and on nonpsychoanalytic (i.e., psychiatric) observations of practicing homosexuals, often including their personal testimonies as recorded by their doctors (e.g., Schrenck-Notzing 1895; Krafft-Ebing 1894). It has not been noticed, in fact, that Freud's bibliographical survey of work on "bisexuality" in the *Three Essays* (1905d: 9 n. 1) was substantively derived (not to say plagiarized) from a review published by the emancipationist lawyer Eugen Wilhelm ("Numa Praetorius") in the 1904 *Jahrbuch für sexuelle Zwischenstufen,* edited by Hirschfeld, even though the intellectual appeal, and to some extent the content, of Freud's notion had derived from his exchanges with Wilhelm Fliess.[5]

The descriptions and classifications proposed in the *Three Essays* were clear, innovative, and convincing. But at an explanatory level the book was notoriously incomplete. Freud tended to indulge a pure metaphysics of original or primal "bisexuality," though the term, at that point, was really an acknowledgment that one did not know the causal origin of adult, manifest or practicing homosexuality: "bisexuality" was a halfway house between the sexologists' claim that homosexuality was originally *hetero*sexual, corrupted by weakness of the will, masturbation, vice, and seduction, and the homosexualists' claim that homosexuality was congenitally homosexual.

An etiological account of infantile and childhood development *from* "bisexuality" *to* overt "homosexuality" did not begin to emerge until Freud's work on "Little Hans" (Freud 1909b) and the "Sexual Theories of Children" (Freud 1908c). Even then, however, the account was not wholly satisfactory. Especially in the latter text, Freud proposed that potential "homosexuals" have placed an inordinately "high estimate of value" on the "universal phallus" in which they believed as children. But this idea did not function as a complete historical explanation. It tended to assume rather than to explain a little "homosexual"'s overestimation of "widdlers," including his own—the mistaken judgment of value which, carried into adult life, supposedly leads to his inability to love creatures who do not possess the phallus (namely, women) and to prefer creatures who do possess it (namely, "youths with a feminine appearance") (Freud 1908c; cf. Freud 1910c). Still, "homosexual" men referred to psychoanalysis by Hirschfeld, practicing in Berlin, were often "impotent" in their marriages, and this finding, made continuously in pre-psychoanalytic sexology, could be made to fit in with the Freudian account. (Hirschfeld himself probably hoped that these face-to-face interactions with practicing homosexuals—whose published personal testimonies frequently insisted on the point—would convince Freud that homosexuality must have a congenital or constitutional basis.) Certainly there was little reason to suppose that any of these homosexual men—whatever the origins and nature of their mistaken erotic value judgments—were substantially disturbed or pre-psychotic. Their intrapsychic troubles flowed from their interpersonal frustration, because they had not, as it were, marshaled the currency to complete heterosexual transactions (specifically, the exchange of women) in the social network. For all that, Freud did not regard homosexual processes in psychic or social life to be intrinsically pathological; homosexuals are poor, as it were, but not evil or sick. The point had been made very firmly in the *Three Essays*. Further investigation of actual cases in the period 1905–14—now, for the first time, Freud actually dealt with a few homosexual patients—did nothing to change Freud's conviction.

However, in the two or three years preceding the beginning of the Wolf Man's analysis in 1910, and in the years 1910–14, Freud and his associates became especially interested in the relations between male or female homosexuality and paranoia. The famous *Memoirs* of Judge Daniel Paul Schreber, Freud thought, provided important evidence here. But actually Freud's conclusions about pathologies of homosexuality seem to have been developed, somewhat earlier than his reading of Schreber, as a response to cases of particular clients and patients. Not surprisingly, these clients were quite different from the "impotent" men referred by Hirschfeld and widely familiar not only from the established sexological literature but also, by this point, from literary representations (see Jones 1990); these new clients, of course, were the troubled neurotic, even pre-psychotic, men and women attracted specifically to psychoanalysis for reasons substantially *unrelated to* their "homosexuality," if any, as such.

For example, Ferenczi's Budapest friend and colleague Philipp Stein, a neurologist who had worked with Jung, seems to have been a practicing, self-acknowledged homosexual, though not a completely "uninhibited" one. Freud called him an "invert"—applying one of the usual sexological labels—to mark the fact that his homosexuality was overt. But Stein apparently consulted with Freud, who in turn recommended an analysis with Ferenczi, because he suffered from a "true anxiety hysteria" (Freud/ Ferenczi 1993: 40 [February 2, 1909]), the causes of which remain unclear. "[It is] strange that most of these inverts are not complete human beings," Freud remarked to Ferenczi with reference to Stein (ibid.: 43 [February 7, 1909]). Unfortunately we do not have Stein's side of the story. Quite possibly he was dissatisfied with the psychoanalysts' attempt to interpret his "anxiety" in terms of his homosexuality as such—etiologically hooking his mental illness to the one area of his being, his "homosexuality," that could be defined as already "incomplete"—rather than simply in terms of well-placed fears about his public exposure: several months later, Ferenczi wrote to Freud, Stein had "turned away from us to a certain extent; he talks in public about the fact that I (and you) 'went too far,' 'want to explain everything in sexual terms,' 'neglect the self preservative drive' " (ibid.: 83 [October 14, 1909]). Stein did attend Freud's lecture on December 1, 1908, when he first spoke about Leonardo da Vinci's childhood fantasy (Nunberg and Federn 1962–75: II, 338–52). Freud relayed the information to Ferenczi because they both understood that Stein would be the natural audience for Freud's speculations in the lecture (cf. Freud 1910c) about the psychological origins of homosexuality. But evidently Stein failed to react as Freud hoped; though specifically remarking that Stein was there, Freud complained that he "didn't get to hear any good response" (Freud/ Ferenczi 1993: 110 [December 3, 1908]). Like many educated homosexuals of his day, and in view of the fact that he was a neurologist, Stein was probably a Hirschfeldian. In late 1910 he invited Hirschfeld to lecture on homosexuality in Budapest, possibly giving Hirschfeld the opportunity to dispute Freud's published study of Leonardo (see ibid.: 226 [October 12, 1910]).

With the publication of the *Three Essays* in 1905, Freud's practice could have taken the same turn as Hirschfeld's—toward running a general "clinic" for sexual diseases (it is not as well known as it should be that in the 1880s Freud had been somewhat involved in syphilis research [Macmillan 1992: 99–100]), sexual dysfunctions, sexual variations, and any related mental illnesses. But his practice remained the more time-consuming, and expensive, depth-psychological one—involving less grungy patients than Hirschfeld would sometimes see—implied by *Studies on Hys-*

teria (Freud and Breuer 1895d) and *Die Traumdeutung* (1900a). One might go so far as to say that whereas Freud's clinical practice remained a fundamentally nineteenth-century investigation of the troubled human soul, Hirschfeld's increasingly became a quintessentially twentieth-century outpatient medical-social service. Hence the "homosexual" patients seen by Hirschfeld and by Freudians were quite different.

Philipp Stein, a busy and probably harried and anxious professional man like Freud himself, was supposedly a "hysteric." Freud did not *equate* Stein's hysteria with his homosexuality but instead apparently tried to conjure the former out of the latter in a fashion that Stein could not fathom and clearly regarded as forced or overdrawn. Consistent with his underlying concept of homosexuality as intersubjectively rooted, Freud avoided equations between homosexuality and individual pathology; he was never enthusiastic, for example, about Ferenczi's (1914) simple identification of homosexuality with "obsessional neurosis" (see Freud/Ferenczi 1993: 507 [September 14, 1913])—for it would seem to miss the historical and etiological point he was struggling to articulate.

Freud's verdict about a homosexually defined pathology hinges on the vicissitudes of the *repression* of homosexuality, not visible, of course, in the overt "invert" Stein—such as Judge Daniel Paul Schreber's supposed reconstruction of his homosexuality in a system of paranoiac delusions. Freud probably overdramatized the extent of Schreber's sexualization of his relationship to his psychiatrist Flechsig (see Fairbairn 1956; Lothane 1989), but Schreber apparently never had a homosexual sexual experience. His only overt "perversion" was private cross-dressing. But irrespective of Schreber's actual erotic experience, "in the world of the unconscious" the judge's "homosexuality"—in both "regression" and "repression"—supposedly determined his fantasy life (Freud 1911c: 43). Freud's study of Schreber (1911c) has sometimes been thought to be claiming that homosexuality and paranoia are essentially linked—that a "homosexual" is necessarily or intrinsically a "paranoiac." But as Freud's interpretation of Schreber's memoirs makes clear, the judge's paranoia resulted from his projection of homosexual desire onto other personages, such as his psychiatrist Dr. Flechsig or various spirits, whom he then imagined to be desiring or otherwise pursuing him. The contrast with Stein and others is crucial: Stein's "hysteria" was unrelated to his "homosexuality," but Schreber's "paranoia" translates—and thus continues—it; where Stein is overt, Schreber, possessed of the same *Instinkt* or *Empfindung,* is not.[6]

Nevertheless, a fine, perhaps imperceptible, line had to be drawn between, on the one hand, a wholly repressed, totally unconscious "homosexuality," the stratum of the subject's primary erotic need for the interest of others of his or her gender as organized in and by their attention to him or her, and, on the other hand, the manifestation of some "detached" component of this homosexuality—overemphasized and distorted—in a conscious awareness or avowal of homosexual fantasies or desires. The first formation can (though it need not) produce debilitating repression— for example, in the paranoid process. But any such pathological manifestation cannot be "cured" if the primary stratum of homosexuality is utterly and irremediably unconscious, that is, cannot be discharged, even in analysis. Thus the analytic "cure" of debilitating repression becomes dependent, paradoxically enough, on discovering some preexisting discharge of repressed homosexuality in the subject's life history—that is, on identifying a second or secondary stratum of homosexuality as it were becoming-conscious or coming-into-consciousness. Plucking at this thread should, in principle, enable the analyst to get the patient to loop back further to the primary stratum and the pathology supposedly leaning on it. Good tugs here would be as good as, or better than, a direct assault on the deeply buried memory of the traumas which had *created* the pathological *Anlehnung*.

In turn, however, this preconscious formation—it might be something mundane such as a predilection for athletic games—cannot be *too* homosexual, for then it would be driven back into repression by the analyst's focus on it. Instead, the analyst has to find just enough of the primary, intersubjectively organized homosexuality in a preconscious domain to start a *recall* of the primary homosexuality and reveal, if analysis is deft enough, an opening into the pathological formation leaning on it. If the subject's homosexual potential subsists in some kind of identifiable secondary discharge—what Freud, in the Wolf Man case history, will call "latency"—then the pathology of his homosexuality can be overcome. Strictly speaking, "latency," as I have suggested, is the continuing partial discharge *from* the primary *into* the secondary stratum of subjective homosexuality. In itself it need and usually does not manifest the pathological excrescence on the primary stratum, but it can become the analyst's "royal road" toward pathology if there is any such formation present.

Once discharge from the secondary into the final or conscious stratum occurs, overtness or blatancy exists—and the temporary therapeutic opening closes again. Here, because psychic energy is now being discharged into the world rather than distributed from one locality to another *within* the subject, very little effective retrospective reorganization of the primary or the secondary stratum could be obtained. Like the utterly repressed homosexual, the fully overt homosexual—but for opposite reasons—cannot be cured of his *homosexuality,* though he might be helped to live more happily. By contrast, the latent homosexual, again somewhat paradoxically, can be rescued from his homosexuality as such by becoming conscious of its primary manifestations and of their excrescences—a consciousness which does not, however, make him into a healthy *overt* homosexual but, as Freud put it, "liberates" him altogether.

The Freudians' work from approximately 1908–1909, in cases such as Little Hans, to 1910–12, including the Schreber, Leonardo, and Wolf Man studies as well as a number of less well known and poorly documented clinical cases, suggests that what we might call the *homosexual preconscious,* the necessary condition for any psychoanalytic therapy, greatly interested them. In fact, handling it delicately enough (as Freud and Ferenczi failed to do in the case of Philipp Stein) was one of the greatest tests of the psychoanalytic possibility itself: we could say that although therapy requires latency, the interests of therapy—of psychoanalysis itself—immediately recognized that latency requires therapy. The sheer possibility that latency could progress to a blatancy of rather than a liberation from homosexuality means that this phase or register of the subject should be placed under continuous surveillance—if not in analysis itself, at least in a psychoanalytically directed social and cultural policy. At the same time, since the therapy of any *particular* latency should ideally result in the identification of the homosexual preconscious and the overcoming of any pathology of the primary homosexual formation, that is, in a "cure," the *final* interest of therapy—attending to the continuity of the practice itself—requires that homosexual latency must be universal. There must always be more of it no matter what society does or does not do with overt homosexuals.

The case and case history of the Wolf Man is the great text of homosexual latency under psychoanalytic review—here, the pathological excrescences of an intersubjectively organized primary homosexuality could supposedly be overcome. But it seems clear that the case is continuous with others in which the same struggle occurred, no doubt with very different results from situation to situation. For example, a little less than a year before the Wolf Man came to Freud, a young man recovering from a venereal infection—just like the Wolf Man—displayed signs of what Ferenczi called "obsessional neurosis," also like the Wolf Man. As a neurotic, in principle he could be cured. But even after a month's treatment, no transference emerged (the Wolf Man's, of course, would emerge during the very first meetings). Now he seemed to Ferenczi to be more like a true "paranoiac," that is, a psychotic beyond the reach of treatment: "he has," Ferenczi asserted, "a very strong but completely unconscious homosexual component that also *can't be made conscious*" (Freud/Ferenczi 1993: 58 [May 1, 1909], my emphasis). His homosexuality was visible in what Ferenczi called the "symbolism" of his speech—but apparently the patient could not be made or persuaded to understand this symbolism, and Ferenczi had to conclude that it was not, after all, in his preconscious awareness. (Of course, like Philipp Stein a month or two earlier, and like the Wolf Man many years later, he just might have thought Ferenczi's interpretations were farfetched.) By contrast, a later patient, "a young, very intelligent woman with jealousy mania," could possibly be cured precisely because she had "conscious homosexual interests *as well*"; "at this point of *cs. homosexuality,* I can gradually pull out everything she has projected up to now" (ibid.: 315–16 [November 26, 1911], my emphasis). In fact, it was at this time that Ferenczi, in particular, began exploring innovative, even wild or dangerous, techniques of analysis itself. Although a full study remains to be written, it seems fairly clear that his researches were motivated by the possibility that the preconscious is speaking in various cases of "thought transference"; although a person is not completely conscious that he has acquired a bit of information, sensed another's interest in a particular topic, or been thinking along lines that have been intersubjectively provoked, he suddenly speaks as if he were contributing to what was consciously on the mind of his interlocutor or even of third parties (see especially ibid.: 205–209 [August 17, 1910], concerning a patient projecting his homosexuality in paranoia).

Complementing the study of Schreber, an account of unconscious but *non*pathological homosexuality—that is, of the vicissitudes of primary, intersubjectively organized homosexuality before and into preconscious discharge, but without the excrescence of a projection into paranoia—was worked out in Freud's 1910 study of Leonardo (Freud 1910c). Freud was still working on the draft in the first weeks of his analysis with the Wolf Man.

Leonardo's image making could not be connected with particularly "perverse" actions, let alone paranoiac delusions. Unlike some historians—including Dmitri Merezhkovsky, whose semifictional biography of the artist Freud used extensively—Freud did not think Leonardo had directly sexual relations with certain of his apprentices (see Freud 1910c: 73). Like Schreber, Leonardo was not (Freud believed) an overt homosexual. In fact, Freud was more reluctant to apply the term "homosexual" as unequivocably to Leonardo as he had to Schreber. Whereas Schreber's homosexuality is merely "unconscious," Leonardo's is supposedly "ideal"; ignoring any intimation that Leonardo had overt same-sex sexual relations, Freud suggests that his repression was partially discharged or "sublimated" in his creative work (ibid.: 80–81). Of course, homosexual sexual activity and sublimation need not be mutually exclusive. But because Freud treats them as such in his study of Leonardo, it is not surprising that Leonardo's sublimation—his painting—should come to carry the whole load of his hypothetical primary homosexuality in its full economy, for which Freud provides an elaborate "maternal etiology," not our topic here (for the term, see Freud/Ferenczi 1993: 156 [April 10, 1910]; cf. Freud 1910h).[7]

Freud considered Leonardo's art principally as an instance of the *sublimation* of the subject's "homosexuality," whereas in Schreber's case he was equally or even more interested in the evidence for *regression* and *derepression* (paranoiac projection), the partly distorted expressions of the subject's archaic homosexuality (see Fig. 52). Thus, in Freud's two psychoanalytic biographies, "repressed" Schreber in one sense appears more "homosexual," as it were, than "ideal" Leonardo—even though Leonardo, in another sense, is much closer to an overt, adult homosexual eroticism than Schreber. The difference arises partly from assumptions Freud accepts but does not explicitly justify. For example, Schreber, but not Leonardo, is already known to be a psychotic—thus more likely to regress. By contrast, Leonardo's images, but not Schreber's writings, are already accepted as creative art—thus more likely to be sublimations.

In contrast to both Schreber and Leonardo, the Wolf Man is supposedly neither regressing and projecting, like Schreber, nor enjoying Leonardo's (and Freud's) creative "overcoming." Instead, he is supposedly a "latent" homosexual, "shackled" by what Freud supposes was his "inherited" prehomosexual predisposition. In Freud's account, the Wolf Man's homosexuality is simultaneously everywhere and nowhere. The peculiarity of his explanation of its origins—and of the concept of "latent" homosexuality in general—can be partly traced to the possibility that Freud was wrong about his patient on both counts. Like Schreber, the Wolf Man probably manifested "psychotic" tendencies, but less dramatically, and like Leonardo, but less dramatically here too, he probably was more creative than Freud believed.

To protect the integrity of the "case" apparently offered by the Wolf Man, Freud *minimized* the patient's psychosis and *maximized* the "apathy" of his obvious intelligence and creativity. And because the case was to exemplify the preeminence of infantile sexuality, it was necessary to in-

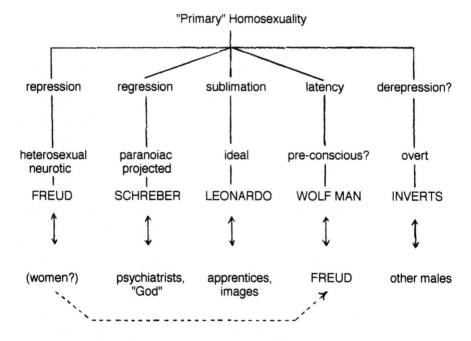

Figure 52. Freud's imagination of the "homosexual" positions of Schreber, Leonardo, and the Wolf Man, showing the elision of the Wolf Man's and Freud's adult repressed homosexuality in relation to "latent" homosexuality

fantilize the patient. His "homosexuality" could not be a childhood, ado-lescent, or adult homosexuality, however organized in repression, stand-ing between the extremes of regression and projection, on the one hand, and sublimation, on the other. Instead, it had to be "latent" in the period of the most archaic sexuality or the childhood years immediately follow-ing it.

VI

FAMILY TREES

> What makes [the analyst] certain in the end is precisely the complication of the problem before him, which is like the solution of a jig-saw puzzle. [. . .] If one succeeds in arranging the confused heap of fragments, each of which bears upon it an unintelligible piece of drawing, so that the picture acquires a meaning, so that there is no gap anywhere in the design and so that the whole fits into the frame—if all these conditions are fulfilled, then one knows that one has solved the puzzle and that there is no alternative solution.
>
> —Freud, "Remarks on the Theory and Practice of Dream-Interpretation" (1923c: 116)

> We are often able to see the schema triumphing over the experience of the individual.
>
> —Freud, "From the History of an Infantile Neurosis" (1918b: 119)

Freud's schematization of the structure of dreams and parapraxes shows that the rooting of repression, of the branches of memory, is the intrinsic doubleness or "bisexuality" of the subject—despite his repression of his memory of the double, homosexualized origins of the idea itself. Activation of the subject's "bisexual" constitution inherently introduces unpleasure into the psychic system. Lateral, deferred discharge—"repression"—will be required to minimize the quantity of unpleasure at any given psychic locality and to defend the organism from an excessive discharge. In the simplest formula, then, bisexuality = repression.

Nächtraglichkeit and *Zurückphantasieren*

This formula, however, was not complete. At some very early historical point in the development of a human subject, the network of lateral, deferred discharge, of "repression," will not yet have been laid down. At this early point, no perceptual impression has activated the intrinsic "bisexuality" of the subject. But at some later point, an incoming perception does activate his or her "bisexuality," generating his or her repressions by laying down the first division in, or branching of, the pathways to direct discharge. A perception of this kind might be called the "primal scene." It *evokes* the subject's double desire—and, for the sake of his or her preservation, in turn enforces an initial division in repression.

In the text of the case history, Freud reconstructs the content of the Wolf Man's primal scene from the material provided by the wolves in the dream. Observing the principle of distortion operating in dreamwork, Freud derives the "violent motion" of the primal scene from the represented immobility of the wolves (35). From the wolves' staring attentively at the dreamer, observing the same principle he derives the little boy staring at the scene. From their whiteness, he derives characteristics of the setting—the parents' white bedclothes, the bedding. From the "several" wolves, he derives the two parents; "as would be desirable," he asserts, the dreamwork avoids showing a couple (42). (In addition to reporting "some" white wolves, the Wolf Man also specified "six or seven," supposedly, Freud thinks, as a result of the way in which the memory of the primal scene had been routed through the fairy tale "The Wolf and the Seven Little Goats." The five wolves in the drawing, as we have seen, represent a correction of this distortion—not, however, to the couple themselves, "two," but rather to the hour of their coupling, "five.") From the attitude of the wolves, sitting high in the tree, Freud derives the sexual act itself, a "climbing up," because the wolves—as yet another of the Wolf Man's fairy tales had it—must have clambered up into the branches (43).

But the imagery of the dream is ambiguous. It does not always seem to support Freud's derivations, and he gives no clear reason why some of them work back through the dream's "distortions" (for example, its change of number) and some do not (for example, its memory of whiteness). In two additions to the case history written in 1918 for his publication of the 1914 draft, Freud acknowledged that the primal scene he had constructed—the Wolf Man's parents making love—could easily be regarded

as a distorted memory of a ram and a sheep or of white sheep dogs copulating on the family estate. In the dream report, after all, the dreamer
specifically stated that the "wolves" look "more like foxes or sheep dogs."
In fact, we have independent historical evidence—an old family photograph now in the Pankejeff Papers (Fig. 53)—that the Wolf Man himself,
as a young boy, was bundled up in wintertime in heavy sheepskin coats,
presumably manufactured by peasants or workmen on the family lands.
Whatever else it might have signified, the dream probably recalled him
to this childhood identity, with its textures, smell, weight, and warmth—
that is, his identity as the little sheep he had actually been imagined (by
his parents or Nanya) and made to be, or perhaps as the wolf who pursues
the sheep, or even the sheep dog who protects the sheep from the wolves.
There need have been no contradiction between all of these possibilities—
and still others we can barely glimpse—in the little boy's imagination.

Taking this general approach, it would certainly be possible to say that
during the night of anticipation before his birthday on Christmas Day,
the four-year-old Wolf Man "transferred" onto his parents a recent sight-
ing of real copulation between animals or other suggestive observations
of or games with the sheep, the sheep dogs, or even his old sheepskin coat.
"The inquisitive child [. . .] based upon his experience with the [sheep]
dogs, [wished] to witness his parents as well in their love-making; and
the scene which was thus imagined now produced [when dreamed] all
the effects that we have catalogued, just as though it had been entirely
real and not fused together out of two components, the one earlier and
indifferent [i.e., "innocent" views of the parents together], the other later
and profoundly impressive [i.e., copulating animals]" (58). Freud's second,
1918 version of the meaning and sources of the dream is tremendously
appealing. But if it were to be fully accepted, of course, it would disprove
the "case" Freud had been trying to make with the Wolf Man from the
very beginning of the analysis, proceeding from the initial "transference"
and his early "conviction" about the infantile sources of the dream.

In fact, the second, 1918 interpretation of the dream might be taken
to confirm Carl Jung's heretical view, target of Freud's polemic in *On the
History of the Psycho-Analytic Movement* (1914d), that neuroses involve retrospective fantasies (*Zurückphantasieren*). According to the Jungian account, later, sexualized perceptions, ideas, or memories have been trans-
planted by an adult neurotic back into his or her childhood past and are
then represented in the analysis as having welled up from that childhood.
Jung's account was a consistent alternative to Freud's belief in an endo-

Figure 53. Very young Serge
Pankejeff in a sheepskin
coat, family photograph, c.
1892–94 (Pankejeff Papers,
LC)

genous, primary, infantile sexuality. On historical grounds, it might seem
even more satisfactory: it could handle the imagery of the wolf dream,
for example, without making strong claims about the deep past of the
subject. It must, of course, make a claim about the more *recent* past of the
subject—for instance, by proposing that the adolescent or adult Wolf Man
had formed sexual thoughts about his parents while watching or remem-

bering animals copulating. This interpretation might be as difficult to confirm as the Freudian claim about the infant's "primal scene": the temporal remove of an event, or fantasy-thought about an event, from the "present-day" reference point of observation says nothing one way or another about the forensic evidence available to show that it really occurred. The virtue of Jung's account, then, lies not so much in its forensic or archaeological plausibility as in its methodological economy: Freud's account makes a claim about *both* the deep past *and* the recent past of the subject—namely, that they are sexual (indeed, that they are part of the *same* sexual history)—while Jung's account limits itself to the recent past only.

Freud was convinced that the Jungian alternative, however it could be developed in its details, would be unsatisfactory. In the case history of the Wolf Man, in contrast to the Jungian he holds definitively "to the more difficult and improbable view [that the primal scene was the parents' intercourse] [. . .] as a result of arguments such as are forced upon the investigator by the case described in these pages or by any other infantile neurosis" (103)—or by the preexisting pictures of repression we have already considered. In Freud's account, the incoming perception of parental intercourse should activate the subject's repression of his constitutional, primordial "bisexuality." Later on, this repression will only be compounded—for example, in the Wolf Man's case, by the dreamer's realization that the anatomical difference between the sexes holds out dire consequences for him if he wishes to assume his mother's sexual position in relation to his father's. Although he initially desires both his father's and his mother's place, a full-blown primordial "homosexuality," his ongoing repression of homosexuality will tend to disentangle and differentially repress his wishes. It might, for instance, suppress any element of the "feminine identification," the desire for his mother's position, and intensify the "masculine protest," the identification with the male position which supposedly guards against the consequences of assuming the female position.

This subtlety maps castration fears and developing (if secondary) narcissism back onto primary bisexuality in an instance of *Nachträglichkeit*. It cannot be achieved in Jung's account, which could probably account for the material of the dream report as such but could not really say why the patient's *childhood* neurosis should ever have arisen. Even more troubling, Jung's account would have later sexuality transferred back into early "memories" but would identify no "root," no forward causation of repression, to explain why any particular early memories should have become the retrospective target of more mature sexuality in the first place. The Jungian subject becomes *nothing but* an architecture of *Nachträglichkeit*—whereas the Freudian subject is a system of *Nachträglichkeit* causally organized *within a historically prior structure*.

To be specific, the longest loop of Freudian *Nachträglichkeit*—before it becomes a causative *Vorträglichkeit* in the "moebius loop" of the subject's history represented, for example, by Jacques Lacan's topologies—must loop back, as we have seen, through the earliest point in that history (see Fig. 38). And this "earliest" point in subjective historicity must also be the *latest* point in the *Vorträglichkeit* of inheritance, a preexisting historicity with its own peculiar temporality. There is no *Nachträglichkeit* in the inherited constitution—an individual organism obviously has no means of selectively and retroactively changing its biological endowment. Therefore this *Vortrag* "imprints" a certain structure which the very next *Vortrag within* the subject's history of "repression," the inaugural distinctions made at the first and earliest "contact-barriers" of psychic arborization, will now carry forward into any future *Nachträglichkeit*. Thus, whatever else occurs in the development of the subject after his or her birth, subjective *Nachträglichkeit* necessarily embodies the structure of the inherited "predispositions."

Throughout his psychoanalytic career, Freud remained fundamentally committed to this "biological" perspective. It can be expressed most exactly, in his case, by saying that the historicity of the subject's ontogenesis—if it is indeed historical at all—cannot be detached from the historicity of his or her phylogenesis. This is not necessarily to say that "ontogeny recapitulates phylogeny," though recapitulationist thought strongly influenced Freud. The fact of ontogenetic *Nachträglichkeit* means that the history of the development of the subject *revises*—not reproduces—the history of his or her ancestors (indeed, if this were not the case there could be no psychoanalysis). But revision, however extensive, occurs in relation to the model or template, and in a particular temporal order determined in the last instance by its configuration.

At the level of theory, Freud's account is better than Jung's. But it is still methodologically suspicious. Freud defined many of the subject's "predispositions" as inherited instincts to tolerate or even to prefer certain eroticisms or sexual pleasures—specific psychic "interests" guiding primary repression and explaining the inaugural movement of lateral binding. In most cases, however, Freud cannot have any evidence for the existence of these dispositions—such as a documentation of their earlier manifestation in the family line—apart from the fact that a later *Nachträglichkeit*, for which evidence has been found in the subject's intrapsychic history, has supposedly derived from them. If Jung's account would be empty, Freud's was patently circular.

Coitus a Tergo, Sodomy, and Bestiality

Freud's theory of repression requires the activation of the subject's intrinsic bisexual constitution in his or her primal scene. The primal scene must provide perceptual material giving pleasure to both the "homosexual" and the "heterosexual" currents within the subject—and it must do so in equal measure, for primary repression has not yet laterally distributed, or arborized, these stimulations. In the Wolf Man's case, Freud believed, the two currents of the patient's bisexuality had remained active throughout his early life. When he was four years old, for example, the little Wolf Man is supposed to have taken his father as his sexual object—the "negative" or "homosexual" form of his Oedipal desire—after his rejection by his nurse: this fantasy underlies his wolf dream at the end of his fourth year, his long-term castration anxiety, and the wolf phobia of his later childhood (32, 35–36, 42, 46). But Freud also claims that the little Wolf Man's object-choices at age two and a half were *heterosexual*— the "positive" form of his Oedipal desire. For example, supposedly he began desiring his mother as a sexual object after being reminded of her position in the primal scene through observing the housemaid Grusha scrubbing the kitchen floor (90–93).

At this point we reach the most central logical difficulty in Freud's account of the Wolf Man's subjective history. Consistent with the theory of repression, Freud insisted on the continuous, simultaneous presence of homosexual and heterosexual fantasies in the patient's life. But, as Adolf Grünbaum (1988: 626) has noted, Freud provides no independent grounds— apart from presumed fit with his "conviction" about the determinants of the patient's neurosis—to explain why the Wolf Man should have had a homosexual rather than a heterosexual fantasy, or vice versa, at any *particular* point. Although the Wolf Man could potentially entertain either kind of fantasy, heterosexual and homosexual, why, in fact, did he *actually* entertain one rather than the other?

The theory of repression, we should remember, requires that the dreamer desires to experience—he "identifies" with—the pleasure had by both parents. Such double identification clearly requires a view, some kind of perceptual impression, of his father satisfied by his mother and his mother satisfied by his father. The little observer, then, must have been able to see both parents simultaneously taking pleasure in making love—even though the face of one of the partners would ordinarily be facing away from the observer and his or her pleasure obscured. Freud specifies an exact scenario—his exactitude is driven by the logical importance of this stage in the argument—by constructing the primal scene as *coitus a tergo*, "intercourse from behind." Apparently he investigated this point especially carefully, perhaps even insisting on it in his "conviction" about the case: according to the case history, the Wolf Man "spontaneously" recollected *three* episodes of *coitus a tergo* but "projected" this memory onto Freud as Freud's own construction (37). In their *coitus a tergo*, the little Wolf Man simultaneously saw the flushed and pleasured faces of both parents—for, of course, they are supposed to have been making love like animals, both facing the same direction from which he could see them. In the *Nachträglichkeit* of the analytic construction, the *animals become the parents*: Freud interprets the white wolves in the dream as the Wolf Man's father and mother. But in the forward *Trag* of Freud's "conviction" about repression and its roots, the matter must have been precisely the other way around: *the parents become animals*.

Freud describes the parents' "intercourse from behind" as being "especially favorable for observation" (36) or "for [making] certain observations" (55, see also 38). The little observer, he claims, "was able to see his mother's genitals as well as his father's organ; and he [retroactively] understood the process [of their intercourse] as well as its significance" (37). He understood, in other words, that in order for him to assume his mother's place in the scene, he would have to possess genitals like hers rather than like his father's. The discovery "terrified" him, for "he saw with his own eyes the wound of which his Nanya had [earlier] spoken" (46) (she had presumably threatened to "cut it off" when she caught him displaying himself). In ongoing *Nachträglichkeit*, then, the homosexual and heterosexual currents activated by the primal scene would be differentially recalled, interpreted, and repressed, as the general theory of repression requires. Anything terrible would become unconscious.

As Serge Viderman has rightly pointed out, however, "the position *a tergo* is the *least* favorable to observe the female genitals, unless the child enjoyed the optimal position *neither* behind *nor* before the couple but at their very juncture" (1977: 306, my emphasis). In fact, Viderman could have added that in *coitus a tergo*—"which alone," Freud says, "offers the spectator a possibility of inspecting the genitals"! (59)—*both* parents' genitals would be obscured from the little observer if, as the account *also* has it, he was simultaneously supposed to be seeing their facial expressions. It is not surprising, then, that for all his effort at reconstructing and describing the specific mechanics of the primal scene, Freud concludes that "it is not clear" ("*non liquet*").[1]

Lee Edelman (1991) has suggested that Freud's description of the primal scene was disturbed by what Freud—as well as the Wolf Man—might have interpreted as its "sodomitical" elements. "Freud's ambivalence about the vision of penetration from behind," Edelman writes, "generates, in consequence, a certain defensiveness about the status of his own analytic hypothesis—a defensiveness that may tell us a great deal about the danger posed by the vision of the sodomitical scene" (ibid.: 99). The possibility of a "sodomitical" primal scene, according to Edelman, "destabilizes" the "definitional barriers" for sex; it "undoes" the conventional "logic of positionality." For Edelman, "this disorientation of positionality is bound up with the danger historically associated in Euro-American culture with the spectacle or representation of the sodomitical scene between men" (ibid.: 103).

Now certainly Freud's description of the primal scene did repeat, even as it partly revised and refused, elements of the homosexual relation between the two participants in the analysis—the patient and the doctor himself—established in the contemporary, intersubjective setting of the initial "transference." As we have already seen, Freud denies us crucial information about the "intercourse from behind" which had come up in the first consultation. And in a larger sense, he effectively subtracts or suppresses the evidence for his own possible "homosexual" position in relation to the patient. This involved not only Freud penetrating the Wolf Man "from behind"—Edelman (ibid.: 100) recalls the "position of the analyst . . . in relation to the man on the analyst's couch"—but also possibly evoked a complementary memory of a time when he himself was penetrated from behind. Much of this material was probably written out of the case history itself—precisely by being written into the peculiar construction of the primal scene—because it would divert attention from the specifically "infantile" causes of the "patient's neurosis."

But we must be cautious in identifying the way in which the "sodomitical" primal scene reconstructed by Freud does or does not evoke the "spectacle of gay male sex." They are not the same thing. Edelman implies that *homosexually* sodomitical elements are somehow intrinsically present in the Wolf Man's primal scene itself. It is supposedly the spectacle—the threat—of these elements that partly forces Freud to suppress or even re-press them even as he (re)constructs them in all their detail—resulting, in the end, in his *"non liquet"*: Freud cannot tolerate his imagination of homosexual intercourse imagined by his patient.

The intercourse "from behind," however, is not inherently an act of *anal* intercourse, even though later the little observer supposedly inter-preted what he had seen according to just this theory (78)—for obviously vaginal intercourse can occur "from behind." For Edelman, the Wolf Man's reconstructed primal scene can be read as a partly disguised scene of homosexual anal intercourse—even though there are no intrinsic grounds to distinguish it as such from other forms of intercourse—because he rightly understands the scene as a displacement of the initial "trans-ference" and of the psychoanalytic situation itself. But even in the initial "transference" (in 1910), homosexual and anal content were not synthe-sized as an unambiguous instance of *homosexual anal intercourse* as such, of the "spectacle of gay male sex" as such. In fact, it was the primal scene reconstructed toward the end of the analysis, in 1914, that probably partly created this "spectacle" by *condensing* initially disparate elements in a retrospective fantasy about the meaning of the four-year-long intersub-jective relationship; this fantasy was projected onto the patient's life his-tory in the writing out of his history conducted in 1914 and supplemented in 1918. Though a homosexual-anal meaning or "spectacle of gay male sex" may have been retrospectively created, then, in the entire *Nachträg-lichkeit* of analysis and writing from 1910 to 1918, the sexuality in the initial intersubjective context itself—the site of the primary intersubjec-tive repression and fantasy image anchoring the whole system of *Nachträg-lichkeit*—has not yet been specified. The homosexuality discovered in the primal scene was probably a complex *reorganization* of the homosexuality present in the initial transference.

From the vantage point of the infant supposedly observing the primal scene, both parents are "believed to possess the phallus"; the primal scene, Edelman believes, "specifically takes shape as a sodomitical scene be-tween sexually undifferentiated partners" (1991: 101). But this construc-tion could not do the work Freud requires of it. Unqualified, it commits the Jungian fallacy: it fails to provide a criterion to explain the selective interests, the backward-reaching attractions and attachments, of retrospection. It depicts the subject to be constructed entirely out of *Zurück-phantasieren*—wholly in *Nachträglichkeit* or "from behind." But, as we have seen, the primal scene must activate both heterosexual and homosexual currents in the subject. It must *create* the very division between hetero-sexual and homosexual desire which henceforth replicates it. In the return movements, the subject retrospectively interprets what was once just "un-differentiated" *as* a scene of "anal" intercourse—one, in this case, which supposedly gratifies the Wolf Man's (and Freud's) "latent" homosexuality even as it terrifies his (and Freud's) mature heterosexuality.

But whence the initial structure, or structuring possibility, in a wholly "undifferentiated" scene? It cannot reside in the genitals of the two part-ners precisely because the little observer, so long as he was not placed at their "very juncture" (Viderman 1977: 306), could not actually see what was really going on—whether he looked at them from "in front" or from behind. And the criterion of differentiation cannot reside in the anuses of the partners. As Edelman notes, the fact that both partners possess an anus is one of the reasons the little boy had for supposing them to be the same, helping to support the "imaginative priority of a sort of proto-ho-mosexuality" (Edelman 1991: 101). Identity *or* nonidentity at this level, then, does not offer the structuring possibility which will create a homo-sexual and heterosexual *difference*—an ongoing history of repression and psychic conflict—once it has become the particular target of retrospective interest and interpretation.

The criterion of specific potential differentiation in the primal scene evidently lies elsewhere. If the parents make love the way animals do—if the parents are "animals"—then there can be no retrospective unclarity or undecidability about which one of the pair is male and which one is female. The differentiation of gender (and it is precisely *not* a differentia-tion of anatomical sex) will be visible *whether or not* the little observer can see exactly what is going on sexually (anal, vaginal, or intercrural intercourse or perhaps simply mutual masturbation) and *however* he is looking at the partners—namely, (a) from "in front" of them making love from behind, as Freud's account seems to require (the child must see their faces to notice the fact that both are taking pleasure), (b) from "beside" them making love from behind (he must see his father's penis going in and out), and (c) from "behind" them making love from behind (he must see their anuses, or, more broadly, their backsides, to believe that both are like him and that their genitals are undifferentiated or indistinct), the triple vision ("*coitus a tergo* three times repeated") that he supposedly registers and repeats by "excitedly passing a stool" (that is, [a] taking an erotic pleasure [b] in something moving, and feeling himself to move something, through [c] his anus). When animals have sex, it is the male that mounts the female; as the case history puts it, in the primal scene the Wolf Man's father is "upright"—the upright wolf with whom the boy initially and strongly identifies but who later terrifies him—but his mother is "bent down" (39).[2]

Most commentators have assumed that it follows from "intercourse from behind" that one partner is "upright" and the other is "bent down." But the reverse logic is more likely. It follows from the implicit differentiation of an "upright" male and a "bent-over" female that their intercourse must be "from behind." As we saw earlier, in the patient's *Nachträglichkeit* supposedly described by the completed analytic construction (see Fig. 13), the parents become animals—but in the *Vorträglichkeit* of the analytic interpretation itself (see Fig. 15), the animals become parents. It is, then, the "imaginative priority"—to use Edelman's term (1991: 101)—of pseudo-*bestiality* in the primal scene which explains why the scene could have supported not only the primary homosexual and heterosexual gratifications but also their retrospective differentiation according to an even more primary supposed distinction between male and female. This imaginative recognition of a founding difference of body posture and behavior between the sexes—this "gendering"—has, of course, been partly displaced in the writing of the text, for it concludes that what actually happened in the primal scene is "not clear." Certainly the text ends up presenting an unrealistic, highly implausible or impossible image of what was actually visible to the little observer in the preferred primal scene of heterosexual and homosexual, male and female intercourse. But nonetheless the text's displacement is highly determined. Freud specifically applies the "*non liquet*"—"it is not clear"—to the possibility that the Wolf Man sees a bestial scene *as* his primal scene not only in order to resist the plausible "Jungian" interpretation recognized in the 1918 footnotes (this would have had a *later* bestial scene superimposed on the primal, ambiguously homosexual one). Freud must also avoid acknowledging that *despite* rebuffing the "Jungian" interpretation, he *still* requires the presence of animals in the primal scene—of human sexuality primordially and primally inflected with animal sexuality. This construction remains outside the manifest narrative or even the implicit reasoning of the case history. To avoid compromising the objectivity of the case, any unclarity must lie, instead, in the Wolf Man's supposedly "clear and life-like picture" rather than Freud's own—for Freud's picture is supposed to be merely an editorial comment on the patient's "perfect likeness of an indestructible past."

Freud was probably partly aware of the ambiguities he had created in his discussion of the repression of bisexuality in the Wolf Man's primal scene as he had finally constructed it at the end of the analysis. In a new footnote prepared for the fourth edition of *Leonardo da Vinci and a Memory of His Childhood*, issued in 1919, he dealt with one of Leonardo's depictions of the position of intercourse (Freud 1910c: 70–72) (Figs. 54, 55). Freud wants us to understand this drawing as one of Leonardo's *Ebenbilder*—one of the artist's "perfect likenesses" of his infantile and childhood past. For just this reason, the drawing supposedly contains a number of mistakes and uncertainties, such as the reversed feet of the two figures, the apparent error in rendering the relation of their legs, and what Freud regards as the excessive feminization of the ostensibly male figure (on the right). According to Freud, all of these features of the drawing indicate the way in which an ambiguous observation of intercourse—or an observation of ambiguous intercourse—allowed Leonardo and his viewers to sustain what would otherwise be contradictory masculine and feminine, and homosexual and heterosexual, interpretations of it. As Jacqueline Rose puts it, Freud used this image to connect Leonardo's "failure to depict the sexual act" with the artist's imagination of "bisexuality"; Leonardo's "confusion at the level of sexuality brings with it a disturbance of the visual field" (1976: 226). Here, then, Freud tries to persuade the reader on a point that he had not quite been able to establish in the case history of the Wolf Man—namely, that the *"non liquet"* applies wholly to the subject's image of the past and not to Freud's own account of it. Though Leonardo's drawing of what is happening in an act of sexual intercourse is, as it were, not at all clear, Freud can clearly specify its unclarity and identify its indications of repression; he can say, with perfect clarity, that the subject's image is "not clear."[3]

As if to confirm the continuing significance of the topic, the Wolf Man's second analyst, Ruth Mack Brunswick, took it up again—with direct reference to the Wolf Man and Freud's case history—in a short paper reporting the case of a patient who supposedly slept *between* his parents as a child and was therefore able to witness their intercourse *a tergo* (Brunswick 1929). If the child is merely placed in front of, beside, or behind his two parents making love "from behind," he cannot, as we have seen, confirm this detail unless he happens to be at "their very juncture"—a requirement

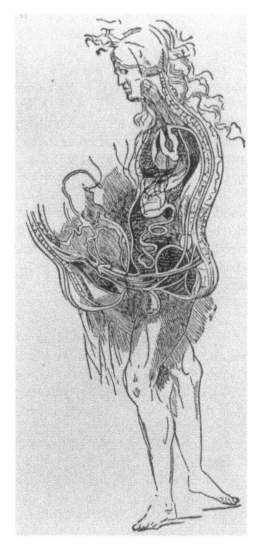

Figure 54. Engraving of human coition in sagittal section, after Leonardo da Vinci, as reproduced by Freud (1919)

Freud had edged toward in his implicit picture of the little Wolf Man receiving three complementary views of his parents' positions. As Brunswick seems to recognize, the position of the child in her study must have been even more peculiar than the little Wolf Man's: the little observer must have been able to see not only the parents' genitals (father's penis and mother's vagina) but also the mother's anus, for it is supposedly part of

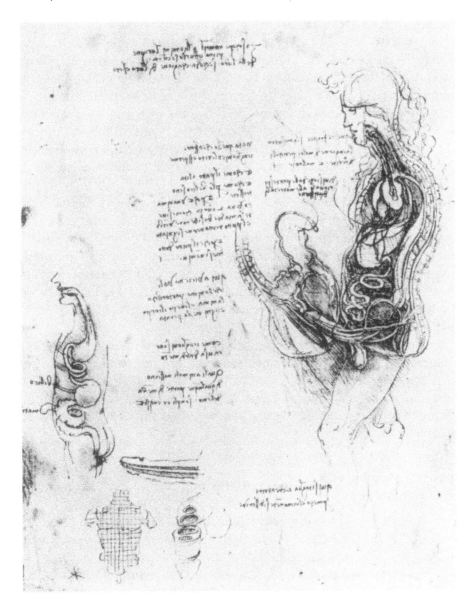

Figure 55. Leonardo da Vinci, drawing
of human coition in sagittal section
(photo Julie Roth)

the retrospective "childish theory of *coitus a tergo*"—the child's defensive interpretation of what had been seen in the primal scene—that in *coitus a tergo* the father's penis is inserted into the mother's anus, an orifice "common to both sexes." According to Brunswick, the male child's idea that "from behind = in the anus" retrospectively means that he denies the existence of the mother's vagina and thus his own possible castration. Brunswick suggests that the Wolf Man held the "childish theory" because the adult Wolf Man "regularly practised not only *coitus a tergo*, but also anal intercourse," information she adds to Freud's account of his sexual life—partly on the basis, it seems, of her own new discoveries (see Appendix). (Notice that Brunswick here specifically distinguishes vaginal intercourse "from behind" and anal intercourse, the point Freud had left utterly vague.) But she continues to believe that it would be physically possible for a child to make the particular observations in question—although, she admits, "only if the room is lighted." She certainly does not explain how the two parents could have had genital-vaginal intercourse "from behind"—later interpreted as genital-anal intercourse—if the observer was lying between them.

Whether or not Freud and his followers could replicate or "supplement and rectify" his account, all of these repetitions, revisions, refusals, and refutations reaffirm the point that behind Freud's manifest interpretation of an inherently ambiguous *coitus a tergo*—the objective historical root of the Wolf Man's divided identity—there lies a complex subjective object of Freud's own.

The Image of Phylogenesis

The Wolf Man's verbal dream report itself, at least as it was recounted by Freud in the case history, gives no basis one way or another for taking the wolves to be copulating animals, the little boy's parents, or some coalescence of the two possibilities. The imagery of the primal scene as it was replicated in the dream—the violent motion, the whiteness, the two partners, and the climbing up—is consistent with all three possibilities. Freud's *preferred* version in the manifest text of the case history, the version of the "case" of an objective Freudian psychoanalysis of the infantile origins of psychic division, probably derived from the drawing of the dream of the wolves presented along with the dream report.

The tree with the wolves is not only the general structure of repressed associations requiring the primal scene of a repression of bisexuality. As Freud's reasoning about the specific content of the Wolf Man's primal scene suggests, it also visualizes the structure of a coalescence of animal and human sexuality—that is, of the individual inheritance of the biologically acquired endowments which the theory of repression ultimately requires. The tree of associations traces or retraces the phylogenetic tree. Freud's sources and memories for this image were probably quite various and complex. Three examples must suffice to make the point.

The phylogenetic tree itself was, of course, the subject matter of Charles Darwin's famous diagram in *On the Origin of Species* (1859: 90–96 = 1988: 94–103) (Fig. 56). Darwin used it in the first edition of 1859 and throughout the later editions published in his lifetime. It appeared in most new printings and translations, including the German translation by Victor Carus, the version Freud probably first encountered as a student and later acquired (Freud's copy of Darwin's works in German [Darwin 1874–76] bears the inscribed date of November 2, 1881). Darwin's diagram (Fig. 56) is considerably more complex than it might initially appear. We should explore it briefly to understand why it should have been attractive—in a retrospective recollection—to Freud's interest in the relations of biological and personal history, of inherited *Vorträglichkeit* and psychic *Nachträglichkeit*, in his assertion of a specifically psychoanalytic, non-Jungian depth-psychological history, one of the principal intellectual motivations driving the analysis and the case history.

As in most "archaeological" or "architectural" diagrams, the vertical axis in Darwin's figure represents the relative antiquity of the different varieties of a species (or the different species of a genus)—from the most ancient at the bottom to the most recent at the top. And as in most typological or seriational diagrams, the horizontal axis represents their relative similarity: the leftmost trunk (labeled A) and the rightmost trunk (labeled I) are the varieties of the species (or species of the genus) least resembling one another. The tree itself is derived by drawing the lines most directly connecting the points plotted on the axes of relative antiquity and relative similarity—by "connecting the dots" of temporal and morphological contiguity. It is understood that only some of the "dots," or actual life forms, have or could ever be observed empirically; the tree reconstructs the whole history—available archaeologically in fragmentary form—at a glance. If new points can be plotted through new zoological observations or archaeological discoveries, the lines—the fundamental rule must be to draw them as short and straight as possible—must be drawn

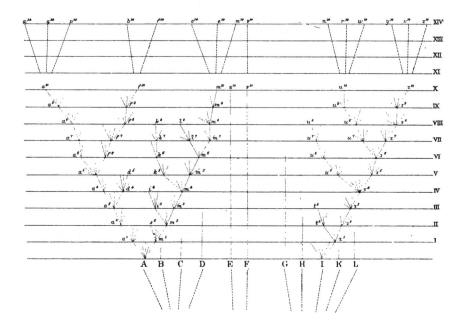

Figure 56. Charles Darwin, diagram of "natural selection" showing "divergence of character" and "extinction," from *On the Origin of Species* (1859)

differently; the resulting tree will be different. One of the problems will be, of course, that the very recognition of the relative antiquity and relative similarity of any new archaeological discoveries will be strongly influenced by the existing total schematic description. For one thing, apparent continuity—a relatively gradual and progressive "evolution"—will seemingly take precedence over discontinuities or entirely new, previously unobserved forms of continuity. Obviously this fundamental evolutionist schema, not original to Darwin, underlies Freud's own variants of it in his notations for the history of psychosexual phenomena.

More specifically, Darwin's diagram shows how natural selection, supposedly favoring organisms best suited to their individual environments at the time of their birth, maturation, and reproduction, will produce—in a wholly nonteleological evolutionary *Vorträglichkeit*—a specific pattern of similarities among the modified varieties and species descended from a common ancestor fourteen thousand generations earlier. The pattern derives from the operation of two *further* processes observed by the Darwinian account of natural selection but not necessarily by other general concepts of evolution as such. First, natural selection supposedly favors the "divergence of character" of varieties and species. Competing for survival in the same environment, the organisms which are most distinct from one another—that is, the least likely to share exactly the same habitat or compete for exactly the same resources—will be favored for preservation and modification in the next generation. Second, natural selection supposedly involves constant partial extinction: in a competitive environment, it completely eliminates some of the organisms (and consequently the possibility of their having modified descendants). These two processes are partly interacting—extinction might derive, for example, from the fact that two varieties are not divergent enough—and partly independent.[4]

As Darwin puts it, "there will be a constant tendency in the improved descendants of any one species to supplant and exterminate in each stage of descent their predecessors and [their] original progenitor"—somewhat, we might say, like Signorelli supplanting Fra Angelico and Michelangelo supplanting Signorelli: at the same time as the later artists "borrow" from the earlier, they also revise, erase, or paint out their predecessors' less adequate inventions. As Darwin pointed out, then, his tree diagram represents not only the growth and divergence of varieties and species from time I to time XIV, that is, the logic of a likely "future" evolutionary history proceeding from a given point of origins, the eleven species A–L existing at time O—a history of "inheritance." The diagram also represents a past history of origins, developments, and extinctions. It is a history not only of planting but also of "supplanting." In Darwin's words, his graphic visualization of natural selection is like "a section of the successive strata of the earth's crust including extinct remains."

As noted earlier, extinction does *not* occur, according to Freud, in the psychic economy. The mind supposedly observes what we might call a principle of nondeletion: everything must be preserved at one or another psychic locality. An approximate psychic analog of Darwin's first principle, "divergence of character," might be the way in which repression supposedly distributes pleasure and unpleasure to different localities in the psychic system. But repression does not necessarily lead to the preservation *of the most disjunct mental contents only* when there is conflict among them, as the Darwinian principle would require. Instead, repression leads to the *most disjunct distribution* of both different and similar mental contents. In fulfilling the two Darwinian principles, then, the purely forward temporality of natural selection—a temporality of modification and *elimination* in the strict sense—is quite different from the simultaneously forward and backward temporality of repression, a temporality of modification and *preservation*. This rule holds in spite of the fact that the structuring principle of psychic repression, which ultimately determines the distribution of differences among mental contents to be selectively and retrospectively modified in the first place, derives from biological evolution.

An organism which preserved extremely unsuitable mental contents, even though it distributed them in repression, presumably would not leave descendants. Therefore any mental contents (or "dispositions") which have been inherited by the next generation, providing the initial structure for its repression, must be regarded as relatively suitable. In other words, one structuring principle of the biological and psychic economies—the selection of environmentally suitable characters—remains constant across the two domains. Its full effects, however, are visible only when biological temporality is observed, that is, when we look at history *through* two or more generations. When we observe purely psychic temporality—that is, the history of a *single* generation, as in the dyad of mother and child or the triangle of parents and child—we cannot see "selection" as such, the instant of *eliminating* what has previously been preserved and modified.

In themselves, the phylogenetic tree (e.g., Fig. 56) and the tree of repressions (e.g., Figs. 33, 38, 46, 51), despite the constancy of the underlying regulatory principle, exemplify processes and temporalities specific to each of them. Their graphic representations appear to be identical; both seem to trace the "forward" historical development of a character and especially its modification and differentiation. But their contents—the directionality of reading—are not. More exactly, their contents are identical only when the biological and the psychic processes and temporalities intersect with one another—that is, in the instant of mating and reproduction itself. Here the phylogenetic tree and the tree of repression must be mapped onto, or mapped through, the family tree.

Darwin's interest was principally in "selection"—the preservation, modification, and elimination of suitable and unsuitable characters. Therefore his diagram was broadly concerned with the relation between inheritance and phylogenesis (or species development), the history in which "selection" could be observed. It was not specifically concerned with the relation between inheritance and ontogenesis (or individual development), the history in which "selection" can be observed, as it were, only in the sheer fact of successful reproduction itself. Thus it is not obvious what Darwin's schema of evolution by natural selection has to say about individual development, beyond providing the image of its determination in the last instance, until we notice that for Freud (though not for Darwin himself) ontogeny supposedly recapitulates phylogeny. In its individual embryonic and to some extent in its postnatal emergence, every organism supposedly retraverses the full phylogenetic emergence of its adult characteristics. To represent this concept, the temporal stages marked in Darwin's diagram, of course, would have to be read (top to bottom) as phases of embryonic and neonatal development rather than read (bottom to top) as phases of varietal differentiation. But any such redirection of Darwin's intention was not really necessary. The recapitulationist argument preferred by Freud already had a well-known visualization which adopted the more conventional bottom-to-top "evolutionist" directionality.

Ernst Haeckel's "systematic *Stammbaum* of mankind" (Haeckel 1874: pl. 15) (Fig. 57) was well known to Freud by the early 1870s. It determined the placement of the topmost, or later, species in relation to one another on the basis of evidence provided both by paleontology and by comparative anatomy (see Gould 1977: 170–73). Needless to say, Haeckel's graphic convention was exactly the one adopted by Freud for his diagram of the "Architecture of Hysteria" (Fig. 38) and other schemas: later structures, dependent on and evolving from earlier ones, occupy the upper parts of the two-dimensional plane. Fossil and anatomical evidence was not available, however, for many of the earlier stages in the history. The lower branches of the tree, then, were placed in relation to one another according to evidence provided by human embryonic development; adopting the "biogenetic law," the law of recapitulation, one could use the development of the embryo to reveal the development of species. Unlike a modern evolutionary "tree" or cladistic chart, which Darwin's diagram (Fig. 56) more closely resembles, Haeckel's *Stammbaum* represents both individual and species history—for it uses the former to derive the latter. More exactly, in addition to its purely evolutionary interest, no different from Darwin's (Fig. 56), Haeckel's *Stammbaum* (Fig. 57) represents the specific conjunction of individual and species history in the ontogenetic recapitulation.

Freud probably became aware of Haeckel's popularizations of Darwinian theory during his student years. Later, as a young scientist conducting

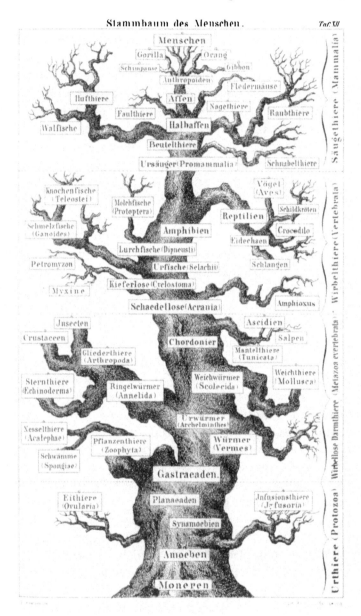

Figure 57. Ernst Haeckel, diagram of the descent
of mankind, frontispiece to *Anthropogenie* (1874)

biological research, he may not have fully accepted all of Haeckel's ideas; he was exposed to strong criticisms of them from some of his teachers (Ritvo 1991: 10–17, 130–31). In his early papers on the nervous system of *Petromyzon*, however, Freud (e.g., 1877) did argue that studying the ontogeny of this organism clarified its phylogeny because the adult organism apparently displays vestiges of earlier stages of its development—a point he also urged in an innovative later paper on the temporal sequence of the myelinization of nerves (Freud 1886). In the twenty-second "introductory lecture" on psychoanalysis, delivered in 1917, Freud actually cited these early research findings to provide a biological analogy for the psychic processes of "inhibition," "fixation," and "regression"—the idea that "in view of the general tendency of biological processes to variation, it is bound to be the case that not every preparatory phase will be passed through with equal success and completely superseded: portions of the function will be permanently held back at these early stages, and the total picture of development will be qualified by some amount of developmental inhibition" (Freud 1916x: 339). Whether or not Freud had explicitly accepted Haeckel's recapitulationist hypotheses (see Ritvo 1991: 74–98), he was apparently interested in the graphic form of the argument. More precisely, when the Wolf Man's replication of its graphic form was presented to him in 1910, he may have recalled those elements of Haeckel's thinking, embodied in his *Stammbaum*, needed to help him make sense of the specifically psychological (and later the psychoanalytic) issue which had concerned him since the 1890s: how does the psyche "know"—how is it organized—to differentiate, divide, and distribute impressions in a way that is not the pure product of some built-in but mysterious homuncular guidance (a problem the 1895 *Project* had raised but could not answer) or the pure result of an entirely retrospective system of Jungian *Zurückphantasieren* (the problem the 1918 case history seemingly solved)? Although the formula may sound paradoxical, evolutionary and recapitulationist biology was Freud's best means of keeping psychology and psychoanalysis on a historical foundation and of resisting what he saw as the idealist, even the mystical, turn of other depth-psychological systems.[5]

A comparative anatomist, Haeckel had concerned himself with the evolution of biological characters, one of Freud's own initial scientific interests. But by the 1880s, twenty years after he had begun biological research, Freud's theory of repression had psychological characteristics in view—namely, as we have seen, the organism's ability somehow to respond appropriately to, to be "interested" in, impinging stimulations. In particular,

Freud needed an account of what the *Project* of 1895 had called the ego's "attention," its apparent abstraction from, reflection upon, and regulation of incoming perceptions according to their pleasurable and unpleasurable "quality."

> If I have on the one hand the ego and on the other hand perceptions— that is, cathexes in P [the psychic system] coming from w [the external world]—then I require a mechanism that causes the ego to follow the perceptions and to influence them. I find it in the fact that, according to my presuppositions, a perception invariably excites w and thus gives rise to indications of quality. To put it more accurately, it excites con- sciousness (consciousness of a quality) in w, and the discharge of the w excitation will, [like] every discharge, furnish information to P, which is in fact the indication of quality. I therefore put forward the suggestion that it is these indications of quality which interest P in the perception.
>
> This would seem to be the mechanism of psychical attention. (Freud 1950: 360)

Some proportion of this "ego" could be conceived merely as the re- sult of previous repression, the branching off (and pooling up) of un- pleasurable stimulations laterally deferred from the routes of direct dis- charge (see Fig. 44). But to avoid a circularity fatal to the whole Freudian theory of mind, at least some proportion of the "attentive" ego has to be given from the beginning. It must be established in the organism as the result of no previous perceptual stimulation and re- pression. In other words, it has to be inherited. As we have seen, Freud thought that the origin of the mechanism of attention in the ego was "biologically determined" (ibid.: 361); "everything that I call a bio- logical acquisition of the nervous system is in my opinion represented by a *threat of unpleasure* [. . .], the effect of which consists in the fact that those neurones which lead to a release of unpleasure are *not* cathected [i.e., are not laterally bound toward discharge]" (ibid.: 370). Freud called this concept his "first biological rule," the rule of "pri- mary defense" (ibid.: 70–71; see Herzog 1991: 43–68).

At least one source proffered a schema, if not all of the details, that provided Freud with particulars—an *image* of the phylogenesis of the ego's "attention"—for this essential final piece of the puzzle of psychic onto- genesis. George John Romanes's *Mental Evolution in Man* (1888), the com- panion volume to his *Mental Evolution in Animals* (1883), was acquired and carefully read by Freud in the early 1890s; Freud's copy of Romanes is "the most annotated work of those that comprise the 1,200-item Freud acquisition of the Health Sciences Library, Columbia University" (Sulloway 1979: 247 n. 7). A follower of Darwin, Romanes was also a committed recapitulationist, though he was not, of course, the only recapitulationist theorist Freud had read. (Darwin himself considered that the embryo is "the animal in the less modified state; and in so far it reveals the structure of its predecessor" [1859: 381].) But for our purposes here, Romanes probably offered the graphic schematization that most impressed Freud—for in the large foldout plate at the beginning of his book, Romanes schematized the psychogenesis of mankind (Fig. 58), completing Haeckel's image of human phylogenesis (Fig. 57) based on Darwin's image of the phylogenetic process (Fig. 56).

According to Romanes, at the age of seven weeks, for example, a human infant—recapitulating evolution through the insects and spiders—is "imagining" and "perceiving" things. In this period Romanes also finds what we could only call infantile sexuality—namely, "sexual emotions with sexual selection," "parental affection, social feelings, sexual selection," and so on. By the eighth month, recapitulating through the birds, "abstraction" appears. At this stage, we would have to place the "ego" of Freud's emerging libido theory—that is, the "lateral binding" or "arborization" of the full discharge of perception, just as Romanes schematizes it, a branching off from the main trunk of perception and imagination (Fig. 58). The eight-month-old infant supposedly also exhibits a "recognition of pictures, understanding of words, [and] dreaming." At fifteen months, abstraction sprouts a new branch, which Romanes labels "generalization." This faculty is roughly equivalent to the more or less stable network of abstractions in the "word concept" Freud diagrammed in *Zur Auffassung der Aphasien* (Fig. 40). In turn, it could be mapped onto the delayed discharges represented in the *Project* (Fig. 44), onto the schemas for repression in dreaming and parapraxis (Figs. 46, 51), in which the unpleasurable elements of a "word concept" are supposedly "repressed," and thus, finally, onto the "unconscious" of *Die Traumdeutung* (Fig. 32), which is a "generalization" that continues to absorb elements of the ongoing arborization of perception, imagination, and abstraction.

The Origins of the Wolf Man's "Homosexual" Predisposition

Introduced into the case history's interpretation of the Wolf Man's psychic history through Freud's comprehension of the drawing, phylogenetic

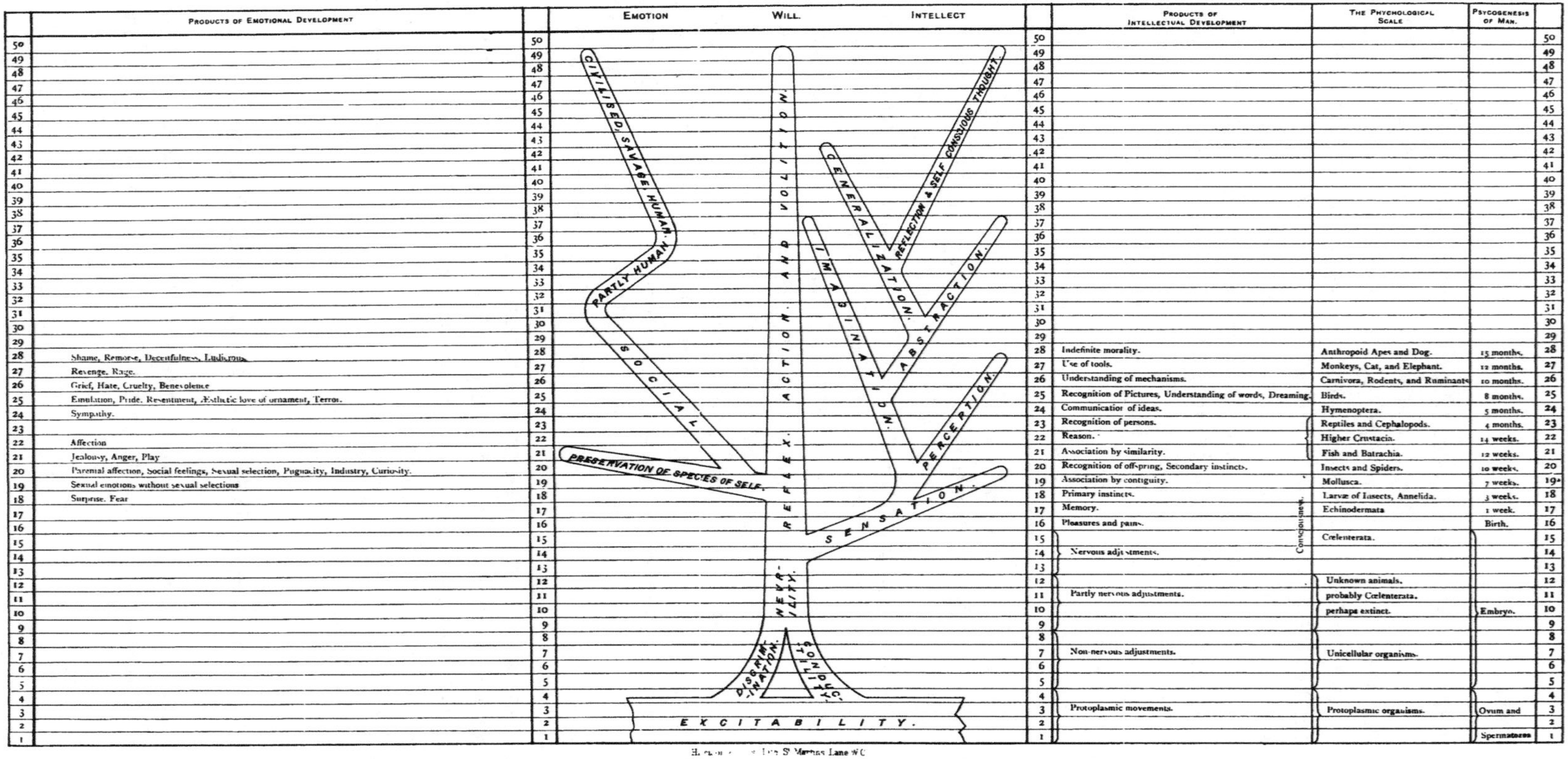

Figure 58. George John Romanes, diagram of the psychogenesis of mankind, frontispiece to *Mental Evolution in Man* (1888)

schemas enabled Freud to solve the pivotal historical problem of the Wolf Man's life story when he came to write out the case in the autumn of 1914.[6] The conundrum itself had been created by assuming—as the dream and drawing had dictated—the human subject's repression of primary "bisexuality." As John Money has phrased it:

> The postulation of bipotentiality, commonly referred to as bisexuality, as an exclusively intrapsychic entity could not, per se, lead to an explanation of sexual inversion or homosexuality as it is now called. At most it could lead only to a declaration of universal bisexuality. Something additional was needed to account for a change from [primary] bisexual equilibrium toward either homosexual or heterosexual predominance [in adulthood]. (Money 1990: 399)

To be specific, Freud needed to explain why the adult Wolf Man was neither a contented heterosexual nor a conscious, let alone active, homosexual. Rather, as the first consultation implied, he was what Freud called a "latent," or "shackled," homosexual whom analysis supposedly "liberates" (71). We have already seen that Freud's interpretation of the Wolf Man's "homosexuality" implicitly imagined him to occupy a position of adult homosexuality midway between the extreme of "regression" and paranoiac projection represented by Judge Schreber, who supposedly ejected his homosexuality into the outside world, and the extreme of "ideal" sublimation represented by Leonardo da Vinci, who supposedly ejected his homosexuality, as it were, into an inside world, a world created by his imagination. In turn, however, Freud denied the Wolf Man this entirely realistic—we might call it self-integrated—position, neither "regressing" nor "sublimating." Instead, Freud deems the patient's "homosexuality" to be merely "latent," ejecting it from his real contemporary life into an archaic and mysterious psychic potentiality. Freud probably displaced the Wolf Man's "homosexuality" in this way because it evoked his own, complementary "homosexual" positioning, especially in the context of the initial "transference," which the case history does not directly represent, which raised the possibility that Freud himself had solicited the Wolf Man's desires— what Freud most fundamentally meant to designate by *Homosexualität*. But if such subjective and intersubjective considerations partly determined Freud's interpretation of the Wolf Man's "homosexuality," a matter to which we will return, how was that homosexuality to be understood objectively in the manifest narrative, model, or theory presented by the case history itself, the text that treated the Wolf Man's subjectivity as a pure object?

All of the material accumulated in the analysis indicated that the Wolf Man had both regressed to an archaic ("pregenital") sexual organization and tolerated—partially repressed but continued in various ways to discharge—homosexually pleasurable thoughts. (They were *partially* repressed because they were not only pleasurable but also "unpleasurable." First, despite their pleasurability, they conflicted with the heterosexual current within him. Second, because they identified him with his mother's sexual position, they conflicted with his "homosexual" identification with his father.) Supposedly these homosexual desires had been activated in the primal scene; by definition, that scene evokes both homosexual and heterosexual currents in primary bisexuality.

But if this was so, then the Wolf Man was a striking anomaly. According not only to sexual stereotype but also to the principles of psychophysics, the two currents of primary bisexuality should have been sorted out by the time the patient's mature object-choices were made—at the cost, no doubt, of an enormous psychic and social labor. Two different excitations toward discharge simply cannot be transmitted in the same laterally bound system of mental contents at the same time; even if the psychic system seeks constancy of energy rather than its discharge, it cannot situate two different contents in the same locality but must distribute them to different places in the entire "network" or "reservoir." One or the other available possibility for sexual object-choice, then, should be repressed in the more or less anxious, neurotic, and unstable achievement of an adult homosexuality or heterosexuality. Because intrinsic and social reinforcements of heterosexual object-choice typically are so great, the path of least libidinal resistance—subjectively painful as it must be—would typically starve homosexual object-choice of pleasure or overwhelm it with unpleasure or both. More rarely, of course, so-called inversions of this pattern might also be found. Here, heterosexual object-choice could be starved, overwhelmed, or both. But the Wolf Man was apparently not an "invert" in the sense implied by contemporary sexology or in the Freudian lexicon.

Paradoxically, despite the splintered condition of the Wolf Man's adult psyche, apparently he somehow had the ability to avoid or resist any unilateral resolution of his primary bisexuality. According to Freud, he *continued* to tolerate (that is, to discharge) homosexually pleasurable unconscious thoughts. There is no sense in identifying a "latent" homosexuality if it always remains completely latent—for the whole point is that homosexuality surfaces from time to time in the subject's history; systemic potentiality must become a real and manifest possibility. It is even possible that the Wolf Man continued to tolerate homosexually pleasurable *practices*, though both Freud and the Wolf Man himself were extremely coy about such matters as the enemas regularly administered to the young man by the mysterious attendant (or orderly, or student, or card player). In her interviews with the Wolf Man, Obholzer—sensitive to the peculiarity of Freud's diagnosis of the patient's "latent" homosexuality—asked him about homosexual encounters. Not surprisingly, he vigorously denied having had any (Obholzer 1982: 84–85). If this was true—if the Wolf Man was not a practicing homosexual, even temporarily, or aware of himself as an "invert"—and if we grant that Freud did not wish to see the adult Wolf Man as a regressed or sublimating homosexual of the Schreber or Leonardo types, how could he, in fact, really be? What continued to keep the young man's homosexuality in an ongoing "latency"—rather than eventually drying it up or cutting it off, as the dynamics of object-choice would seem ordinarily to require?

It was, Freud reasoned, the Wolf Man's *inherited* predisposition—his "congenital sexual constitution" (81, 103)—that had firmly soldered in place at least two unusual but (we can now see) utterly determining relays in his psychic circuitry. First, the patient was congenitally disposed to experience pleasure in imaginarily accepting the male partner in a sex act—an inclination toward what Freud usually calls "feminine identification" but which he sometimes also describes as a "homosexual" wish. Second, the patient was supposedly constitutionally disposed to take erotic pleasure in his anal region (41, 56, 81). Here Freud was carefully separating what had tended to run together in some of his and his students' previous work: the emerging concept of "homosexual anal erotism" did a good deal of work for psychoanalysis (for example, in its growing body of theory about the origins of paranoia in a man's simultaneous desire for and fear of a painful, but possibly also pleasurable, anal assault). But, strictly speaking, to say that an instinctive or congenital "homosexual anal erotism" could have provided the psychic foundations for the Wolf Man's ongoing "latent" homosexuality would have been tautologous; the patient's ongoing latent homosexuality simply is the manifestation of his "homosexual anal erotism."[7] This psychic formation must be broken down, then, into its constituents, identified as "feminine identification" (relating erotically to other men in a passive fashion) and "anality," each independently asserted to have an instinctive, congenital basis.

On this account, the formation of "latent" homosexuality can be understood as emerging developmentally in the differential preservation, interaction, and repression of more primitive elements. (According to Freud, the Wolf Man's "propensities" toward "ambivalence" and "fixation" [27, 188–19] were also congenital. They are major mechanisms of his psychic history as Freud constructs it. But they are less directly involved in accounting for the patient's "latent" homosexuality.) In themselves, "feminine" passivity and anality are neither homosexual nor heterosexual. But in the Wolf Man's primal scene they became the relays of same-sex desire within the entire system of primary bisexuality. Because of their inherited, intrinsic strength, throughout his life they continued to transmit his "homosexuality," evoked in the primal scene, toward discharge.

Freud's objective argument is ingenious and appealing. But it is not an entirely satisfactory solution. First, the hypothesis about the Wolf Man's "hereditary predisposition" to passivity and anality was produced only *after*—and as an explanation of—Freud's discovery of the little Wolf Man's actual object-choices. Logically, then, it should not be used to explain the observations from which it derives—at least without securing some kind of independent evidence about the Wolf Man's disposition. But Freud nowhere provides such evidence.

For example, the case history barely considers any men apart from the father in the Wolf Man's life. Thus it has little means of distinguishing general and early pre-homosexual "disposition" from a specific and later homosexual "identification." Because his father is represented to be the only outlet for the Wolf Man's alleged predispositions, it is not surprising that he should be said to attract the Wolf Man's homosexual fantasy. If Freud speculated about the adolescent or adult Wolf Man's "homosexuality," no trace of it appears apart from his private representation of the initial "transference." Just as the adolescent Wolf Man liked to watch serving girls bend over, did he like to be bent over while being watched by a male attendant, as his reliance on enemas suggests? One possible point of departure, the account of the Wolf Man's teacher "Herr Wolf," remains underdeveloped in this regard. For Freud, Herr Wolf is simply a replication of the Wolf Man's father, the "upright wolf" in the primal scene. But he is not really treated as a personage who might have retroactively sexualized elements of earlier stories and scenes in the boy's life (one wonders if he might ever have beaten his boy student [Freud 1919e]), pulling the boy's homosexual "latency" into a new phase of his life—as Freud's implicit story of the continuing nondeletion of the Wolf Man's homosexuality would seem to require.

Second, Freud's account rides on tendentious assumptions about gender. Throughout the case history, for example, he assumes (often without directly saying so) that the patient's wolves are *male* wolves—especially the "upright" wolves in the picture book and in the fairy tales, who supposedly remind the Wolf Man of the father's position in the primal scene. Neither the dream report nor the drawing, however, provides any evidence about the wolves' gender, at least in the dream of the wolves. It is in the patient's later associations to the fairy-tale wolves that he refers to male wolves. But why should Freud take these indications at face value when he regards the number of the wolves, their positions, and their activities as distortions requiring interpretation? The constructed primal scene actually seems to require the wolves in the dream and drawing to be both male and female, for the dream and drawing must represent *both* parents. But stating this directly would undermine Freud's later hypothesis that the little Wolf Man had unconscious homosexual fantasies evoked by the "male" picture-book and fairy-tale wolves. It would raise the underlying question, again, why his particular fantasies should have turned out to be homosexual instead of heterosexual.

In light of all this, it was probably the homosexual content of the first consultation which was brought forward, by Freud, to the dream report and the drawing to suggest that "biologically determined" relays should be sought in the Wolf Man's sexuality. The drawing was not a clear "confirmation" of the dream report. But we can now recognize that it probably did "confirm" the first consultation. It pictorially exemplifies the idea that Freud should seek an ultimate explanation of the Wolf Man's homosexuality in phylogenetically acquired endowments, such as the theory of repression finally required.

Prehistoric Experience

For Freud, the trees of phylogeny and psychogenesis, the descent of particular biological and psychological characteristics (Figs. 56–58), support the tree of repression (Figs. 30–44, 47, 51) precisely by determining—in the last instance—why the subject's repression should take the individual historical direction that it does. More exactly, the tree of descent provides the seed that grows up as the tree of repression. The tree of repression becomes a tree of descent when it provides a seed, in turn, for yet another tree of repression.

To be sure, Freud was well aware that some kind of historical explanation must be offered for the "phylogenetic motives and productions themselves." What produced the "biologically determined" circuitry of repression, traveling down through family lines by inheritance, which an individual will use, as Freud puts it, "to fill in the gaps in individual truth with prehistoric truth" (97)? Freud's essay *Totem and Taboo* (1912x) provided a partial account of phylogenetic events to explain the general outlines of human repression—assuming, of course, a recapitulatory psychogenesis. In this essay, and still deep in the analysis of the Wolf Man, Freud greatly elaborated Darwin's notion of the "primal horde" with a complicated story of his own about prehistory (see further Wallace 1983). His scenario, which will not be reviewed here, is intended to explain not an individual case of repression but the general (Oedipal) form of all human repressions. Individual repression, of course, is partly determined by much more particular inherited relays (specific, in principle, to an individual family line) and instinctual vicissitudes (specific, in principle, to an individual life history) such as the ones Freud infers for the Wolf Man.

The recently discovered draft essay "Overview of the Transference Neuroses" (Freud 1987), discovered among Sandor Ferenczi's effects, indicates that by 1915 Freud had refined his approach considerably. Setting aside his story of the primal struggles and attachments between fathers and brothers-sons reconstructed in *Totem and Taboo*, in this paper he focused on the sheer experience of privation in forming the *Vorbild* of the psyche: the primal "anxiety" aroused in coping with scarcity prompted—in an evolutionary teleology—the adaptation Freud would often call the *Reizschutz*, or "shield against stimuli," namely, the defense system of repression. Naturally enough, Freud dates the "great privation" to the Ice Ages: the advancing glaciers drove hominids into increasingly intense competition for increasingly scarce necessities. (Freud's scenario can be traced back, in part, to Felix Wittels's paper "The Natural Position of Women," presented at the Vienna Psychoanalytic Society in March 1908; at this meeting, Freud expressed pleasure at Wittels's "fantasy" about the origins of repression in the glacial period [Nunberg and Federn 1962–75: II, 347–51].) Here we should recall that the Wolf Man's dream was dreamed, as he reported, in "winter time." In the text of the case history, Freud never offers a single interpretive speculation about this element of the dream, despite his great attention to all of the other details. But, as already suggested, he seems to have been quite interested in it; in later paintings, the Wolf Man located the dream events themselves in "winter time." Indeed, both Freud and the Wolf Man had probably been taking the drawing to be depicting a wintertime event all along; the black-and-white ambiguity of the image, of course, would be most readily resolved by supposing that we are seeing white wolves on a bare (black) tree in winter (white) time. In theory, then, the waiting wolves looking at the little boy as if they are about to "eat him up" could be seen as a *direct* or unmediated phylogenetic memory—the "prehistoric truth" that fills out individual experience—of Ice Age antiquity, precisely as the case and case history most fundamentally require. Freud does not make this argument in the case history, drafted before "Overview of the Transference Neuroses." But the "Overview" both logically and rhetorically begins, at least in part, at the logical point where "From the History of an Infantile Neurosis" had left off.

In "Overview of the Transference Neuroses," Freud makes a point of asserting that obsessional neurotics—the Wolf Man, of course, was one— struggle against a complete regression "to phases that the whole human race had to go through at some time from the beginning to the end of the Ice Age." Their neurosis is supposedly a "compromise" between the "primevally old" (the source of their basic fears) and the "demands of the culturally new" (especially the ritualizations that enable them to ward off their fear). "But," Freud concludes, "neurosis, insofar as the repressed has been victorious in it, must bring back the prehistoric picture" (*das urzeitliche Bild wiederbringen*) (1987: 13, 46). Indeed, Freud's "Overview of the Transference Neuroses" is in many ways a meditation on the problem of pictorial (*Bildliche*) resemblance and reproduction; "die Bilder können sich natürlich nicht völlig decken": the prehistoric and the culturally new pictures, Freud says, "naturally cannot fully coincide" (ibid.: 46)— but they have been and can be *made* coincidental or coterminous in several forms of *Übertragung*, or "transference," from prehistory to history, from biology to psychology, from myth to narrative, from pictures or visual thinking (the earliest modality of a human being's thought) to words or binary logic, from patient to analyst, and from the *Vortrag* of evolution to the *Nachtrag* of memory.

Freud's method for reconstructing the psychogenetically meaningful events of prehistory combined recapitulationist logic and outright speculation. Many post-Freudian theorists, despite their involvement with a psychoanalytic theory of the subject, have hoped to avoid this enterprise. Some would like to understand the "prehistoric" context of individual psychogenesis to be the structure of the language—or, more broadly, of the symbolic system of a culture—preexisting an individual's birth and into which he or she gradually enters (see especially Laplanche and Pontalis 1968). In principle, however, this project undertakes an inquiry just as problematic as Freud's. Whence this "language" or "symbolic system"? Prehistorians cannot simply take it for granted as determining human social interaction (Davis 1995a). Other post-Freudian thinkers hope to ignore the so-called biological dimension and implicit prehistoric archaeology of Freudian psychology altogether. They would take the historical analysis of the formation of subjects back only as far as the Oedipal triangle between a child and its two parents, the pre-Oedipal dyad of mother and infant, or the earliest "undifferentiated phase" of the infant's cognitive and affective integration. But in Freud's theory a person's psychic relay of *particular* inherited predispositions is the *sine qua non* for his or her history. Subjective and intersubjective events cannot be fully explained by examining the social-historical relations of the individual, such as the Wolf Man's desires for his mother, father, Nanya, teacher, serving girls, medical attendant, and so forth. Ultimately they require the differentiating criterion which only the biological-historical relations can supply. This component of the theory cannot be waved away as unessential to most applications; like Marx's assertion that human consciousness is determined "in the last instance" by the forces and relations of production, Freud's view that it is determined in the last instance by the biological history of psychogenesis is both foundation and capstone: without it, we have virtually nothing, or nothing new, to say.

Perhaps confusion has arisen about the Freudian *theoretical* requirement that the biological-historical differentiates the individual-historical in the last instance because the theory can be satisifed most easily by applying a *methodological* rule which works in reverse. The individual-historical is our best means of identifying the biological-historical. In writing his 1918 additions to the case history of the Wolf Man, Freud considered that incidents of "[witnessing] parental intercourse, of being seduced in childhood, and of being threatened with castration are [all] unquestionably a phylogenetic inheritance, but they might just as easily be acquired by personal experience" (97). Consequently one must determine through historical investigation exactly how descent and repression were in fact related to someone's particular "personal experience." This history must observe a "methodological" rule (97), a "correct order of precedence" of inquiries (121): it proceeds *as if* the subject's life history is a result of his or her "personal experience" as it impinges upon his or her existing repressions and his or her inherited endowments.* Methodologically reversing the temporal direction of the construction of subjectivity proposed by the theory, it works *back* through personal experience *to* existing repressions *to* primary repression (the "first rule" of "primary defense") *to* descent.

The *Nachträglich* order of psychoanalytic history is adopted not just because it is generally convenient to retrace the flow of causes in the opposite direction. It is based on the specific insight that a *Vorträglich* history—such as a biologist might pursue in observing the fertilization, flowering, and withering of a plant—would, as a history without hindsight, miss the hindsights *within* the history of subjectivity itself. In other words, psychoanalytic method must be *Nachträglich* because the subject was formed in *Nachträglichkeit* in addition to *Vorträglichkeit*. Personal experiences retroactively animate earlier events with the significance of repression or discharge. Further, primary repression retroactively animates earlier inheritances—such as the Wolf Man's "predisposition" to passivity and anality—with the very potential to constitute repression or discharge in the first place.

Working from inheritances forward to repression and experience—or from repression forward to experience—we could not know *which* inheritances, repressions, or experiences to track because we could not know in advance which formations would ultimately prove to be retroactively animating. It was for this reason that in the twenty-third "introductory lecture" of 1916–17, Freud organized his diagram of the "causation of neurosis" (Fig. 59) to indicate that psychoanalysis works downward (temporally backward) from particular "fixations" of the "hereditary sexual constitution," formed in relation to "accidental experience," toward more archaic experiences ("infantile experience") and finally to constitution itself ("prehistoric experience"). In a footnote, the editors of the *Standard Edition* have inverted Freud's order of presentation (Fig. 60) because they suppose that it is "easier to follow" the diagram according to the convention of a "genealogical tree" (Freud 1916x: 362). But although Freud was implicitly mapping his diagram onto a *Stammbaum*, his concern in this diagram was quite specifically "methodological." Sitting at the very top

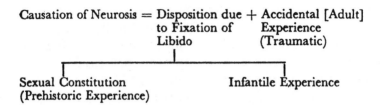

Causation of Neurosis = Disposition due + Accidental [Adult]
                        to Fixation of   Experience
                        Libido   (Traumatic)

Sexual Constitution   Infantile Experience
(Prehistoric Experience)

Figure 59. Freud, diagram of the "path of symptom formation," from *Introductory Lectures on Psychoanalysis*
(1916–17)

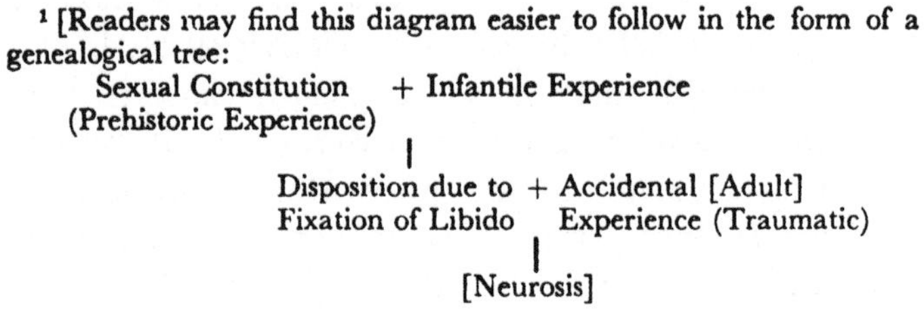

¹ [Readers may find this diagram easier to follow in the form of a
genealogical tree:
        Sexual Constitution   + Infantile Experience
        (Prehistoric Experience)

        Disposition due to + Accidental [Adult]
        Fixation of Libido   Experience (Traumatic)

                    [Neurosis]

Figure 60. James Strachey et al., inversion of Freud's diagram of "symptom formation" (Fig. 59) for the *Standard Edition*

of the tree, we can tell which branches to climb down to get to the bottom.
But sitting at the bottom, we could not tell which branches to climb to
get to the very top.

Put another way, the tree of descent scatters many seeds that we could
try to investigate, like a descriptive botanist or evolutionary biologist. But
only a few trees of repression will actually grow up from some of them;
and, at least if we are psychoanalysts, there is no point in looking at the
seeds that did not flower. Each tree of repression will necessarily be a member of its species. But it will also be historically unique, its particular
form—stunted or towering, oriented this way or that—a product of the
historical environment, *both* biological *and* social, in which it grows.

The Family Portrait

There is, then, yet another term to consider in the rooting of repression. The context in which the tree of descent plants a seed that will grow up as the tree of repression is, of course, the family tree (see Figs. 61, 62).

Graphic conventions for drawing kinship diagrams were well known to Freud. He based the ones he used in *Totem and Taboo* (1912x: 13) (Fig. 63), for example, on Wilhelm Wundt's *Elemente der Völkerpsychologie* (e.g., 1913: 160, 167) (Fig. 64). Although Freud may not have read Wundt until 1912 (Wallace 1983: 61)—and regarded his ethnologies as "rubbish" (Freud/Ferenczi 1993: 411 [October 17, 1912])—the conventions in question had been widely used earlier. Even if they had not existed, we can be fairly certain that the family tree—and, more literally, the family portrait—completed Freud's schema in the Wolf Man's drawing as his "confirmation" of the arguments of psychoanalysis about repression.

A family tree of the Freud family (Fig. 65)—a *Stammbaum des Hauses Freud*—was prepared from tombstone inscriptions in the Jewish cemetery in the family's original home town in Galicia, Buczacz on the Moravian border, and probably from other sources, sometime after Freud's appointment to his professorship in 1902 (Krüll 1986: 233, Table 2; Krüll says that the family tree was "probably drawn up in 1914" by its compiler, but does not give a reason for this dating). The drawing has the names of members of the family placed where the Wolf Man's wolves would be sitting. Their relations are depicted by a bare and peculiarly lopsided tree, suggesting amputation or even extinction. More stump than growth, it is quite unlike the weatherbeaten—but very much alive, even noble—trees of Romantic convention, such as those painted by Friedrich or Carus (Figs. 22, 23, 25–27), partly lying behind the Wolf Man's drawing. But its dramatic truncation recalls the cut-off or blasted appearance of the Wolf Man's tree. Although it seems very likely, it is not possible to confirm whether Freud knew this genealogical picture—whether it had even been produced—at the time the Wolf Man case commenced.

A painting of her children was in Freud's mother Amalia's possession for many years (Fig. 66). Probably produced about 1868 or a little later, it hung in her drawing room until it was lost during the Nazi invasion of Austria. A photograph of the painting was apparently first published and described by Freud's son Martin (1958: 14–15, 28), who did not know the painter's name, though earlier Ernest Jones (1953: frontis.) had reproduced

Figure 61. N. Buvneuov, portrait of Serge Pankejeff's father, c. 1890 (Pankejeff Papers, LC)

Figure 62. "Wolfman" (Serge Pankejeff), portrait of his mother, c. 1920 (Pankejeff Papers, LC)

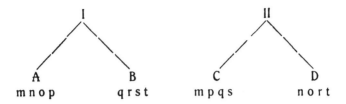

Figure 63. Freud, diagram of kinship
structure, from *Totem and Taboo* (1913)

Phrathrien

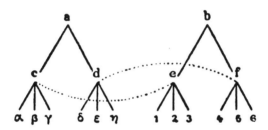

Figure 64. Wilhelm Wundt, diagram of
kinship structure from *Völkerpsychologie*
(1912)

a detail. Apparently it has never been compared with the Wolf Man's drawing of his dream of the wolves. The painting portrays young Sigismund
(his name at birth) in the upper left, his younger brother Alexander in
the center foreground, and their five sisters, five little girls in their dresses
and white petticoats, or "six or seven" children in all, depending on how
we group them—five, counting all the girls; six, for all the girls plus Freud's
brother; seven, for all the girls plus the two boys. Freud referred to the
six initial members of his "Secret Committee" as his "adopted children"
(Grosskurth 1991: 52). The later collective photograph of this group, as
we have seen, may have prompted Otto Rank to suppose that pictures of
members of the committee lay behind the Wolf Man's drawing. But there

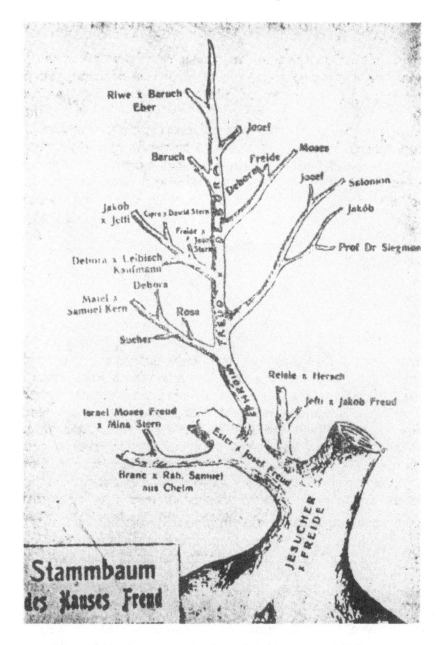

Figure 65. Family tree of the Freud family, attributed to Hell-reich, c. 1902–14 (after Krüll 1986)

Figure 66. Portrait of the Freud children, artist unknown, c. 1868 (photo Julie Roth)

is a better chance that an image of the group of five, six, or seven children, brothers, or followers lay behind *Freud's* drawing, Freud's construction of the drawing presented to him in analysis.

When they could afford it, Jewish families in Galicia, where Freud's family on his father's side came from, traditionally commissioned paintings of the children (Nelken 1991: 129). In preparing a detailed analysis of the Freud family's relationship to its Eastern European origins, Emanuel Rice has concluded:

That self-consciousness about one's East European origins (due to the most intense prejudice on the part of the established middle class who looked upon *Ostjuden* as primitive and inferior) motivated a pressing need on the part of the Viennese Jewish middle class to overcompensate by being as German and middle class in their cultural and intellectual interests and values as the non-Jewish middle class, if not more so. The Freud family even went so far as to create a myth, a family romance, in which their background was elevated to a most noble status. (Rice 1990: 7)

In 1869–70, in entering his name into the records of the new *Sperlgymnasium* in Vienna—opened in 1864 and which he joined the following year—Freud changed his given name, Sigismund, to Sigmund. "In this manner," Rice argues, "he presumably severed his tie with his provincial [Eastern European or Galician] Jewish background and identified with the progressive German-liberal culture" (ibid.: 193; see further Klein 1985). In his 1925 *Autobiographical Study*, for example, Freud wrote, "I have reason to believe that my father's family was settled for a long time on the Rhine (at Cologne), that in the fourteenth or fifteenth century they fled to the east from an anti-Semitic persecution, and that in the course of the nineteenth century they retraced their steps from Lithuania through Galicia to German Austria" (Freud 1925b: 7–8). The Freud family had resided in Galicia for at least four generations. Freud's evidence for the earlier *German* origin of the family appears to have been a fresco in the Cathedral of Bressanone (Brixen), in the South Tirol, supposedly signed "Freud of Cologne," which Freud and his brother Alexander visited after its discovery in 1910.[8] It may be impossible to say whether Freud actually attached any conflict to the Freud family portrait as such. But, as he would have argued, the histories of congenital constitution and of psychic repression intersect in the time and place represented in family portraits—a time and place largely forgotten by most persons and possibly by Freud himself, but remembered, we might suppose, when in 1910 the Wolf Man presented its replication, with its five, six, or seven wolves. Because of its predecessors, the Wolf Man's drawing immediately explicated itself, for Freud, as the psychic history of man—child, infant, family, and species.

VII

INTERSUBJECTIVE TRANSFORMATION

What we are in search of is a picture of
the patient's forgotten years that shall be
alike trustworthy and in all essential respects complete. But at this point we are
reminded that the work of analysis consists of two quite different portions, that
it is carried out in two separate localities,
that it involves two people, to each of
whom a distinct task is assigned. It may
for a moment seem strange that such a
fundamental fact should not have been
pointed out long ago; but it will immediately be perceived that there was nothing
being kept back in this, that it is a fact
which is universally known and, as it
were, self-evident and is merely being
brought into relief here and separately examined for a particular purpose.

—Freud, "Constructions in Analysis"
(1937d: 258)

Was it only the patient who should not
make a graven image?

—Peter Heller (1990: 1)

The meaningfulness of Freud's iconography for the history of minds and
persons had been established well before the psychoanalysis of the Wolf
Man commenced. It was probably activated during the psychoanalysis.
And apparently it provided the forward impetus by which the case resolved itself as the exemplary case history for that very iconography,
that very picture of the mind.

In spite of the importance of the case history, however, the Wolf Man's drawing seems to have been largely overlooked. Freud's essentially vulgar procedures in his 1910 monograph *Leonardo da Vinci and a Memory of His Childhood* (Freud 1910c) remain the usual illustration of psychoanalytic reasoning about images. In the case history of the Wolf Man, an image could be interpreted through the artist's own associations, recollections, and transferences in the specifically psychoanalytic situation—a context entirely lacking for Leonardo. In *Leonardo*, then, Freud was constrained to construct Leonardo's subjectivity—including, for his example, his theory of Leonardo's homosexual "narcissism"—as a pure object for him.

By contrast, in the Wolf Man case Freud's interpretation was constructed intersubjectively. At least in principle, the subject could speak back to the ostensibly objective observer attempting to interpret him—confirming, supplementing, correcting, and resisting his interlocutor. The drawing, for example, was "added" as a "confirmation" of the Wolf Man's report of his dream (*er gibt dann noch eine Zeichnung . . .*)—an act that we can imagine only as having had some kind of intersubjective sense. Perhaps the Wolf Man was determined to convince Freud of the importance of the dream, whether or not he already sensed Freud's "conviction" about his case as a whole. Perhaps, of course, Freud actively solicited the drawing, even demanding that it be drawn. However the graphic response was determined, the observer could pursue this replication of the dream report, as we have seen, in even further direct exchanges with the subject. In the end, this exchange—we should probably conceive it as lasting from the very beginning of the analysis in 1910 until long after its technical completion in 1914—decisively reorganized both partners' subjective identities and positions.

Freud's past enabled him to comprehend the Wolf Man's past. More accurately, an object produced by the Wolf Man was already part of Freud's past. This conclusion might tempt us to accept Stanley Fish's proposal, popular in a number of similar literary-critical studies of the case history, that the "Wolf Man is, in short, a piece of language," "the perfect rhetorical artifact"—a construction made by Freud in order to persuade a reader of the fitness of Freud's own interpretive preconceptions. "At bottom," says Fish, "the primal scene is the scene of persuasion" (Fish 1989: 540–50).

What has been described here so far, however, is not just more evidence for what we already know—namely, that a historian's own subjectivity is an inescapable touchstone for his or her reconstruction of the subjectivities of others. To be sure, Freud's construction of his patient was wide-ranging and penetrating. But the relation cannot be reduced to the construction of one subject, the "Wolf Man," *by* another, Freud.

We should not forget the *Wolf Man's* share in the construction of Freud's interpretation of him. Freud certainly made the "Wolf Man" who was the subject of his case history; this "Wolf Man" is almost entirely a figure in Freud's narrative construction of him. Even his most intimate manifestations, such as his report of his childhood dream, come to us through Freud's transcription of them. But I say *almost* entirely, for the Wolf Man, Serge Pankejeff himself, made something Freud needed to complete—to reproduce and reinvent—himself as a subject at that point. And although that object necessarily became Freud's own subjective object, it was distinguished from Freud's representation, the "Wolf Man" presented by the case history; it was a representation not written *by* Freud but rather by the Wolf Man himself. It was written *into* Freud. More exactly, these very terms—representation "by" Freud or "by" the Wolf Man—break down completely in certain domains; and it is this effective intersubjectivity which is of interest.

The Wolf Man's Werewolves

To obtain a complete picture of this exchange, we would need to investigate elements in the intersubjective relation of Freud and his patient quite different from what has so far been considered here to be Freud's construction of the Wolf Man's drawing on the basis of his own iconography for the history of minds and persons. If we are to measure Freud's subjective construction of the Wolf Man's drawing—let alone the intersubjective constructions created jointly by the two of them—we need to acknowedge the many determinations of the *Wolf Man's* drawing of his dream of the wolves apart from *Freud's* drawing of the dream of the wolves.

To identify all of these determinations would require a broader historical inquiry than the one pursued here. In some ways it would be the kind of familiar "art-historical" investigation—pursuing the artist's intended meanings or at the least the meanings specifically attributable to him as an agent, person, or consciousness—that have deliberately been set aside in this book so that we might pursue *another* art history. But we have already seen, for example, that the Wolf Man's drawing probably replicated certain motifs and themes in a network of pastoral and landscape imagery which he probably knew through his experience as an amateur painter (Figs. 2, 4, 6–10, 16–18, 22, 23, 25–27). In their seeming contrast between "wild" trees and *Parkbäume,* his paintings—and possibly the drawing of the dream of the wolves—apparently depended on and perhaps even referred to this iconography. It is worth pursuing a similar example in order to reiterate, however, that what might seem to be the independent historical determinations of the Wolf Man's drawing, in and for his own life history, cannot be disentangled from the intersubjective relationship between Freud and the Wolf Man—for it is, of course, the primary art-historical fact about the Wolf Man's drawing that it was made precisely for Freud's interpretation and in response to his attentions.

As Melanie Klein recognized, the little Wolf Man's supposedly profound fear of his father, represented in the wolf phobia of the four- and five-year-old, need not be reduced—as Freud had it—to his fear of being "castrated." Instead, the little boy's fear could be seen "as a *primary* anxiety" which "persisted in an unchanged form *along with* later, modified versions of it" in a retrospectively developed fear of castration by his father. The little boy's idea of being devoured by the father does appear to be a formation of Oedipally organized thought. But actually it could well be a "relic," to use Klein's word, of a pre-Oedipal or pregenital stage of psychic development (Klein 1932: 223, my emphasis)—a construction, then, of the Wolf Man's first two years of life, contemporary with and not wholly the product of the supposed primal scene. A similar point was made by Otto Rank in his review of Freud's *Inhibitions, Symptoms, and Anxiety.* According to Rank, Freud overemphasized the castration anxiety of the Wolf Man, oriented toward his father-"wolf," at the expense of the patient's fear of being devoured by the *mother-*"wolf" (Rank 1927: 182). This fear should have been connected less with the boy's Oedipally aroused anxieties about his genitals and more with archaic anxieties about fusion with or separation from the mother. As we have seen, Freud's reasons for presuming the wolves in the dream and drawing to be male were probably determined partly by his own subjective object in the drawing. It was not surprising, then, that he tended to ignore the possibility that they symbolized the exceedingly ancient fears identified by Klein and Rank; such fears would probably have been represented, in the dream and the drawing, by female wolves that Freud did not see there.

If the Wolf Man's "primary" anxiety—supposedly one of his earliest and certainly one of his most persisting ideas—was a fear of being devoured, his attitude makes best sense in the light of his family's cultural symbolism, whether or not Freud, Klein, or Rank correctly explained it in depth-psychological terms. As Carlo Ginzburg (1989) has argued, the meaning of the Wolf Man's "wolves" should probably be partially situated for him (if not for Freud) in Central European and Russian folk traditions of lycanthropy. Ginzburg explicitly notes that these traditions cannot fully explain the patient's neuroses; they provide what he calls a "cultural context" for the Wolf Man's dream (Ginzburg 1989: 149). But he goes on to offer the more specific hypothesis that the little Wolf Man, who had been born with a caul, might have heard from his superstitious Nanya (see Fig. 71) about "what extraordinary (not necessary negative) powers were conferred by th[at] fact." In Slavic folklore, the caul conferred, or at least indicated, the bearer's ability to become a werewolf (ibid.: 147–48; cf. Jakobson and Szeftel 1966). Ginzburg might have added that the Wolf Man was born on Christmas, another traditional attribute, in Slavic cultures, of a person capable of becoming a wolf-man (see Senn 1982: 75). In view of the significance of the number seven in the Wolf Man's representations and in Freud's analysis, it is also worth remarking that in the Transcaucasus—which shares cultural traditions with Russia bordering on the Black Sea, where the Wolf Man was born—female werewolves supposedly wander for seven years, during which time they must devour first their own children and then whatever other children they can find (Haxthausen 1856: 322).

The likelihood that lycanthropic stories were widespread and could sink into the memories of young Russian men and women brought up on them finds some support in work by the Hungarian psychoanalyst Nandor Fodor (1895–1964), who treated a number of Eastern European and Russian émigré patients in New York in the thirties and forties. In a little-known essay, Fodor recounts the case of "a Russian woman who presented for analytic consideration as her very first problem a recurrent nightmare about wolves" (Fodor 1945: 312). The nightmare returned repeatedly throughout her childhood and recurred after she had emigrated, as an adult, to America.

> I was standing in a hollow. In front of me was a hillock which looked like the crest of a wave. It was of red clay with green grass on top. I heard my mother's voice: "Here come the wolves." With that three figures appeared on the crest of the hill: two wolves with my mother in the midst. To her left was a male wolf with black mane and golden yellow belly; to her right a gray female wolf. My mother's face was ferocious, although human. (Now that I think of it, she also looked like my

sister Anna, with whom I had a feud all my life.) My mother said: "Now shoot!" I picked up a rifle, aimed at the female wolf and shot it dead. My mother disappeared and I was now on top of this wave, looking down into the hollow. In front of me were two square kitchen stoves with rounded edges, a gray one made of hams and a black one, nearest to me, made of iron. Suddenly I realized that these stoves were the wolves. The next moment I was sitting on the lampshade.

In supplementation of the dream, she stated:

There were times when I could not keep my windows open for fear that somebody would look in, stretch in a hand and grab me. One day I saw a hand, the fingers slowly opening. Later, in another dream, I discovered the identity of this hand. It was the hand of the physician who delivered me, and the physician was my mother's father.

The patient added that her sister, Anna, used to frighten her with stories about wolves and eyes. (Ibid.)

Compiling the memories the patient attached to her dream, Fodor discovered that in addition to fearing the wolves, she also dreamed about making wolflike killings, conversing with putrefying bodies, tearing at her own entrails with her teeth, and changing shape and sex—a network of associations "the grim horror of which may well compete with medieval chronicles on lycanthropy" (ibid.: 314). Fodor's primary interest, like any psychoanalyst's, lies in elucidating the personal erotic significance of these fantasies. But he assumes that they were culturally rooted in a very specific tradition.

In her childhood [he discovered], Russia was still rife with werewolf superstition. Many people believed that by certain practices men could change their bodies into the shape of beasts. She vividly remembered a story about a certain prince and his servant which she herself had been told. The servant threw himself three times on the ground and became a wolf; whereupon the prince sprang on his back and rode away on some nefarious business. The story sent cold shivers down her spine. When her growing intelligence rejected it, it receded into the hotbed of her unconscious fantasy life from where it flowered into nightmares. (Ibid.)

Fodor does not specify the source of the patient's recollection. She may have been thinking of stories such as those drawn by Ivan Bilibin (1876–1942), the great illustrator of Russian fairy tales (see Golynets 1982) (Figs. 67, 68); his images of the grey wolf with bright eyes might have influenced the Wolf Man's visual and verbal reports to Freud in 1910–14, though Bilibin's books were produced somewhat after the Wolf Man's childhood dream itself.

Fodor buttresses his point about his patient's cultural memory by briefly

Figure 67. Ivan Bilibin, drawing of the prince and the grey wolf (photo Northwestern University Library)

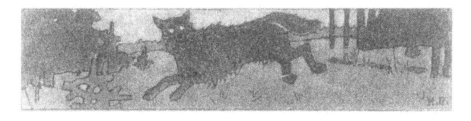

Figure 68. Ivan Bilibin, drawing of the grey wolf (photo Northwestern University Library)

describing another case in which a young woman of Hungarian extraction believed herself to be a werewolf. She fantasized about destroying her little sister, whose name, Piroska, was the Hungarian equivalent of "Little Red Riding Hood." Indeed, like the Wolf Man tracking down his childhood book of stories to show to Freud, this patient insisted that Fodor read a book which she had taken from a previous analyst, David Garnett's novel *Lady into Fox*, which recounted a thrilling lycanthropic story (Fodor 1945, 1959: 202–207).

If he had been imbued with the notion that he could be a werewolf, from his own cultural vantage point what the little Wolf Man dreamed, Ginzburg suggests, was really an "initiatory" dream calling him to his werewolf's "vocation." On this account, presumably the wolves in the tree staring "attentively" at the dreamer would have to be the werewolf's familiars waiting for him, which the traditional stories would have led the dreamer to expect. Ginzburg concludes that the Wolf Man "became a neurotic on the brink of psychosis" instead of "turning into a werewolf," as he might have done "two or three centuries earlier" (Ginzburg 1989: 148). At the most general level, a new cultural script, the modern script of psychiatry and psychoanalysis, had partly replaced the archaic script the Wolf Man had encountered in his earliest childhood and which supplied the imagery of the wolf dream in its original setting.

There are a few holes in this very typically culturalist or culturological analysis. Ginzburg does not fully acknowledge, for example, the twenty-one-year gap between the dream itself and the Wolf Man's written and drawn reports of it. Though the childhood experience could well have expressed the lycanthropic ideas, the adult representations were produced as partly *psychoanalytic* ideas—that is, in the context of the psychoanalytic encounter. We might even say that it was the Wolf Man's psychoanalysis—not his Russian childhood—which turned him into a werewolf; this is certainly true at the most literal level, of course, to the extent that the text of the case history (possibly replicating the intersubjective positions emergent in the analysis itself) transformed a sophisticated, multilingual, widely traveled twenty-four-year-old man into an infantile "Wolf Man" who remembered that once, long ago, he had dreamed of wolves. It was not so much that the modern script had replaced the traditional one in the Wolf Man's growth from four and a half to twenty-four years of age; rather, the twenty-four-year-old Wolf Man found the traditional reference which suited his immediate need to be charged, now, and in part retrospectively, with significance it would never have had. The little Russian boy would never have become a werewolf, even "two or three centuries earlier"; the twenty-four-year-old patient in Vienna was the only "wolf man" in this story. In all of this we would, of course, be guessing at the exact balance of true *Vorträglichkeit-Nachträglichkeit* and mere *Zurück-phantasieren* in the Wolf Man's psychic history. But the fact that there is a balance at all does not sufficiently enter Ginzburg's account.

Even on its own terms, Ginzburg's proposal fails to explain why the little dreamer—if he was unconsciously assuming his "cultural" identity as a werewolf—should have been *terrified* by his own dream. Why was it not deeply satisfying or sexually stimulating, gratifying grandiose fantasies about his real identity or "family"—especially when we notice that in Russian folk tradition the werewolf is often a creature with a princely lineage? Because the dreamer feels that the wolves in the dream are about to "eat him up," it is not the *dreamer* himself but the wolves in the trees looking at him who must be the werewolves which the little boy had heard about. In other words, Ginzburg's rereading of the Wolf Man's dream as a fantasy of becoming a werewolf does not seem to locate the dreamer's distinctive sense about the werewolves/dream wolves—they eat people up—in quite the right place. If Ginzburg's scenario is to work in the way he has in mind, the Wolf Man, who "two or three centuries earlier" might have turned into a werewolf, should not become a "neurotic on the brink of psychosis"; instead, in assuming, himself, the fearsome wolves' power—in becoming a werewolf—he should actually become a sociopathic psychotic, at least in his fantasy life. Though the Wolf Man probably was on the edge of psychosis at times, there is no evidence that it was psychosis of this kind—that the Wolf Man behaved, even in fantasy, like a werewolf. To be sure, Fodor's Russian patient feared wolves, like the Wolf Man, but also made "wolflike killings"; but Ginzburg gives us no reason to suppose that the Wolf Man was the same kind of neurotic. Indeed, the thrust of the case is quite the reverse: the Wolf Man's "psychotic" response is a partial, in some cases extremely dangerous, disintegration and paralysis in the face of a powerful or overwhelming outside authority.

On the one point most relevant to his argument, Ginzburg provides no specific evidence that the little boy associated his caul—if he even knew about it at the age he had his dream—with being, himself, a werewolf. (In fact, there is a strong Jungian element in Ginzburg's underlying psychological assumptions, such as his apparent willingness to entertain the idea of what must amount to an inherited cultural memory in the subject—not just a "cultural context" for his representations, admittedly a practically empty concept—where the Wolf Man's individual experience would not have afforded him the knowledge and beliefs in question.) More likely, the little boy vaguely heard about wolves which are more dangerous and terrifying than ordinary wolves. In the Wolf Man's boyhood, for example, the peasants from the villages near his father's estate organized wolf hunts "several times every summer." According to his later recollections, "these hunts always ended with a festive evening, for which my father paid the bill"; at this point in the hunting ritual, "the village musicians appeared, and the boys and girls danced their native dances" (Gardiner 1971: 12). In this setting, the little boy, presumably accompanied by his parents or Nanya, might have encountered various stories about wolves and werewolves, which make an appearance in numerous traditional Russian songs (Ralston [1872: 409–12] collected some examples which could have been current in the Wolf Man's boyhood).

For the Wolf Man listening to Freud interpret his dream in 1914, the wolves in his dream could be legibly rendered—following but not necessarily *due to* Freud—as his parents, particularly his father, because in his folk tradition the werewolf was already a punitive father transformed into a beast who will "eat you up," like the wolves in the dream. (We can safely assume that parents, older siblings, and nannies tried to manage the youngest children in the family by frightening them with fairy-tale threats, partly in jest. The stories themselves frequently identified the werewolf with a figure of authority, like the prince in the Vseslav epic or Bilibin's version of the story of the grey wolf.) It was fully consistent with Freud's findings that the Wolf Man adopted the werewolf's identity not so much because he believed *himself* to be a werewolf but because he partly identified with the father's position. Indeed, within the analysis itself, the Wolf Man behaved like a wolf or a werewolf—he continually threatened to "gobble up" Freud (106–107)—precisely because Freud actually occupied the desired position of paternal authority, even "wolf doctor," in relation to the patient.

Whether or not his rereading of the Wolf Man's dream is on the right track, Ginzburg believes that the particular folkloristic sense of the dream—and, by extension, its wider cultural sense—"eluded" Freud (Ginzburg 1989: 149). Freud probably did not know anything about the Russian traditions to which the little Wolf Man might have been exposed. But he was surely familiar with the comparative material on werewolf beliefs collected in J. G. Frazer's *The Golden Bough* (Frazer 1913: 308–10) and E. B. Tylor's *Primitive Culture*, both of which he owned. In particular,

Tylor (1903: I, 308) explicitly referred to the lycanthropic delusions which sometimes appear in "various forms of mental disease," an idea with roots in Burton's section on wolf "madness" (*lupinam insaniam*) in the *The Anatomy of Melancholy,* itself synthesizing many earlier sources (see Burton 1989: 133–34). Considering his own education and interests, Freud might also have been familiar with Jakob Grimm's philological introduction to northern European werewolf lore (1875: I, 915–18) and with the classical traditions, most famously represented in Petronius's werewolf story (*Satyricon,* 61–62) and Ovid's tale of Lycaon in the *Metamorphoses* (Bk. 1). After all, Freud's way of dubbing his patient, "Wolf Man," was not unmotivated; the name was chosen as much for the general connotations it would have for readers of the case history—presumed to have knowledge something like Freud's—as for its specific denotation within the interpretation itself.

Indeed, because Freud had made a special point of changing his own name from Sigismund to the more Germanic Sigmund, he probably recalled that Sigmund and Sinfjotli, in the story of the Volsungs, donned wolfskins with a "weird power" which enabled them to howl like wolves and understand the sounds of the beasts (*Volsungasaga,* chap. 8; see Byock 1990: 44–45). Moreover, Sigmund, imprisoned in the forest, tore out the she-wolf's tongue:

> For nine nights in a row that same she-wolf came at midnight and each time killed and ate one of the ten] brothers [imprisoned in a tree trunk] until all but Sigmund were dead. And now before the tenth night [Queen] Signy [wife of King Siggeir] sent her trusted man to her brother Sigmund. She gave him some honey and instructed him to smear it on Sigmund's face and to put some in his mouth. Her man went to Sigmund, did as he had been instructed, and then returned home. As usual the same she-wolf came in the night, meaning to bite Sigmund to death as she had his brothers. But then she caught the scent of the honey that had been rubbed on him. She licked his face all over with her tongue and then reached her tongue into his mouth. He did not lose his composure and bit into the wolf's tongue. She jerked and pulled back hard, thrusting her feet against the trunk so that it split apart. But Sigmund held on so tightly that the wolf's tongue was torn out by the roots, and that was her death. And some men say that the she-wolf was Siggeir's mother, who had assumed this shape through witchcraft and sorcery. (*Volsungasaga,* chap. 5; Byock 1990: 40–41)

Because of the importance of these episodes in the story of Sigmund, in many Nordic traditions he was frequently described as wearing a wolfskin mantle or girdle (see Hertz 1862: 80). In failing to entertain the kind of possibility *for Freud* that he is willing to entertain for the Wolf Man, Ginzburg, like Fish, does not really come to terms with the intersubjective dynamic of the case. He fails to appreciate that Freud almost certainly responded to the implication—built into both the general social structure and the specific text or iconography of the analysis—that both he and the Wolf Man could be construed as "wolves" in relation to one another.

Freud's Criticism of the Patient's Culture

It would certainly be possible to identify other aspects of the cultural roots of the Wolf Man's subjective object, the drawing projected for Freud, which Freud might have partially or wholly missed. We have already seen, for example, that the icons and rituals of the Russian Orthodox Church might have played a part in shaping both the graphic form and the personal meaning of the Wolf Man's drawing. To take a similar example, Florence J. Levy (1968–69) has proposed that the Wolf Man's "father phobia," supposedly expressed in the dream he had on Christmas Eve, might have to be interpreted differently when one knows that in some Russian folktales the giftgiver is not Saint Nicholas (= the father) but an old woman, "Babushka" (= Grandmother), whom the Wolf Man may have represented in his "butterfly" dream (Russian *babochka* = "butterfly" = *babushka*, "granny"?). Such information might tend to confirm Klein's and Rank's argument that Freud concentrated on the patient's paternal identifications and fears (special relays of his "homosexual" desires and anxieties) at the expense of maternal ones.

Nevertheless, it is difficult to know whether additional background knowledge would have substantially changed the course of Freud's reconstructions. Levy's point is well taken; but the paternal (and masculine) images for possible subjective identification were certainly as deeply rooted in the Wolf Man's culture as maternal (and feminine) ones. In fact, Freud could have made much more of them than he actually did. Freud saw the period of "obsessive piety" in the Wolf Man's childhood, for example, almost exclusively as a defensive formation abetted by the superstition of the boy's Nanya and by local priests. But he noticed only the obvious identification between the Wolf Man (born on Christmas Day) and Christ rather than the other cultural images for possible identification which might have organized the Wolf Man's religious practice. Little Serge was evidently named after St. Sergius (c. 1314–92), who saved Russia from the Tartars and whose piety and miracles must have been recounted to him, most likely by his Nanya; the saint's life was the subject of a famous medieval Russian chronicle by Epiphanius the Wise (see Zenkovsky 1963: 208–36). In his adolescence and adulthood, the Wolf Man's identification with the great Russian poet Lermontov, whom he supposedly resembled physically, led him into various entanglements (Gardiner 1971: 21; and see Halpert 1975). In the case history, Freud had a very vague knowledge of this association. The Wolf Man credited the adolescent revival of his interest in picture making, rooted in his very early childhood enthusiasm for drawing trees, with a visit to the spectacular mountain site where Lermontov had been killed (Gardiner 1971: 9, 34). Who can say exactly how Freud might have taken account of this information had he acquired it?

Certainly Freud often minimized or did not fully grasp such major aspects of the Wolf Man's native language and ethnically specific symbolism. But he was not wholly blind to the patient's cultural experience. He *also* recognized and criticized certain aspects of it, however partially— and despite, indeed because of, the patient's deceptions and defenses. We should be careful to distinguish Freud's lack of knowledge of his patient's culture, whether unwitting or willful, from his refusal to indulge the patient's myths. His partial, fluctuating recognition, acceptance, and refusal of the Wolf Man's culture operates throughout the case history on many levels.

One striking example has not been noticed by commentators. It would seem that the Wolf Man himself was largely unaware of the ways in which his own narrative—recounted to Freud and later to the readers of his *Memoirs*—reproduced a stereotyped narrative about childhood produced within his own society. Instead, he discovered this narrative in, or as, the history of his own real childhood.

According to Andrew B. Wachtel, who has examined more than fifty autobiographical or pseudo-autobiographical texts written by members of the Russian gentry between 1860 and 1940, before the publication of Ivan Goncharov's story "Oblomov's Dream" (1849) and Tolstoy's *Childhood* (1852), the memoirs "give no indication that they felt that the places, persons, and memories of childhood were in some way privileged." Conceptually and socially, "childhood leads directly into later life without being considered a qualitatively different stage" (Wachtel 1990: 224 n. 3). But *after* the success of Tolstoy's book, Russian memoirists "selected, organized, interpreted, and even verbalized their memories of childhood experiences in accordance with a pattern drawn from works of literature" (ibid.: 86)—what Wachtel calls the Russian "myth of childhood."

Although, oddly enough, Wachtel does not include it in his survey of "memoirs," the Wolf Man's story of his childhood on the Odessa estate in the 1880s and 1890s—we have its two versions in Freud's reports and the patient's *Memoirs*—conforms closely to this general "myth." The Wolf Man's Nanya (see Fig. 71), for example, was clearly one of those nannies who were said to leave "an indelible positive mark on the life of almost every Russian gentry child" (ibid.: 106). Indeed, the two major roles which the Wolf Man retrospectively assigned to his Nanya—she provided him with the intimate, maternal love his mother did or could not offer to him, and she awakened his intense religious feelings, sentiments his freethinking father, in particular, probably disliked—are the two roles most commonly ascribed to nannies in the "myth." In the "myth," the nanny also passes on fairy tales, folklore, and superstitions. Ginzburg (1989) supposes that the Wolf Man's Nanya was the intermediary in the dream supposedly calling him to the "vocation" of werewolf; certainly, as we have seen, the Wolf Man's report of his dream gives a peculiar place to Nanya—as if she both provoked the nightmare by telling scary stories and rescued him from it when he woke up screaming. Similarly, the Wolf Man's story of his relations with his foreign governesses and tutors finds many echoes in gentry memoirs. As a final example, the world of the servants on a landowner's estate "provided material to pique and to satisfy the early sexual yearnings of slightly older male children" (Wachtel 1990: 109), at least as they later recollected and represented their boyhoods. In this regard, the Wolf Man's encounters with Grusha, the serving girl who supposedly replicated his mother's position in the primal scene, and with other servants are absolutely stock elements of the "myth." According to Wachtel (ibid.: 84–86), at a time when a nonaristocratic, urbanized bourgeois began to compete with the landed gentry, the "myth" of gentry childhood enabled memoirists to define themselves according to a special distinction that no *arriviste* could share.

In this light, Freud's analysis of the Wolf Man's narrative of childhood—whether or not he knew anything about its specifically literary lineage—can be seen as an attempt to interpret, even to explode, this mythology. In February 1910, when the Wolf Man appeared for his first consultation with Freud, Freud's Russian-born disciple Max Eitingon (later a member of the "Secret Committee") presented Freud with a twenty-one-volume German edition of the collected works of Dostoevsky; Freud already owned a 1908 German edition of *The Brothers Karamazov*, as well as Dmitri Merezhkovsky's critical study of Tolstoy and Dostoevsky (Merezhkovsky 1902). It is likely that Merezhkovsky's book was received warmly by Freud. In addition to working out an elaborate parallel between Tolstoy and Dostoevsky, on the one hand, and Michelangelo and Leonardo da Vinci (two of Freud's other great artistic interests), on the other, Merezhkovsky couched his description of Dostoevsky's achievement in a remarkably "Freudian" language (e.g., 1902: 241, 255, 307–308). All of this reading might have disposed Freud to be skeptical of his new patient's reminiscences. He had read enough to suppose that a *counter*narrative or *counter-myth* could be juxtaposed with the obviously superficial story of the Wolf Man's privileged and carefree Russian upbringing—namely, a counterhistory of repressed homosexuality, trauma, fear, and obsession which he later synthesized in an essay called "Dostoevsky and Parricide" (Freud 1928b).

Indeed, Freud seems to have glimpsed that his patient may have been ill *because of* his privileged way of life. This possibility had been represented in the Russian literary tradition in Goncharov's 1859 novel *Oblomov*. The paradisiacal country-estate childhood of Oblomov, the novel's main character, had been depicted in Goncharov's story "Oblomov's Dream," published ten years earlier; according to Wachtel (1990: 119–21), this tale became one of the fundamental texts of the "myth" of gentry childhood. In the later novel, however, the adult Oblomov has taken up residence in the city. Here he lives an infantilized life of social malaise and erotic indecision. The narrator makes it clear that Oblomov's condition is rooted in his childhood. The fairy tales which his Nanny had told him long ago now cripple him; they fill him with erotically charged yearning, nostalgia, and vague but peculiarly pleasurable frustrations in relation to his real-life activities and obligations: his "mind and imagination, imbued with make-believe, remained enslaved by it till old age." In fact, "the fairy tale had become confused with life in his mind and at times he was sad that the fairy tale was not life and life not a fairy tale," though some of the horror stories he had heard also created in him "a residue of fear and unaccountable anguish" (quoted by Lyngstrad and Lyngstrad 1971: 81–82). An active, realistic adult could have escaped such fantasies. But having been coddled by servants all of his life, Oblomov is comparatively defenseless. As another character in the novel tells him, Oblomov's malaise "began with your not knowing how to put on your socks and ended with your not knowing how to live" (quoted ibid.: 94). In sum, as commentators have put it, "the ethos of patriarchal life is at the root of Oblomov's malaise" (ibid.: 79), echoing the judgment of the mid-nine-teenth-century critic Dobrolyubov, who suggested in a famous essay of 1859, *What Is Oblomovism?*, that "being saturated with the spirit of serf-dom, Oblomov in his freedom from work paradoxically becomes the slave of everyone" (quoted ibid.: 94).

There is no evidence that Freud had read *Oblomov*. But in the very first section of the case study, he presents a characterization of the patient that reads like a catalogue of Oblomovisms. The first page of the case history tells us that the young man who had arrived for a consultation in 1910 was "entirely incapacitated and completely dependent upon other people" (1). Although thenceforth Freud concentrated on the patient's childhood disorder, the adult Wolf Man's way of life—including his behavior in anal-ysis—was marked, above all, by what Freud calls "an obliging apathy." It turned out to be nearly impossible for the analyst to penetrate it without taking very strong measures, such as imposing a time limit on the analysis. Indeed, the Wolf Man's "shrinking from an independent existence was so great as to outweigh all the vexations of his illness" (5).

We do not know whether Freud recognized that his patient was partly living out well-defined and (within his own social milieu) well-known scripts. He could probably piece some of them together from his own read-ing and experience. But seemingly he did discern where the *disjunction* of the patient's narratives might lie and thus where psychoanalytic "work"—the editorial review and, where necessary, revision—could begin. At least for an outsider to late-nineteenth-century Russian gentry society, the pa-tient's manifest Oblomovism was inconsistent with his own mythology of a privileged, happy childhood—leading Freud to look, in turn, for a history of Dostoevskyan turmoil, that "Russian censorship" which he had already identified as the basic mechanism of unconscious defense.[1]

In sum, Freud did not have the resources he would have needed to in-terpret the Wolf Man's myths fully. But it is hard to imagine what kind of historian, ethnographer, or psychologist would have full information in this sense. Throughout the case, Freud largely had to take the Wolf Man at his own word with regard to what actually occurred in his life and works. There are points in the case history, of course, where he questions the reliability of the Wolf Man's memory—but they always concern events that should have actually occurred which the Wolf Man does not remember (what is *left out*) rather than events that did not actually occur which the Wolf Man supposedly does remember (what is *represented in*). That the Wolf Man was not only telling his own story but also, and necessarily, expressing a more general cultural construction is a possibility Freud never systematically entertained. It is not clear, however, what benefit this inquiry would have had; among other things, for example, the culturalist investigation probably would have deflected attention from the material history Freud hoped to reconstruct—namely, the specific form of the patient's tree of repression in the context of childhood, infantile, family, and species history conceived as epigenetically linked.

As Ginzburg puts it, Freud principally wanted to know how the patient's general cultural myths were (or were not) replicated in the "individual contexts within which the myth comes into being and functions" (1989: 155). Ginzburg would adopt this attitude for cultural history or psycho-ethnography, despite the Jungianism of his own case study of the Wolf Man. As matters stand, it is almost impossible to gauge the Wolf Man's attitudes, conscious and unconscious, to the scripts he replicated. Any ironical or other attitudes he might have sustained—for example, his story of his childhood could be seen as a parody of the Russian "myth" of happy childhood, a sardonic version of Oblomovism, or a theatricalization of Dostoevskyan gloom—were more or less lost on Freud, at least in just these terms. But investigating them might have enabled him to buttress his basic insight that the Wolf Man's neurosis was in part a malfunction of language itself, which had too long afforded him an ideal—defensive, magical, and unrealistic—narrative that did not permit him to say, or perhaps even to think, what had happened.

Freud's Wolf Doctor

These examples indicate the kind of partial recognitions, revisions, and gaps that necessarily occur in any intercultural or intersubjective exchange. Freud could probably divine some elements of the Wolf Man's fairy tales or folklore, his literary or social references, on the basis of his own armchair experience. After all, the Wolf Man helpfully provided some of the documentation itself, such as an actual copy of his childhood picture book. But what triggered Freud's response to his patient's representation of himself was not really a product of an exact or objective knowledge of the Wolf Man's culture; such knowledge is never fully available. More important, Freud subjectively responded to many aspects of the other's history precisely as it was presented to and perceived by him. Just as Freud projected his subjective object onto the Wolf Man's drawing, so too did he incorporate the Wolf Man's subjective objects—whatever their determinations—into his own representations.

An example drawn from material we have surveyed already will make the point. Immediately following his introduction of the drawing, in the text of the case history Freud recounted how the Wolf Man associated the wolves in the dream with a wolf he had seen in a picture book as a child. In the picture book, the Wolf Man reported, the wolf was supposedly depicted "standing upright, striding out with one foot, with its claws stretched out and its ears pricked" (30)—just like the wolves in the dream and drawing, which had "their ears pricked like dogs when they are attending to something" (29).

As we have seen, though Freud initially supposed that the picture illustrated the story of "Little Red Riding Hood," he quickly decided that "some other fairy tale" lay behind it. The Wolf Man, presumably anxious to "confirm" Freud's latest "conviction" in the same way he had "confirmed" his dream and aroused Freud's initial "conviction," managed to find an old copy of the picture book in a Viennese secondhand bookstore. It turned out at this point that the story "The Wolf and the Seven Little Goats" was the one that he had once seen illustrated with a picture of a wolf—and here Freud repeats his initial phrasing—with "one foot forward, with its claws stretched out and its ears pricked" (39).

But predictably, we might now say, it was also *Freud* who had a treasured childhood picture book; it had been awarded to him for his excellence in school and was later passed to his own son Martin to become a Freud family "heirloom." And this book, Friedrich von Tschudi's *Animal Life in the Alpine World* (1865), contains a striking illustration (Fig. 69) of an Alpine rescue dog, striding out with one foot with its ears pricked, saving a little boy lost in the snowy mountains (see M. Freud 1958: 21; Ginsburg and Ginsburg 1987: 478–81). Toward the very end of the case history, a phrase from his twice-repeated description of the wolf appears yet again; the exact words, and the specific image relayed, would appear to be both the Wolf Man's *and* Freud's, an intersubjective superimposition or palimpsest. At this point, Freud is explicitly discussing the "delayed confirmation" of material introduced, like the wolf dream, much earlier on in an analysis.

Figure 69. Illustration from Friedrich von Tschudi, *Animal Life in the Alpine World* (1865)

It happens in many analyses that as one approaches their end new recollections emerge which have hitherto been kept carefully concealed. Or
it may be that on one occasion some unpretentious remark is thrown
out in an indifferent tone of voice as though it were superfluous; that
then, on another occasion, something further is added, which begins to
make the physician prick his ears; and that at last he comes to recognize
this despised fragment of a memory as the key to the weightiest secrets
that the patient's neurosis has veiled. (89)

The Wolf Man's wolf—or werewolf—may be a terrifying gobbler, which
he partly conflated with sheep dogs on his father's estate and partly assimilated in his "curious behavior" in the transference, trying to "gobble up" Freud (106). But this subjective object was seemingly incorporated and reprojected by Freud—Sigmund the wolf-hero—as a wolf-dog
doctor, the attentive listener who will save the patient from the consequences of his childhood trauma by chasing away the terrible wolf-parents (see Fig. 70).

Probably based on Freud's own childhood pictures (Figs. 69–70), this
conversion was necessary because the Wolf Man's initial "transference"
and later associations—and Freud's technique in interpreting them—potentially cast Freud as an aggressive homosexual wolf-physician who,
"pricking his ears," connects up childhood imagery with the patient's history in the devouring activity of analysis. The Wolf Man confirmed his
second verbal association ("Seven Goats") to the drawing introduced as
a "confirmation" of the dream report by seeking out another picture, even
though this deferred historical research could not yet have taken place
when Freud formed his "conviction" that the first verbal association ("Red
Riding Hood") was inadequate and that "some other fairy tale"—some
other kind of wolf—lay behind it. But if what lay behind the patient's
fairy tale was Freud's Christmas or scientific fairy tale, as suggested earlier,
then Freud himself was nothing but a wolf sitting behind and looking
attentively at his patient and offering interpretations—even though (or
precisely because) the patient wants to use *him* from behind, shit on *his*
head, and gobble *him* up.[2]

Following the Wolf Man's associations, Ruth Mack Brunswick (1928:
289–90) interpreted the wolves in one of the patient's later "wolf dreams"
as "all the fathers or doctors" trying to destroy him. One of the Wolf
Man's associations in the reanalysis exhibited his conflict. The wolves in
the childhood dream he had reported to Freud, he now told Brunswick,
remind him of Romulus and Remus—and he then thinks both of "Rome"

Figure 70. Illustration from Friedrich von Tschudi,
Animal Life in the Alpine World (1865)

and the "persecution of the early Christians" (he himself was born on Christmas Day) and of the she-wolf who suckled the two mythological infants and saved their lives when they had been left in the wilderness. Freud's text, especially if it was partly determined by his own picture of the dog-rescuer (Fig. 69), shows that he was probably alert to roughly the same texture of meanings construed from his own position *as* the desiring, and desired, doctor. (We might remember, too, that "Rome" was Freud's preferred disanalogy—his heuristic model—for the mind [e.g., Freud 1930a], and that a "she-wolf" was his namesake Sigmund's enemy in the saga, from which "Sigmund" was rescued by his sister and the manservant who smeared honey in his mouth.) If it is Freud who "tears" the "veil" which the Wolf Man's dream and drawing represented for him, permitting the patient to see the world clearly, then Freud was potentially cast in the position of the attendant who administered the Wolf Man's enema, satisfying the patient's desire to be homosexually relieved. To tear the veil in the devouring activity of analysis was to give the patient what he wants sexually. Despite (in fact, because of) all this, "pricking his ears" and "striding out with one foot forward," Freud will try to save the patient from his repression of bisexuality. As Freud incorporates and projects it, the analysis is neither homosexual assault nor homosexual flight but precisely a homosexual rescue.

Homosexuality and the Drawing of the Wolves

In the most general terms, then, two objects, the Wolf Man's drawing and Freud's writing, became absorbed into one another in the lateral, deferred actions of psychoanalysis and writing. This intersubjective transformation must be distinguished from any merely unilateral construction of one subject "by" another. Freud was not the same subject, observing and interpreting other subjects, that he was before his encounter with the Wolf Man took place. His own subjectivity—that discharge of partially unrealized desire which constituted his own historical identity—was reorganized by the incorporation and transformation of an object from the other, even as that object was the support for his own projections. Fish is right, of course, that the "Wolf Man" is a "piece of language." But that language is not wholly Freud's—and it speaks of *both* subjects as "wolf men" in terms partly absorbed from the other. It is a language forged between two subjects seeing and speaking with one another. They jointly created a new, intersubjective image out of their separate histories—a partial but nonetheless usable palimpsest of all the separate images, from Freud's childhood picture book, family portrait, scientific education, and creative notation (e.g., Figs. 69, 66, 57, 43) to the Wolf Man's childhood picture book, family portrait, artistic education, and creative notation (e.g., Figs. 67, 61, 27, 12), all of which had been brought to, were evoked in, and were substantially reorganized in the history of their address, interpretation, and response itself.

At the same time as the analytic situation includes this subjective incorporation and projection, a supposedly therapeutic intersubjectivity, it also claims, of course, to identify and explain it objectively, because the analyst, at least, has been previously analyzed. The analyst supposedly knows how he or she incorporates and projects subjective objects from or into the other. Therefore the analyst qualifies as an objective historian of the other by knowing what to *subtract* from seeing and speaking with that other, knowing how to *reserve* his or her subjective objects from an objective interpretation of the other because he or she objectively observes the countertransference—the moment when a personal subjective object materializes in response to the patient's representations, the ostensible object of analytic observation in the first place. But whence the emergence of an objective observation of countertransference, permitting objective identification of the observer's subjective object emerging in response to the other's transference?

The analyst's objectivity was itself supposedly obtained by having *another* analyst subtract his or her subjectivity, in turn, from addressing that of the analyst-in-training. The analyst-in-training, to find objective subjectivity, awaits the "training" analyst's objective subjectivity—and so on, indefinitely. The moment of objectively observing and interpreting the subjective objects in the history of the historian's intercourse with the other, then, is at least laterally bound—if not infinitely postponed—in the deferred action of the retrospective inauguration of psychoanalysis itself. It is referred to a place and time at the absolute horizon of historical interpretation—that is, to the "self-analysis" of Freud, in which the objective recognition of someone's subjective objects, his own subjectivity, was supposedly secured *without* being addressed by another. But the existence of this time and place is only a mythology of an objective subjectivity supposedly preceding intersubjectivity itself.[3]

Because Freud's history of visualizing psychic history was replicated for him in the Wolf Man's drawing, to *subtract* these schemata would have been to eliminate the basis on which the Wolf Man's drawing could have been rendered intelligible to Freud in the first place. Without the observer's subjective object in interpreting the other's representation, he would not attain an objectivity at all but rather encounter an illegibility. Despite the historian's cathexis to a horizon in which history was or becomes objective, there is no final subtraction or reservation of the subjective object—and this object, when it materializes for observation and interpretation, is always intersubjectively constructed.

This is not to say, in turn, that the case history of the Wolf Man is based on *nothing but* that kind of intersubjectivity within the psychoanalytic situation which an "authentic" interpretation seems to require. In Freud's conceptualization of homosexuality and masculinity in the case history, for example, he often depended on evidence or concepts developed in earlier, "vulgar" interpretations—including his knowledge of "homosexual" patients analyzed not by himself but, among others, by Isidor Sadger, by Sandor Ferenczi, by Karl Abraham, and by Alfred Adler (with whom he officially disagreed but whose doctrine of the "masculine protest" he appropriated) and his study of the notebooks of Leonardo da Vinci and the memoirs of Judge Schreber, whom he had never met. Indeed, the case could be made that psychoanalytic "authenticity," whatever it might be, actually *requires* psychoanalytic vulgarity as well as unanalyzed subjective objects on the part of the supposedly analyzed or self-analyzed observer. But the difference between this state of affairs in the Wolf Man case and "psychoanalytical" applications such as Freud's *Leonardo* (1910c) is simply that the vulgarity and subjectivity of "authentic" analytic interpretation exist in, and are motivated by, an intersubjective exchange between observer and observed. And this is all the difference in the world.

It has been practically axiomatic throughout this investigation that an interpreter's preexisting subjective sexuality must be brought to, evoked in, and reorganized by the intersubjective exchange in which a jointly, if differentially, meaningful history is being jointly, if differentially, constructed. In the very first session, the Wolf Man proclaimed his desire to "use [Freud] from behind and shit on his head"; we have considered some of the possible determinations—even the varying possible senses— of this statement, including the possibility that it was partly a speech act of Freud's own reported to us as being the patient's. In developing his interpretation of this "transference," inaugurally including his subject response to it, Freud apparently carried over its homosexual content (in his own further transference or *Überzeugung*) into a complicated theory of the "inherited" origin of the Wolf Man's homosexuality, a thesis derived in turn, as we have seen, from Freud's schemata for the repression of bisexuality replicated for him in the Wolf Man's drawing.

The dynamic of such intersubjectivity—of schema and interpretation, transference, subjectivity—was probably at least partly within the horizon of Freud's overt awareness in the early weeks of the analysis, possibly provoked by the immediate significance for him of the patient's first solicitation and by the extraordinary fit between his own emerging "convictions" and the patient's first "confirmations." It was in these weeks that Freud—so far as we know, for the first time—began to think of the psychoanalyst's "countertransference," as he called it, as an emerging formation within a psychoanalysis and requiring interpretation in itself. (In this book, then, it is not appropriate to describe the case and case history of the Wolf Man as "countertransferential" phenomena—of course they are—in just that terminology because the Freudian concept of countertransference would seem, at least in part, to be *the product* of the Wolf Man case, yet another manifestation of Freud's use of the case to grasp and reorganize his own "homosexual" position. It should not be used, then, simply as an available concept to describe and explain the fundamental structure and themes of the case.) In early March 1910, Freud called his students' attention to the fact that "while the patient attaches himself to the physician, the physician is subject to a similar process, that of 'countertransference.' " Explicitly, of course, Freud's attitude toward this formation—one of the precipitates of analytic intersubjectivity—was that it must be subtracted from the analysis in order to preserve the analyst's objectivity. "This countertransference," he went on, "must be completely overcome by the analyst; only this will make him master of the psychoanalytic situation; it makes him the perfectly cool object, whom the other person must lovingly woo" (Nunberg and Federn 1962–75: II, 447 [March 9, 1910]). In the first few weeks of the analysis, the patient's hot, fluctuating desires to seduce the doctor have stimulated, and are being invoked by, the doctor's subjective erotic heat. But it is Freud's fantasy—to some extent his sense of his possible achievement in analysis and his prescription for others—that he can "overcome" his heat to become the "perfectly cool object." And what must be "overcome," what must be cooled down, is, of course, his homosexuality—stimulated by, but also provoking, the patient's demand to "use him from behind." And if the doctor cools down sufficiently, so—perhaps—will the patient; instead of "shitting on his head," the patient will come to "lovingly woo" his physician.

The conflicted, homosexualized origins of his own theory of repression itself, as we have seen, had generally been ignored or actively suppressed by Freud—for instance, in his explication of the Signorelli slip (Fig. 51). But apparently by the second half of the year 1910, this tendency had shifted markedly. In September 1910, for example, Ferenczi traveled with Freud in Sicily while the latter was working on Schreber's memoirs and, more specifically, the theory of homosexually determined paranoia which Ferenczi himself had helped to develop. Freud proved, however, to be unwilling to share this intellectual labor, as he had initially offered to do and as Ferenczi had expected in joining him on the trip. Especially in view of their comparatively stable friendship up to this point, Freud's sudden flash of fear, rivalry, and hatred—possibly a fear that Ferenczi would detract from his originality or steal the credit—was immediately and openly acknowledged by both men, shortly after their return from the south on September 26, to have had "homosexual components" (see Freud/Ferenczi 1993: 214, 217–18 [September 28 and October 3, 1910]). Indeed, the trip was partly perceived as an attempt at "living together" rendered difficult by the discovery that Ferenczi's "fantasy ideal," Professor Freud, was really just an "ordinary old gentleman"; on the trip, or soon afterward, Ferenczi dreamed of Freud "standing naked before me (naturally without feeling the slightest conscious [indeed, also in the dream still unconscious] sexual arousal)" (ibid.: 218 [October 3, 1910]; brackets in original). The two men's recognition of their "unc. homosexual tendency and [. . .] longing for absolute mutual openness" (ibid.), even if it was difficult and somewhat embarrassing to make when it involved confessing a certain amount of physical distaste for one another, was more or less explicitly understood to defuse the situation and to permit both men to cool down.

With a few more days' distance from the unfortunate trip, Freud went on to say:

> This need [for a full opening of my personality] has been extinguished in me since Fliess's case, with the overcoming of which you just saw me occupied. A piece of homosexual investment has been withdrawn and utilized for the enlargement of my own ego. I have succeeded where the paranoiac fails. (Ibid.: 221 [October 6, 1910])

And a few days later, he added:

> Perhaps you are imagining completely different secrets [from] those I have reserved for myself, or you think there is a special suffering connected with that, whereas I feel myself to be a match for anything and

approve of the overcoming of my homosexuality, with the result being greater independence. (Ibid.: 227 [October 17, 1910])

Freud's sense, in late 1910, that he had "overcome" his homosexuality—"working through" his homosexual feelings toward Fliess, as he told his friend Max Schur (1972: 256–57) about this time—was a matter of interest, of course, to the entire Freudian group. By 1912, Freud claimed to be entirely free of the "homosexuality" that he acknowledged had disturbed some of his earlier relations with friends and students. In December 1912, Ernest Jones claimed to perceive a connection between Freud's fainting at Munich and Freud's "older affects," that is, Freud's friendship with Fliess (Freud/Jones 1993: 184 [December 23, 1912]). But in reply, Freud wrote: "You are right in supposing that I had [once] transferred to Jung homosex. feelings from another part but I am glad to find that I [now] have no difficulty in removing them for free circulation" (ibid.: 186 [December 26, 1912]).

"Free circulation" meant intellectual work and the general administration of psychoanalysis. Indeed, from Freud's vantage point by late 1910, the troublesome form of "homosexuality" in the Freudian group—suspiciousness, competitiveness, overdependence—was placed entirely where it belonged, namely, in the colleagues and students who were offending Freud or psychoanalysis in one or another way. They were reenacting the original "paranoid" homosexuality of Fliess, that forceful desire both to imitate and to resist Freud which Freud supposed had lured him into his own passively "homosexual" dependence on such interest and attention in the first place. Freud himself was now free of this need. He was, he imagined, neither assaulting anyone nor fleeing—merely curious, in a cool and objective psychoanalytic fashion, about the others' fantasies. As he wrote to Ferenczi: "I have now overcome Fliess, which you were so curious about. Adler is a little Fliess *redivivus,* just as paranoid. Stekel, his appendage, is at least called Wilhelm" (Freud/Ferenczi 1993: 243 [December 16, 1910]).

In fact, the students' very interest in homosexuality itself, compared to Freud's own *dis*interested interest, manifested their infantilism. "It is strange, and certainly no coincidence," he told Ferenczi, "that both Fliess and Adler emphasize *bisexuality* in this way; the homosexual origin of their character is expressed therein" (ibid.: 245 [December 19, 1910]). Freud meant that Fliess and Adler had, for whatever personal reasons, been unable to come to terms with *homo*sexuality, which Freud now believed he could trace in its full development *from* an original bisexuality guided, he would propose in the Wolf Man case history, by homosexual "predis-positions." The students continued to invoke, and depend on, the thesis of bisexuality, but the idea was just a disguise or a placeholder (as Hirsch-feld among others had urged all along) for the real discussion, an avoid-ance of the "overcoming" which they had proved—in their relations with Freud—that they really required.

Exactly why the whole matter should have been so much on Freud's mind at this time will probably always remain somewhat unclear. Indeed, *"non liquet."* But it seems apparent that between late 1909 and late 1910, Freud's attitude toward his own "homosexuality" was transformed. He more or less consciously understood his homosexuality to have been fun-damentally reorganized. In the fall of 1909, for example, Freud had ex-perienced what he later described to Jung—a few days before meeting the Wolf Man—as an "Indian summer [*Johannistrieb*] of eroticism" (Freud/ Jung 1974: 292 [February 2, 1910]). Freud may have meant that he was experiencing a second bloom, even a sexual renaissance, in his marriage with Martha. More likely, however, the "Indian summer" was the tumul-tuous friendship with Jung himself, brought to a crisis during the trip to America they had taken along with Ferenczi. But again, by the autumn of 1910, as Freud's letters to Ferenczi imply, Freud thought that he was able to "overcome" the "homosexual" position—demanding, flirtatious, solicitous, dependent, frequently aggressive—he had held earlier.

Although the historical evidence can be only circumstantial, we might say, then, that the Wolf Man's representations (the drawing of the dream of the wolves was presented in April or May 1910) and the conditions and possibilities of the case in general (beginning in February 1910) allowed the partial discharge of Freud's sexual repression.[4] The case, its whole di-rection strongly projected and predicted by the highly determining initial "conviction," enabled him to appropriate Fliess's idea of inherited psy-chic bisexuality, to combat his followers' doubts, and to settle many out-standing questions concerning his originality, authority, probity, and ra-tionality—that is, to "overcome the homosexuality" that the Wolf Man's first consultation and initial transference had elicited. Freud later worked out at least one complex model for one *pathological* form of a male subject's "overcoming" of his homosexuality: in his essay "Fetishism" (Freud 1927e), he interpreted heterosexual male fetishism not only as a species of perverse heterosexuality but also as what "saves the fetishist from his homosexuality." The details of this account are not relevant here (see Davis

1995a: chap. 12), for by this point Freud's language and imagery had a well-established lineage in his writing. In 1910, Freud did not suppose that he had "saved" himself from his homosexuality by becoming a fetishist. But the verbal, written, and visual text of the case and case history of the Wolf Man—whether or not Freud would have consciously acknowledged it—suggests that he believed he had rescued himself from his homosexuality by trying to rescue the other from *his* homosexuality; they were both saved from being "gobbled up."

As proposed earlier, by way of a complex tissue of schemata, metaphors, and images, Freud incorporated and projected the case in such a way as to convert his "homosexual" aggression and feared "homosexual" solicitation into an objective, but also decisively masculine and heroic, "homosexual" concern for the other man's psychic welfare—for the rediscovery and repair of his heterosexuality. Needless to say, the irony would be that although Freud would claim to save the "Wolf Man" from the prehistoric and infantile past—from the persistence of homosexualizing "predispositions"—represented by his "wolves," he would cast the patient as the "Wolf Man" of psychoanalysis for ever and ever, constructing him in the published case history as the "latent" homosexual for perpetual citation and interpretation. Whether or not Serge Pankejeff ever was or continued to be "shackled" by his latent homosexuality and whether or not he had been "liberated" by his analysis with Freud, it is certainly true that in his eighties he was interrogated about the homosexual experiences he supposedly might or must have had in his teens and twenties. He might write about psychoanalysis and "freedom of the will"; he could express some of his own tastes and interests—quite distinct from anything Freud ever knew or cared for—in a study of Aubrey Beardsley. But he would always be the "Wolf Man."

In sum, that the Wolf Man desired Freud was matched, practically point for point, by the fact that Freud desired the Wolf Man. But over the course of their exchange, their two different homosexualities apparently were intersubjectively reorganized for each subject as an overcoming of his homosexuality—mediated by the drawing that evoked those two different pasts. Indeed, the drawing laterally bound or siphoned off the subjective desire of each into the objective history of the other. For the Wolf Man, Freud's interpretation of his dream and drawing resituated his homosexuality, manifested in the contemporary intersubjective context of the first consultation, in an objective archaic past. Once identified, this prehistory could be surmounted. And for Freud, the Wolf Man's dream and drawing seemingly allowed *his* receptive, paranoid relation to the desires of other men, again evoked in the intersubjective context of the first consultation, to be resituated as an objective analysis of what other men really want. Freud's subjective object, the primal repression of bisexuality, was placed into the Wolf Man as the Wolf Man's objective history, now surmounted through therapy. And the Wolf Man's subjective object, a homosexuality that threatens to gobble him up, was placed into Freud as Freud's objective history, now surmounted through the exemplary "case" of and for psychoanalysis itself—for he could now believe that the Wolf Man's desire for him wholly derived from the Wolf Man's prehistoric and infantile history rather than from Freud himself in their actual and contemporary intercourse. Thus a sexuality was intersubjectively constituted—in this case, a particular homosexuality somewhat paradoxically resisting itself by rescuing itself from its own repression, or what Freud called latent homosexuality. Derived from originally separate histories, like any sexuality it was realized only mutually with an other who could represent and interpret it in the intersubjective exchange of subjective objects. No doubt this exchange was a relation of misrepresentation and misinterpretation, of asymmetric (though not necessarily unequal) needs and powers. But there could never be a fully mutual absorption of subjective objects in the first place—a complete, objective recognition of the other as a subject. Intersubjectivity is not objectivity. The question, rather, is whether and how subjectivity, "homosexual" or not, can, or does, become intersubjective, and with what consequences for the balance of our lust, rage, guilt, and fear. In the case and case history of the Wolf Man, these consequences were not, of course, wholly or even largely positive ones: Freud's transference was surely organized as a homophobia, as we might have expected, structurally transferred, in turn, to the theory and the practice of latent homosexuality, while the Wolf Man was hardly "liberated" if all he could do, in the end, was acquire a new focus for that dependence on the other's attentions which Freud was so pleased to believe that he himself had overcome. But just as we cannot expect intersubjectivity to become objectivity, neither can we expect intersubjectivity to become equality or community; manifest sexualities—the effective intersubjectivity established between people—are obviously not sciences of or ethics for intersubjective forms.

If there is anything worth rescuing from the Freudian metaphysics of "sexuality" and its theories of erotic potentiality, including, for example, its histories of homosexual "latency," it is the Freudian recognition that *effectively* sexuality is the actual intersubjectivity in which the latent becomes manifest, a potential is realized, and a transformation occurs. It would require a science to explicate this process and an ethics to evaluate but not, one would hope, to regulate it; but as our case study has suggested, any such science and any such ethics must, themselves, relay a historically specific intersubjective sexuality. Although the manifest text of the case and case history of the Wolf Man is, as we have seen, a theory about and a therapy for sexual potentiality or sexuality, its latent text was the production *of* a sexuality itself. Most exactly, when sexuality pictures itself to itself—through the desire and the provocation of another—the merely latent becomes manifest, words of authorization and identification are spoken, the speakers, partners, or lovers review and revise their schemes, and a new history begins. We can only picture what lies beyond that.

APPENDIX

Ruth Mack Brunswick's Draft
for a Clinical Study of the Wolf Man
(Gardiner Papers, Library of Congress)

Note: This printing reproduces Brunswick's text exactly, without
amending her punctuation or correcting her spelling errors; the text
is obviously a rough draft. Remarks in square brackets are the present
author's.

[A. Outline]

The History of an Infantile Neurosis, A Psychosis, and An Adult Neurosis
theoretical: 1. the child's *first relations* (nurse or mother) as the prototype
for all later hetero- and homosexual relations, as well as the basis *in
reality* for all sexual understanding . . . of the Urszene and for all phantasies; masturbation . . . it is the fundament of the psychic life.
2. the problem of passivity, *conversion to activity, etc.,* in the male.

[B. Fragmentary Text]

The Wolfman

I. Introduction.

   The wolfman has already provided the psychoanalytic literature with
two clinical histories. In "The History of an Infantile Neurosis" Freud describes for the first time the passive relation of the neurotic male child to
the father. The passivity which lead at first to the development of a severe
and paralyzing neurosis later, under the stress of circumstance, found expression in a hypochondriacal form of paranoia, which, accessible to analytic treatment, corroborated the hypothesis that passive homosexuality
is the etiological factor in male paranoia. However, at the end of the second
analysis [i.e., Brunswick 1928], it was impossible to state definitely what
factors were responsible for the cure of the paranoid process. It was held

215

that the working-through of the remnants of the father-transference constituted the principal treatment.

Six years after the analysis of the paranoid illness in 1926–27, the Wolf-
man again presented himself. The ensuing portion of analysis, which
comprised sixteen hours, will be given in the following pages. But the
span of more than twenty years from the beginning of the Wolfman's
first analysis in 1910 and this most recent bit, which I abstain from calling
the last, in 1932 has witnessed a large measure of development in the
psychoanalytic theory itself. There have been few changes but many en-
largements to the body of our knowledge. And, curiously, the case of the
Wolfman almost seems to have kept pace with the increase. It is perhaps
not an accident that the patient in whom the passive relation of the neurotic man to the father was first classically presented should now be available for the demonstration of the earliest and, in its origins, most passive
of all relations, that of the child to the mother or mother-substitute.

In order to facilitate matters for the reader of this material, which, in
the course of extensive treatment has become cumbrous, the clinical
history of the Wolfman will here be given in its entirety. Parts of it have
never before appeared. It will be recalled that "The History of an Infantile
Neurosis" was exactly what its name implies: the history of the infantile
neurosis which lay at the root of the adult neurosis. Now, however, it becomes necessary to describe the case as a whole, including thus the neurotic manifestations in the adult patient. Before proceeding to the clinical
history, we shall, however, consider certain theoretical problems, which
we hope later in the light of the clinical material to bring a step further
toward solution.

[This, apparently the first page of Brunswick's manuscript, is followed
by a gap, probably of at least two pages. The next surviving page is num-
bered 4.]

enormous wave of virility in the adolescent boy, and along with it the
need to penetrate the vagina. And it is the installation of the menses
which awaken the vagina in the girl. Thus the coitus concept of the
phallic phase, in which the vagina is unknown, and the need of penetration not yet formed, is the mutual touching of the genitals. This is
indeed what children for the most part do amongst themselves, when
attempting to copy the coitus of the parents. The position of the parents
is often reproduced, both in masturbation phantasies and in the mutual

Figure 71. The Wolf Man's Nanya, c. 1903 (Pankejeff Papers, LC)

masturbation of children: but the content of the scene, which is outwardly that of coitus, is inwardly one might say, masturbatory. The persistence of masturbation at a time when coitus is possible, and when the situation demands coitus and not masturbation is not infrequent in neurotic individuals, and played, as you will perhaps remember from my history of the W. an important part in his sexual life.

I wish now to return to the clinical material on which in part I base this idea. Unfortunately because of the need for brevity I can give you only one fragment of the analytic material concerned with the patient's relations to his Nanya [Fig. 71]. The remainder must be left for publication. But that fragment is perhaps the most important element that came to light in our sixteen hours of the most concentrated analytic work.

This fragment is a memory which suddenly appeared, and which was entirely unknown to Professor Freud and to me, as well as to the patient, from our previous analyses. The patient is very small, less than three, almost surely less than 2 1/2, the age at which the Gruscha scene occurred. He goes with his Nanya to the toilet. This toilet seems to have had two seats, although this is not certain. In any case, both the patient and his Nanya have bowel movements. The patient is constipated—as he was during all his adult life; for years he was given daily enemas by a male attendant. His Nanya tries to help him defecate; she inserts her finger into his anus, and teaches him that by pressing with the finger in a certain way, defecation will be made easier.

We should call this anal masturbation of the little boy by his nurse. And indeed [portion of sentence missing] neurosis which show the cardinal importance of this scene—which [was?] undoubtedly not an isolated incident [?]. But I would remind you of the connection of one or two facts broughout in in the "History of an Inf. Neurosis." They are in connection with the seduction of the Wolfsmann by his sister. Freud says: "The pt. suddenly called to mind the fact that, when he was still very small, 'upon the first estate,' his sister had seduced him into sexual practices. First came a recollection that in the water-closet, which the children used frequently to visit together, she had made this proposal: 'Let's show one another our bottoms.' Subsequently the more essential part of the seduction came to light, with full particulars as to time and locality. It was in spring, at a time when his father was away; the children were in one room, playing on the floor, while their mother was working in the next. His sister had taken hold of his member and played with it, at the same time telling him incomprehensible stories about his Nanya, as though by way of explanation. His Nanya, she said, used to do the same thing with all kinds of people—for instance, the gardener: she used to stand him on his head, and then take hold of his genitals."

We drew the conclusion, the pt. and I, that his open seduction by his sister was also a cover memory for an earlier, far more prolonged and more generalized seduction by his nurse. And we felt able also to understand his sister's strange stories about Nanya. His sister was always jealous of Nanya's affection for the younger child. She after all had had Nanya's exclusive care for the two years before the Wolfsmann was born. Her telling him these things is therefore to be interpreted as a statement of Nanya's faithlessness: Nanya, she said, used to do the same thing with all sorts of people—in other words, don't think you are the only one. Moreover what the Wolfsmann's sister the seduction of the pt. by his sister [*sic*] was the little girl's attempt to identify herself with her lost Nanya, and to replace that Nanya in the affections of Nanya's present love object, the little brother. From these facts we may deduce how strongly seductive this primitive old nurse, who later became insane, was in her influence upon both children particularly in the anal field. What I here trace back to the influence of the nurse, Freud, at a time when the role of the nurse was less well known, traced back to the influence of the primal scene. He says: We cannot fail to be struck by the idea that perhaps the sister, at a similar tender age, also witnessed the same scene as what [was] observed by her brother later on, and that it was this that had suggested to her her notion about 'standing people on their heads' during the sexual act. This hypothesis" Freud goes on to say, "would also give us a hint of the reason for her own—the sister's sexual precocity."

What seems likely, in view of all the facts, is that both children witnessed, at a very early age—under two years in both cases—a coitus on the part of the parents; that both children, at this very early age, were being cared for by a particularly devoted nurse, who was very anally-erotic in character; and that the children interpreted the coitus of their parents in terms of their own experience with their Nanya. Only at the time of the wolf dream, when the pt. was 4 yrs old did his full awareness of the fact of castration appear, with the resultant anxiety, and far fuller understanding of coitus observed. Whether the parental coitus was really a coitus a tergo it is impossible to determine. The entire family of the pt was so anal in character—anal intercourse was for years the sole mode of coitus with the pt—that it may very well have been. On the other hand, we must remember that Freud says elsewhere—in the Vorlesungen—that when the primal scene is reconstructed in any given case it is almost invariably a coitus a tergo: and that this mode of sexual relations is much less common than would appear from the phantasies of our pts. We might say that in the present case, it need not have been coitus a tergo, although it may well have been. The pts. constitution, plus his anal seduction by his Nanya—who refused to seduce him phallically, as you will remember—, and above all, and this I should say applied to all cases, the importance of the anal care of the child in the anal regression which comes as a reaction to the discovery of castration, and the fact that coitus a tergo, or anal intercourse obviates the necessity for the existence of the vagina, is adequate explanation for this most common form of the coitus phantasy.

NOTES

I. **Freud and the Wolf Man**

1. There is an extensive literature on the Wolf Man in psychoanalytic, psycho-therapeutic, and psychiatric publications. The most influential diagnostic recon-siderations were three essays published in the 1970s—Offenkrantz and Tobin 1973; Blum 1974; and Meissner 1977 (compare Frosch 1967; Abrahamson 1980; Magid 1992; Winer 1993). These are all English-language (specifically American) contributions; for a quite different tradition of response, see the *Revue française de psychanalyse* 35, no. 1 (1971), a special issue devoted to the Wolf Man. Ricardo Bernardi (1989) has presented a thoughtful comparison of Freud's, Melanie Klein's, and Jacques Lacan's means of reading and rereading the Wolf Man's rep-resentations (as presented by Freud). His essay helps steer a reader through the American, British, and French literature.

II. **The Wolf Dream**

1. A partial text of this letter, translated slightly differently, was provided by Masson (1982), who had special access to the Freud/Ferenczi correspondence well before its official publication (Freud/Ferenczi 1993). Earlier, Ernest Jones had sum-marized the letter misleadingly by saying that the Wolf Man "initiated the first hour of treatment with the offer to have rectal intercourse with Freud and then to defecate on his head!" (Jones 1955: 274). In view of the importance of the "first meeting," I should note that dating and even identifying it poses some historical problems. According to Muriel Gardiner's notes of her correspondence and conversations with the Wolf Man, Serge visited Freud, seemingly for the first time, in January 1910. This visit would have been a "consultation"—a personal meeting between a client and his potential doctor at which both parties could determine whether they would pursue the relationship. Gardiner's notes date the beginning of the "psychoanalysis proper"—i.e., what Freud, in his letter to Ferenczi, called the "first session"—to January or February 1910 (Gardiner Papers). The correspondence with Ferenczi enables us to date the first session more pre-cisely to the first week of February 1910. It is not clear in any of this when the famous initial "transferences" were made—for Freud says that they were made "*after* the first session," possibly in the *second* session of the psychoanalysis proper, that is, in the second week of February 1910 (between February 8 and 13). The likelihood that the Wolf Man had already had two meetings with Freud before his expression of his "transferences" should be kept in mind when we consider their "homosexual" dimension—for example, when we consider whether the Wolf Man projected them at Freud *ex nihilo,* as Freud seems to suggest to Ferenczi, or whether Freud at some level suggested or solicited them, as the Freudian theory of "homosexuality" actually requires.

2. Although its Adlerian source has generally not been acknowledged or even recognized, the concept of "masculine protest" against—or, more generally, male anxiety about—perceived effemination has reappeared in recent cultural

analysis. Here the virtue of Adler's model of "psychic hermaphroditism" is its specifically sociological or even culturalist perspective. Unlike Ulrichs's embryological thesis of a "man's soul in a woman's body," an influential idea among late-nineteenth-century homosexualist emancipationists (see Kennedy 1988), or the general Fliessian/Freudian concept of a biologically given "bisexuality," Adler needed only to observe "the antithesis in the valuation of male and female as it actually exists" in a social system—for example, in the classification and management of ideals of masculinity and femininity (Adler 1917: 105–106). A society's devaluation of the feminine role would lead to the reaction among men of "masculine protest" if and when their bodies or identities are perceived, by them or by others, as contaminated by femininity or even as becoming female. At the most general level, we might say that Adler's thought tended toward recognizing what today would be called "gender"—and in specific opposition to his teacher's insistence on and theory of "sexuality." My formula is, of course, a simplification; Adler did need, for example, to investigate the biologically given properties and history of "organ inferiority" itself—for perceptions of relative masculinity and femininity lean on the differentiation of bodies in human development due in part to forces utterly outside social and cultural control. Moreover, Adler—unlike some contemporary cultural theorists—was alert to the body's self-perception of what he called its "organ identity" independent of, and sometimes utterly contrary to, existing cultural ideals and social classifications of "masculinity" and "femininity." The body arrives at its judgment of itself not only in relation to human categories but also in relation to its nonlinguistic perception of its inherence in and movement through the gravitational field, the field of illumination, and so forth, irrespective of (but attentive to) the ways in which these relations could be organized in human occupations of lifting, running, and so on, distributed in the gender division of labor. Adlerian "protest," then, is as much a biophysical as a socially constructed psychic formation.

3. In this and the following paragraphs, though my interpretation departs from theirs, I have learned from the thorough scrutiny of the case history by Mahony 1984; the elegant analysis by Lukacher 1986: chap. 4; and the general reflections by Culler 1981: 172–82; de Certeau 1981; Brooks 1984; and Fish 1989. The latter writers, especially de Certeau and Brooks, have pioneered an approach to the text and the other case histories in which Freud is said to have "perilously destabilize[d] belief in explanatory histories," turning the case history into "an unspecifiable network of event, fiction, and interpretation" (Brooks 1984: 277–78). For a judicious response, see Cohn 1993, with which I am in considerable sympathy.

It is certainly true that Freud's case histories do not wholly embody the canons of scientific argumentation. But, Cohn argues, neither do they become merely coextensive with the novel, whether traditional or "modernist." Instead, as Cohn has well put it, the Freudian case history can be seen as "enlightened—demystified—historiography applied to the biographical genre" (1993: 40). In explicitly *avowing* his own interpretive "uncertainties in telling his patient's mental history," Freud produced a text quite different from the "hyperomniscient novelistic discourse" propagated by writers such as Virginia Woolf, whose "characters are invariably given life by a narrator who knows them in magically intimate ways" (ibid.: 39). To simplify, while Brooks sees Freud's case histories as basically a species of modernist *literature,* Cohn sees them as basically a species of modernist *history.*

This debate fundamentally turns on the apparent or supposed place of fantasy (or personal fiction) and fiction (or social fantasy) in the case history and on the problem of its authorship(s). As Cohn points out, "the analyst's discourse is no more fictional—no less referential—when it traces the origins of the patient's neurosis back to infantile fantasies (or 'fictions') than when it traces it back to a verifiable biographical point" (ibid.: 40). In other words, whereas the Wolf Man was supposedly the author of the "fiction," Freud maintained a separate role as historian-observer *of* that fiction-producing operation and was the author of an account of his conclusions and uncertainties about what he had heard. Of course, Freud's "history" of the Wolf Man's "fiction" of his historical life may itself be a "fiction"—but Cohn's point here would be that the two fictions are clearly not the same. Naturally Cohn must disagree, then, with "critics who have sensed a fictionlike fusion, or confusion, of voices (or perspectives) between analyst and patient" in the case history. For Cohn, it is not really "undecidable," as some would contend, which voice—Freud's or the Wolf Man's—is speaking (ibid.: 44n. 19).

At this point, however, I will be diverging from Cohn. Whether or not it is "undecidable" which voice is speaking at a given point in the text, the voice that *does* speak—readily identifiable by the reader as "Freud" or the "Wolf Man"—is *effectively intersubjective,* though this is *not* recognizable to the reader on purely internal textual grounds, however "deconstructive" (the province of the literary-critical approach largely shared by Brooks and Cohn). To hear or read the effective intersubjectivity of the case and the case history requires, I believe, a historical excavation of the process of the production of the text in which the text itself is not the only kind of evidence we should mobilize. Most important, the text *replicates* other texts, and it belongs to an *assemblage* of other artifacts with which it was subjectively linked (for the general concepts, see further Davis 1995a). And in fact, as we will see, what counts as the *text* of the case history of the Wolf Man has not been fully identified by any of the writers I have cited here. They have all, for example, completely ignored the Wolf Man's contribution to what Freud published—his drawing of the dream.

In this study, then, the problem of genre as such does not really interest me very much. The genre of the case history of the Wolf Man—"science," "interpretation"; "history," "narrative"; "biography," "novel"—is so obviously mixed, and probably unique, that although generic criticism might help us to recognize textual formations, it ultimately can tell us very little about their motivation, content, or interrelations. Disentangled from and seen as logically prior to the problem of genre, the problem of authorship and intersubjectivity—who is speaking, where, and why, in this text?—will be my principal critical focus.

Several important analyses indebted to the deconstructive, narratological, and rhetorical studies I have just cited have developed particular interpretive inflections: see especially Kartiganer 1985; O'Neill 1989; Møller 1991; and Edelman 1991. I will not attempt to assess all of these sometimes incompatible accounts of argument and proof, of "conviction" and "confirmation," in Freud's case history. In every case, the authors have asserted, as I will, that "Freud's insistence upon the 'infantile factor' [in the Wolf Man's neurosis] merely introduces fantasies or dreams of his own" (O'Neill 1989: 155). But there remains a need for a detailed specification of these "fantasies or dreams"—the tissue of images or schemata organizing Freud's thought. There has been a tendency to see them as general fantasies of mastery, of masculinity, of bisexuality or homosexuality, and the like, common not only to many of Freud's texts but also (we could easily argue) to late-nineteenth century psychological discourse, to Freud's Viennese Jewish and medico-scientific culture, to modern science as a whole, or to the entire Western imagination of sexuality or history—an approach which is not terribly useful in explicating the letter of this particular text as such. In an area which will especially interest me, for example, it hardly needs saying that Freud's and the Wolf Man's imagination of their "homosexuality," actual or possible, was homophobically organized—that it manifested a fear of and resistance to erotic and sexual relations between men. Homophobia is a structurally defining condition and built-in property of all modern homosexualities. As we will see, the Freudian concept of latent homosexuality, then, has a homophobic derivation, function, and significance. But again, without further analysis this tells us hardly anything about the particular history and identity of our text. What are the social, psychic, historical, and textual dimensions of homophobic sexuality in the case and case history of the Wolf Man?

As this footnote may have suggested, I will try to hold to the concept, and attempt an interpretive recognition, of "sexuality"—the historically specific effective intersubjectivity of people representing themselves to themselves and to one another as desirable.

4. Later Freud asserted that Adler's concept of "masculine protest" (see above, n. 2) was the same thing as his own concept of "castration anxiety" (for example, Freud 1937c: 252–53), an argument proposed as early as 1914 in "On Narcissism" (Freud 1914c: 92–93). This statement was a somewhat misleading theoretical shorthand as well as a denigration of Adler's originality. In the case history of the Wolf Man, Freud clearly distinguished between the two terms. He regards Adler's "masculine protest" as a useful way of characterizing psychic *response to* "castration anxiety": the "anxiety" is the cause and the "protest" is an effect. As later clarifications such as "Fetishism" (1927e) took pains to point out, "castration anxiety" responds—*as* "masculine protest," if you will—to a preexisting "castration threat." The Adlerian "masculine protest," then, is the male's protest about his protest—his dislike of having to be or being disturbed about his masculinity. This feeling, of course, characterizes the wholly stable, "normal" condition of adult male heterosexually neurotic masculinity. For precisely this reason, the masculine protest is not really a "crisis of masculinity," as some recent writing has had it. More exactly, if it *is* a crisis—a male drama?—it is so predictable and permanent, and in some ways so gratifying (affording a *frisson* of uncertainty) to the male's by-now-established conviction about his integrity and power, that it hardly challenges a man's basic agency in any fundamental way. A man's "crisis of masculinity" brings with it nothing like the utter derealization or nonattainment of selfhood permanently created by a woman's inaugural psychic disenfranchisement. And although the "crisis of masculinity" might involve an encounter with homosexuality, it cannot be compared with the *Ichspaltung* endured by men whose "crisis" it is to live homosexually—to be on the *other* side of the wall which "masculinity in crisis" thinks itself to have come up against.

In any reasonably Freudian scheme, the real male "crisis," the threat of and anxiety about castration itself, logically precedes the "masculine protest." It cannot, in itself, involve the male's disturbance about his "masculinity"—for "masculinity," in a Freudian scheme, is the *product* of surviving castration anxiety, letting go of the phallus (and [per Freud 1910c] avoiding becoming homosexual), and entering genital heterosexuality. If "masculine protest" is the thrilled annoyance a man feels in any challenge to his achieved gender, the male crisis is the agony some men must experience in merely partially achieving the sexuality which will enable him to have his expected gender in the first place. In view of all this, it is not surprising that Freud evidently thought Adler's attention to the masculine protest dealt with relatively superficial dimensions of the psychic history of the male.

III. **The Drawing of the Dream of the Wolves**

1. Lubin refers, however, to works that he saw in 1961–62 in the Wolf Man's apartment in Vienna; I may not have seen or identified all of them. In addition, the psychoanalyst B. D. Lewin, who saw some of Gardiner's "Wolf Mans" in 1967, considered them possibly to display "a progression in bringing in more color if not more action," which he thought might tie in with the "anal" meaning of the primal scene. The interpretation implies that Gardiner knew, and told Lewin, the dates of at least some of the different paintings—information now apparently lost. Another analyst, William G. Niederland, concurred that "the landscapes by the Wolf Man represent basically a continuation and psychological documentation, however modified and artistically elaborated, of his first 'artistic' experience that Freud uncovered" (Gardiner Papers).

2. Recently the psychoanalyst Robert Winer has offered a hypothesis somewhat parallel to Rank's. He too emphasizes the partly transferential construction of the Wolf Man's dream and implies that the Wolf Man must have sensed Freud's emerging construction of him. Winer recalls a passage in the Wolf Man's *Memoirs*:

> [Freud] was a genius. Just imagine the work he did, remembering all those details, forgetting nothing, drawing those inferences. He may have had six, seven patients a day. (Gardiner 1971: 32)

He goes on to wonder

> if the [six or seven] wolves represented for the Wolf Man Freud's daily patients, six or seven, depending on whether he included himself. We are aware of his intense rivalry with his sister for his father's affection, and it is easy to imagine that he felt a similarly intense competition with his analytic siblings; he asked Freud about the people he saw coming and going, and Freud identified them to him by occupation and circumstance, although not by name. [Presumably this technique—now considered a "violation of technique" and certainly a "violation of privacy"—partly expressed Freud's construction of his patient. One might recall that Freud twice drew attention to his patient's great wealth.] At the point at which Freud finally succeeded in analyzing this dream, might the Wolf Man have been retelling it because he was facing rejection by Freud, imagining the siblings poised outside the consulting room door, motionless, ready to spring, a projection of his own wish to break in on Freud's life and make his claim, a protest against the exclusions, both the forced termination date and the Sunday absences, the one day of the seven Freud didn't receive him, the omission blurred by the phrase "six or seven"? (Winer 1993: 155)

This interpretation is appealing. But it does not have the comprehensiveness of Rank's: it deals only with the "six or seven" wolves in the Wolf Man's verbal report of his dream and not with the "five" in the drawing, which Freud had made an object of special attention precisely because they were a potentially revealing "correction" of the dream report. Moreover, Winer seems to suppose that the Wolf Man was anxious about his "sibling rivals" among other patients and intent on making his claim on Freud because of the imposed termination date of the analysis. But the termination date was imposed in 1914, a few weeks or months before the end of the analysis, while the verbal report of the dream and the dream drawing were produced in the first weeks or months of the analysis, in 1910. In these early weeks of the analysis, is it likely that the Wolf Man had any clear idea about the "six or seven" other patients Freud was seeing?

3. For his part, Freud may have been especially sensitive to Krafft-Ebing's words not only because they uncannily replicated the title of the draft essay for Fliess but also because he may have believed that he had had a similar professional experience a decade earlier. On October 15, 1886, after his return from Paris, he presented a paper to the Viennese Society of Physicians introducing aspects of Jean-Martin Charcot's observations on organic symptoms, such as "stigmata," in male hysterics, and suggested that the well-known phenomenon of "railway spine" should be included under this umbrella. Later—perhaps even at the time—he believed that he had met with a cool, even hostile, reception (see Freud 1925b: 15–16). Freud attributed the criticism to intellectual disagreement and defensiveness on the part of the senior doctors in his audience. But their motives might have been quite different: papers to the society traditionally presented original or firsthand work, which Freud's did not, and the clinical phenomena he presented as novelties probably were both more familiar and more contested in Vienna than Freud had brashly believed. Although some of the senior doctors did, indeed, dispute Charcot's interpretations, they may have been more annoyed at Freud's attitude toward them—he was assuming their total ignorance of the whole matter—than at his workmanlike account itself (I follow Ellenberger 1993, but compare Eissler 1971: 351–58).

IV. **Pictures for Repression**

1. This is not the only place in Freud's model of the mind where one psychic system exerts superordinate control on, even a kind of observation of and dialogue with, another psychic system. The very first point of "contact" between the psychic system and the outside world, the point of perceptual stimulation itself, seems to contain such an agency. Because this point of contact is, of course, at the opposite end of the system from the point of discharge, it is, in Freud's terms, deep in—or, more properly, at the beginning of—the "unconscious." (Thus the unconscious should probably be regarded as existing materially at the *surface* of the body, located in the nervous proprioceptors and the body's integument, rather than being somehow buried deep in the brain, as Freud's archaeological metaphor—intended principally to apply to *psychoanalytic method* rather than *psychical reality*—has sometimes been taken to imply.) We should properly refer to any instance of the selection of stimulation at proprioception itself as "primary repression," to distinguish it from the temporally and causally "secondary" repression enforced by any later (or "deeper") branching or blocking, however temporary, of the energy which has survived initial selection and has been routed toward the terminus of ultimate discharge. Needless to say, however, the very existence of primary and secondary repression cannot be intelligibly explained in a purely mechanical model of the mind. The necessary homuncular, intentionalist, or

Cartesian hypothesis—some agency actively intervenes in the "processing" of proprioception—decisively differentiates Freudian metapsychology from preceding and contemporary materialist psychophysics.

2. Freud's entire account, of course, is hardly credible. It implies among other things that sensory stimulation received *during* sleep should result, perhaps after a delay, in the sleeper's perceptual discharge of it—that is, in a dream. But we know perfectly well that motor discharge—or a speech act—can also occur. And Freud offers no evidence whatsoever to show that when there is no dreaming there is no sensory stimulation—as the theory would seem to require—and in fact such evidence could not be found: during sleep, the body is constantly stimulated.

3. The original manuscript of the *Sexualschema* is reproduced in Freud, Freud, and Grubrich-Simitis 1978: 157, fig. 146; a transcription (by Gerhard Fichtner), reproduced here, is published in Freud 1986: 571; an English translation (which simplifies Freud's graphic) is published in Freud 1950: 354.

4. The original manuscript of the *Normalschema* is reproduced in Freud 1985: 103, fig. 4, and Freud 1986: 103; a transcription (by Gerhard Fichtner), reproduced here, is published in Freud 1986: 572. The other side of this diagram had a further, quite cryptic explanation by Freud. For the original manuscript, see Freud 1985: 104, fig. 5, and Freud 1986: 104, and for a transcription (by Gerhard Fichtner), see Freud 1986: 573.

5. An influential analysis is Amacher 1965, but see also Andersson 1962; Sulloway 1979; Solms and Saling 1990; and especially Hirschmüller 1989, 1991, which will surely prove to be the foundation for any further work on the matter.

6. There is no space here to consider how Lacan's remarkable graphic and quasi-mathematical explorations of the torus produced an elegant notation for—if not a solution of—the problem of the "topologically possible" total lateral arborization of psychic *Verbindung* that nonetheless embodies its fundamental gap or fissure. (For one brief and helpful account, see Rose 1986: 184–90.) Earlier, in explicating his Freudian semiology in "The Agency of the Letter in the Unconscious, or Reason since Freud," Lacan had reproduced the "classic" diagrammatic example of the meaning of the word "tree" (Lacan 1977: 151). It embedded Saussure's notation for his concept of the sign, S/s or Signified/signifier—where the bar designates a relation *not only* of "arbitrary" morphological or natural connection *but also* of necessary cognitive reciprocity or mutual inherence. But Lacan was not, of course, a Saussurean. As the essay itself makes perfectly clear, he juxtaposed this model of the sign with a *counter*-Saussurean concept of signification, intending especially to establish the bar as the site of a founding division or resistance (or repression)—that "order of spacing according to which the law is inscribed and marked as difference, . . . even the *structural hole*" (see generally Nancy and Lacoue-Labarthe's elegant and precise discussion of the Lacanian schemas in their chapters "Algorithm and Operation" and "A Tree of the Signifier" in *The Title of the Letter* [1992: 33–59; this quotation is from p. 46]). What Nancy and Lacoue-Labarthe call the Lacanian "structural hole" was visualized by Lacan in the torus diagrams. Like Saussure's graphic notation for the concept of the sign, these representations are graphic notations for the concept of the subject. The "algorithms" that would "operate" the torus—that would show how it "turns" in history and around the hole—are not, however, the referents of Lacan's notation as such. As a very crude formula, which I adopt simply for its pictorial value, we could say that the torus turns on the structural hole penetrated by the phallus.

In a remarkable passage later in "The Agency of the Letter," Lacan illustrated the figurative properties of language by remarking on the "symbolic contexts" in which the signifier "tree" can circulate. Here, as Lacan's wordplay suggests, it is no coincidence that it should be this signifier (in both written and pictorial forms) which is, literally speaking, the signifier of the unconscious as such.

Let us take our word "tree" again, this time not as an isolated noun, but as the point of one of these punctuations [i.e., the "anchoring points," or *points de capiton,* in which the "letter," the signifier as such, "dominates" or creates the subject], and see how it crosses the bar of the Saussurian algorithm [i.e., how the figurative possibilities of the signifier in the language create what is signified in both conscious and unconscious domains]. (The anagram of *"arbre"* and *"barre"* should be noted.) [Lacan is probably referring to Saussure's own studies of "hypogrammatical" possibilities at the level of the signifier, especially anagrams.]

For even broken down into the double spectre of its vowels and consonants [two "r"s = Fr. *"double-air"*?], it can still call up with the robur [double-"r"] and plane tree (*planar* = *"plein r"* = *"plein air"*] the significations it takes on, in the context of our flora, of strength and majesty. Drawing on all the symbolic contexts suggested in the Hebrew of the Bible [Tree of Knowledge, Tree of Life, Tree of Jesse, etc.], it erects on a barren hill the shadow of the cross [i.e., an "X"]. Then reduces to the capital "Y," the sign of dichotomy [= X and Y chromosomes = sexual difference] which, except for the illustration used by heraldry [the blazon used to divide "houses"], would owe nothing to the tree however genealogical we may think it. Circulatory tree [a reference to Harvey's image of the circulation of the blood in the "trunk" and "limbs" of the body?], tree of life of the cerebellum [= spinal cord and brain, = the unconscious itself?], tree of Saturn, tree of Diana, crystals formed in a tree struck by lightning, is it your figure [i.e., both physical form and linguistic representation] that traces our destiny for us in the tortoiseshell cracked by the figure [= divination, = psychoanalysis?], or your lightning that causes that slow shift in the axis of being to surge up from an unnamable night [Hegel] into the "`Enpqnta of language:

No! says the Tree, it says No! in the shower of sparks
Of its superb head

lines that require the harmonics of the tree [i.e., the musical stave or "staff"] just as much as their continuation:

Which the storm treats as universally
As it does a blade of grass. [Valéry]

For this modern verse is ordered according to the same law of the parallelism of the signifier [i.e., the rhyme between the lines = musical harmony] that creates the harmony governing the primitive Slavic epic or the most refined Chinese poetry. . . .

But this whole signifier can only operate, it may be said, if it is present in the subject. It is this object that I answer by supposing that it has passed over to the level of the signified. . . .

What this structure of the signifying chain discloses is the possibility I have, precisely in so far as I have this language in common with other subjects, that is to say, in so far as it exists as a language, to use it in

order to signify *something quite other* than what it says. . . .
I have only to plant my tree [cf. "sow my seed"] in a locution; climb
the tree, even project on to it the cunning illumination a descriptive
context gives to a word; raise it (*arborer*) so as not to let myself be imprisoned in some sort of *communiqué* of the facts, however official, and
if I know the truth, make it heard, in spite of all the *between-the-lines*
censures by the only signifier my acrobatics through the tree can constitute [i.e., the unconscious], provocative to the point of burlesque, or
perceptible only to the practised eye, according to whether I wish to be
heard by the mob or by the few. (Lacan 1977: 154–56; interpolations in
parentheses are by Lacan's editor and translator, and interpolations in
square brackets are the present author's)

Freud identifies the reconstructed primal scene—even though it is "unclear"
what it contains—as the ultimate "reality" of the Wolf Man's history. For Freud,
it is the real event to which the Wolf Man's words and images refer. But Lacan
treats the primal scene as "successive and repeated subjective visions of the event
in the different moments in which the subject re-structures himself" (Bernardi
1989: 346). In one Lacanian interpretation of the Wolf Man's history, the Wolf
Man's desire is structured in many linked signifiers of "opening" distributed
throughout his life history—the open window; the wolves' open mouths; opening
the eyes; the repetitive writing of open letter forms, "V" and "W," and so on
(Leclaire 1958; for a brilliant application of the Lacanian insistence on the "letter"
of signification, see Fineman 1987).

Outside the Lacanian tradition, contemporary psychoanalysis has been less interested in a semiological reading of Freudian metapsychology, which tends to be
highly conservative with theory. It turns instead to cognitive approaches; they
enable more radical revisions. (For example, supposedly fundamental Freudian
principles of psychic structure and dynamics, such as the principle of systemic
unifunctionality or the principle of nondeletion of mental contents, need not be
observed.) But even here, Freud's schemas tend to remain embedded in the analysis. As Marina Warner has noted,

[A] quest for order underlies the popular mediaeval and renaissance representation of knowledge; and after some centuries of neglect, this kind
of figura, or visual mnemonic, is receiving attention again, perhaps
because the schemata in question appear to imitate the linear, but multi-
branching model of information storage in a computer, which itself provides a simple and useful image of the working of the brain itself. The
anthropomorphic perception of trees does not just match trees' form to
the outer and whole human body—the crown, the trunk, the limbs—
but the imagery is also internalised, mapping the pathways in the head.
(Warner 1989: 24)

7. In order to focus on the role of graphic or imagistic schemas in Freud's account, I have drastically simplified the questions arising out of these passages in
the *Project* and related texts. See further Holt 1989; Sulloway 1979; Laplanche
1976: chap. 1; Herzog 1991; Brennan 1992. After my own work was very far along,
I was able to read the discussions of Freud's visualizations and schematizations
in Morris 1992 and especially Moran 1993: 30–53. Morris emphasizes how Freud's
schemas enabled him to establish the "narrative" coherence and the "allegory"
of Freud's "fiction of a pure primary process" (1992: 61). Moran considers the

problem of agency—what motivates or empowers the system of consciousness to make decisive distinctions about incoming stimuli, whether external (in the reflex arc) or internal (in hallucinatory wishing). Both writers deal very ably with the textual role and logical status of Freud's schemas, but neither addresses their visual or graphic form as such.

8. Scientists, engineers, and artists have often testified that their most productive intellectual work began—and often ended—with a highly schematic intuition of an otherwise unknown or undetectable process or structure. It frequently takes the form of a "sudden picture," "vision," or dream, such as Kekulé's dream-vision of the ring structure of benzene (see Shephard and Cooper 1982; Brown and Herrnstein 1981), a hallucination psychoanalytically interpreted in the first issue of *Imago* by Kekulé's student Alfred Robitsek (1912). Even Karl Popper's (1959, 1962) philosophy of science, which calls for the rigorous "falsification" of scientific hypotheses, prescribes nothing about the initial source of the hypothesis. According to E. H. Gombrich, artists depend quite literally on an initial, arbitrary "schema," embodied in a graphic or other notation, serving as a preliminary "substitute" for the thing itself (see esp. Gombrich 1961; Rogers 1964; Novitz 1977; Richter 1976). Gombrich never specifies the origins of the schemata. They are supposedly arbitrary creations, strongly influenced by existing traditions of representation—even as they establish the very possibility of a tradition of representation. For Gombrich, it would seem, artists choose to use one of the available schemata for purely instrumental reasons. For our purposes, the schema must be understood to organize the subject's very identity and desire. Although it determines a subject's representations and the possibility of their replication, it is itself a representation. As such, it becomes the target of retrospective thought in ongoing intersubjective history (for a more general view of such "replication," see Davis 1995a).

I am not suggesting, of course, that Freud's psychoanalytic theories derived merely from replicating the schemata identified here. Rather, the availability of certain visual schemata—we probably will never identify all of them—enabled Freud to make sense of the Wolf Man's drawing by recalling and working back through his remembered stock of them in the terms which had already relayed his intellectual, professional, and personal ambitions and desires. The replication of the schemata occurred, in the forward direction, because Freud constantly depended on and added to them; but it also occurred, in the backward direction, because Freud *needed or wanted* to depend on and add to a schema of a certain kind. Reaching back to the very earliest version of a schema in order to make sense of its apparently latest replication would not make much sense in the purely forward sense; in its subject matter or ostensible content, the earliest schemas, such as the ones I am considering in this chapter, are quite far away morphologically, generically, and thematically from the latest, the Wolf Man's drawing (Fig. 12). (Indeed, definitively establishing that a "chain of replications" exists among these replications would require both physical and psychological evidence of a rather precise kind [see further Davis 1995a].) But precisely because the latest replication does not possess any determined or definite "meaning" at the very moment of its introduction into the entire series, it is the reaching back through the series, as far as the earliest replications, that renders it intelligible. That Freud *should* reach back through the series in the first place, however, derived from his needs and desires in the contemporary intersubjective situation in which the latest replication was produced. Thus this situation, as much as the "meaning" accumulated in the earlier replications, determines the construction—the present, intersubjective significance—of the latest replication, positioning it, in turn, for any possible future replication.

V. **The Homosexual Roots of Repression**

1. On the basis of Jones's bare mention of it, this statement has often been quoted in histories of psychoanalysis and in gay studies or queer theory; it has long been regarded as a clue to understanding some of the central dynamics of early psychoanalytic theory and practice. Because the Freud/Jones correspondence has been fully published only very recently, however, it is worth quoting the immediate and fuller context. After and *à propos* of a recent meeting of psychoanalysts in Munich, Freud wrote (in English in the original):

> The letters I get from him [Jung] are remarkable, changing from tenderness to overbearing insolence. He wants treatment, unfortunately by my last attack [Freud's fainting attack, in a hotel room in Munich, in Jung's presence] I have lost [a] portion of my authority. There must be some psychic elements in this attack which besides was largely fundamented on fatigue, bad sleep and smoking, for I cannot forget that 6 and 4 years ago I have suffered from very similar though not so intense symptoms in the *same* room of the Parkhotel; in each case I had to leave the table. I saw Munich first when I visited Fliess during his illness (you remember: "Propylaeen" in *Die Traumdeutung*) [see Freud 1900a: 294–95] and this town seems to have acquired a strong connection with my relation to this man. There is some piece of unruly homosexual feeling at the root of the matter. When Jung in his last letter again hinted at my "neurosis" I could find no better expeditive than proposing that every analyst should attend to his own neurosis more than to the others's. After all I think we have to be kind and patient with Jung and as old Oliver said, keep our powder dry. I restricted myself to the remark against Jung, that I do not think *he* has been a sufferer by my neurosis. In any case, there is a suspicious amount of dishonesty, want of simplicity and frankness I mean in his constitution [. . .]. (Freud/Jones 1993: 182 [December 8, 1912])

The "homosexual" dimension of the episode seems to have been obvious to those who heard about it at the time. Later on Jones, for example, claimed to have sensed its connection to Freud's "older affects" (ibid.: 184 [December 23, 1912]).

This fainting episode was associated with a previous one. At a luncheon in Bremen before his, Jung's, and Ferenczi's departure for America, in late August 1909, Freud (as he noted in his private travel diary) "broke into a bad sweat with a feeling of faintness"—perhaps, as Jung believed, because Jung's table conversation covertly expressed a death wish toward him. (On the series of fainting attacks, see further Jones 1953, 316–17; Jones 1955: 146–47; Schur 1972: 264–72; Rosenzweig 1992: 52–55, who quotes from Freud's as-yet-unpublished diary.) When Freud was experiencing the final stages of his personal relations with Jung, Ferenczi could point out that this incident with Jung on the trip to America in 1909 had manifested the "deep aftereffects of the Breuer-Fliess experiences." At the same time, he acknowledged that both Jung's and his own "dissatisfaction with the incomplete intimacy with his teacher" had expressed "a piece of sexual curiosity at play in me and Jung. But shouldn't this be permitted in its sublimated form?" (Freud/Ferenczi 1993: 305 [October 19, 1911]). In making the final break with Jung, according to Freud, "I spared him nothing at all, told him calmly that a friendship with him couldn't be maintained, that he himself gave rise to the intimacy which he then so cruelly broke off; that things were not at all in order in his relations with men, not just with me but with others as well" (ibid.: 434 [November 26, 1912]).

For further discussions of Freud's "bisexual" and "homosexual" conflicts, although debatable in points of detail, see Schur 1966; Swan 1974; Krüll 1986; McGrath 1986: 278–88; and Harris and Harris 1984.

2. Symonds's side of the correspondence has been fully published (Symonds 1969). Ellis's side, though it has been partly quoted in biographies, has not been published (I have consulted the manuscripts in the British Library).

3. Hirschfeld resisted developmentalist analysis, such as Freud's picture of postnatal infantile sexuality and its subsequent vicissitudes, and embraced what I have identified as Ulrichs's general and specific hypotheses. Freud thought that Hirschfeld's theories were "tendentious deliria" (Freud/Ferenczi 1993: 147 [March 3, 1910]). In particular, Freud objected to Hirschfeld's continuous conflations of, and supposed confusions between, homosexuality and transvestism—the "inversion of object and of person" only partially clarified in his 1910 book on transvestism (Hirschfeld 1991; see Freud/Ferenczi 1993: 175 [May 20, 1910]).

4. Friedlaender's perspective is readily intelligible; it was shared by writers such as Elisar von Kupffer (1899), many of the members of the circle of Adolf Brand and *Der Eigene,* the nascent *Wandervögel* movement (see Blüher 1922), and others, probably including the monarchic homoeroticists among the Kaiser's intimates. Noble homoerotic sentimentality and chivalry would be tarnished, such homoeroticists thought, by any kind of association with a fundamental pathology of instinct or a perversion of psychological interest. And even if congenital *Homosexualität* was *not* pathological, as Ulrichs or Symonds and Ellis urged, the homoeroticists had no desire to limit homoerotic attitudes and practices to groups of "Urnings" (Ulrichs's term for homosexuals before the latter term was coined) or "inverts" in their sense—for this restriction would rule out most of the schoolboys, cadets, college men, sportsmen, and others whose beauty and manliness (symbolized at least in part by their heterosexual procreativity) they idealized. From their vantage point, Hans Blüher—strongly influenced by Freudian psychological theory though never fully embracing psychoanalysis (see Blüher 1917)—was an apostate; for them, Blüher's study of the *Wandervögelbewegung* as an "erotic phenomenon" (Blüher 1922) excessively *instinctualized* what they saw as their aesthetic, moral, and political concern for certain possibilities of masculine feeling or *Kultur* in the established sense.

Hirschfeld's position is a little more difficult to appreciate. Freud's approach went a great distance toward an acceptance of his overarching commitment to the general theory espoused by Ulrichs: homosexuality is a congenital or instinctive condition. Thus Hirschfeld was quite drawn to psychoanalysis, for at least in the first phase of his work (in and immediately after the *Three Essays*), Freud seemed clearly to be moving to locate homoerotic *Empfindungen* in basic psychological *Interessen* (congenital or not) and ultimately, at least in some cases, in congenital *Inversion.* At this point, then, Hirschfeld avoided getting into any disputes with Freud about the actual neuroanatomy of inversion; he had accepted Ulrichs's specific as well as general hypothesis and proposed a complex picture of sexual variations resting on the embryological possibility of "intermediate types" (*Zwischenstufen*). Symonds and Ellis had already recognized this to be a blind and probably counterproductive alley, for it implicitly presented inverts as "sports" or monsters of nature. Freud was equally dismissive—though it is worth remarking that implicitly his own neuropsychology depended partly on a Jacksonian model of embryonic as well as phylogenetic and neonatal cortical differentiation and neuronal arborization ("variation"). But because Hirschfeld's and Freud's approaches were compatible at other levels, there was no need to split hairs when larger, more public battles had to be fought (for example, in 1905 newspaper interviews reported in Hirschfeld's journal, Freud spoke out publicly in favor of granting full civil rights and better legal protections to homosexuals).

In the period 1908–14, however, Freud's psychogenetic model filled out, and its logical implications were more vigorously pursued by psychoanalysts. Now Hirschfeld found himself in an awkward position. When psychoanalysis detected the possibility of an un- or preconscious homosexual *Inversion* in the apparently *non*homoerotic conscious feelings of adult men and women, it had the salutary effect, from Hirschfeld's vantage, of reminding people that same-sex interests are probably much more common than they supposed. But the focus unavoidably shifted from Hirschfeld's primary concern for congenital inverts and other "intermediate types," largely rejected by society, to the Freudian homosexualization of *all* psyches, including those psyches idealized by society—an extension finally realized in the full-blown concept and case history of "latent" homosexuality (Freud 1918b). Though Freud himself might have seen this concern as emancipationist—consistent with Hirschfeld's—his return from *Instinkt* to *Interessen* and *Empfindungen* left the crucial legal and social questions of rights and responsibility oddly up in the air: *Empfindungen* potentially remain within the reach of criminal prosecution as facts of individual morality, volition, and responsibility, however "unconscious"—though now the punishment might not be imprisonment but rather psychoanalysis! (An understudied but crucial aspect of this history, which I cannot take up here, concerns the surprisingly close relation between Freud's psychoanalytic sexology, in the period 1905–14, and forensic psychiatry and psychotherapeutics in criminology. In general, the relation between late-nineteenth-century theories of sexuality and changing legal frameworks needs thorough re-examination.) Hirschfeld's emphasis on congenitality, after all, had been partly designed precisely to get away from the stereotype that a defendant accused of sodomy "basically knew what he was doing—he's a moral pervert." Psychoanalysis threatened to replace this stereotype with the equally problematic stereotype, from a juridical standpoint, that the defendant "basically *didn't* know what he was doing—he's a latent homosexual." In either case, though in somewhat different ways, the rights of "homosexual" men and women—that is, of people charged with homosexual acts—were threatened; their best defense—of true irresponsibility—was undermined by the peculiar psychoanalytic concept of an *unconscious* responsibility. Hirschfeld never wholly resolved his attitude toward psychoanalysis or the way in which it, as well as his own perspective, boxed him in. For the rest of his productive career, he continued to refer, sometimes interchangeably and sometimes not, to sexual variations and intermediate types, to "homosexuality," and to sexual pathologies. The legacy of this troubled relationship has, of course, been terribly debilitating for the relation between contemporary gay and lesbian or queer "theory" (substantially Freudian) and contemporary gay and lesbian or queer "activism" (for much of this century, substantially Hirschfeldian).

5. It seems that Freud did not even check all of Numa Praetorius's references, though he inserted them into his own text. For example, had he examined James Kiernan's articles, which he cites as early examples of the medical-scientific recognition of "bisexuality," he would have discovered that they were actually quite conventional accounts of sexual "perversions" incorporating homosexual actions and an underlying homosexual-criminal motivation. There is no mention of "bisexuality," and certainly Kiernan's point was diametrically opposed to the one Freud wanted to make. Freud's real interest in citing this literature was probably to establish, however fictitiously, that the intellectual priority of the concept of bisexuality did not lie with Fliess—that it had an intellectual lineage, as his references seem to imply, well back into the early 1880s. Those readers who knew the literature were not deceived by Freud's smokescreen. Fliess could suspect and publicly object that Freud had transmitted his ideas to others because he knew quite well that he was the principal, if not the sole, scholarly originator. And Numa Praetorius (1906) himself, reviewing Freud's *Three Essays,* knew quite well that Freud's plethora of citations did not deliver a single shred of independent evidence for the Freudian (Fliessian) theory of biologically given "bisexuality"; thus he could properly say that the theory was provocative, possibly even revolutionary, but not yet "confirmed" by others. Numa Praetorius had the good grace not to protest that Freud had lifted and twisted his own researches.

6. The full publication of the Freud/Ferenczi correspondence (1993) suggests that Freud's monograph on Schreber, begun in September 1910, was conceived in relation and response to the cases of particular "paranoid" clients, about whom we unfortunately know very little. Among them were cases accepted or acquired by Isidor Sadger (see Freud/Ferenczi 1993: 147 [March 3, 1910]), but to my knowledge he did not publish on the topic. In March 1908, Freud briefly examined a client referred by Ferenczi, one Frau Marton, who was suffering from "a still rather fresh paranoia with a predilection for delusions of jealousy" (ibid.: 3 [February 10, 1908]; see also 5–6 [February 11 and March 18, 1908], and see further Ferenczi 1916a). Although she believed herself to be "absolutely not perverse," Frau Marton had transposed her earlier attractions to girls in her boarding school onto her husband, whom she now suspects of having affairs with other women whom she fears (and desires). Because "she can no longer become homosexual, [. . .] she detaches her libido from the woman," but the sublimatory connection to her husband was ruptured by the paranoid fantasy and once again "the homosexual component in particular comes to the fore" (Freud/Ferenczi 1993: 7 [March 25, 1908], and cf. 113 [December 12, 1909], referring to another patient). In such cases, "the homosexuality which had been repressed undergoes a subtle strengthening, that is to say, overemphasis, so that it must press forward into consciousness, but as a consequence of resistance it is presented with a negative sign and as a projection, if only symbolically" (ibid.: 22 [October 12, 1908]). This and related cases (e.g., Ferenczi 1916b, and a case published by Maeder [see Freud/Ferenczi 1993: 223]), recalling Freud's Dora case of 1901 (Freud 1905e), provided the background to Freud's reading of Schreber, but unfortunately there is no space to take them up in detail here.

7. Elsewhere I have tried to show that Freud's account of Leonardo's "narcissism" and the complex history of relations and identifications between the boy and his mother derived from aspects of the Freudian imagination of homoeroticism I have not been able to consider here. In particular, the concept of narcissism was taken directly from Sadger's work with homosexual patients apparently asso-

ciated, quite intimately, with the homoeroticist traditions in art, athletics, and the military (see Davis 1995c).

VI. **Family Trees**

1. At this point it is worth underscoring yet again the underlying importance of visuality in Freud's account. The little boy's ability simultaneously to see his parents' genitals and flushed faces is a question of optical sightlines and visual impressions. The patient's dream, relaying the memory and retrospectively constructed meaning of the primal scene, was a "clear and life-like picture"; the primal scene as reconstructed, however, "is not clear" (*non liquet*): it is, and was, literally or materially unseeable. By contrast, of course, the little boy could easily have seen animals copulating on the family estate. Thus Freud's very reference to this possibility—though he rejects the Jungian model of *Zurückphantasieren*—in some ways helps him sustain his "more difficult and improbable" reconstruction precisely by putting the parents' and the animals' actions on the same footing *as* visual facts. The question becomes not whether the little Wolf Man could ever have seen any of the sexual acts proposed but which ones he *did* see—the parents' or the animals' or some visual memory overlay of both. But in fact the primal scene, as reconstructed, could not have been a visual fact at all—though textually it may be, as I am urging, a palimpsest of visual schemas, notations, and projections. Despite Freud's continuing and perhaps fatally debilitating difficulties with the "clarity"—the very visibility and hence the historical reality—of the primal scene, it is striking that he remains entirely committed, as if reflexively, to pursuing a visual model of and visual evidence for it. He does not stop to consider, for example, that the little Wolf Man's perceptual evidence for the sexual actions and feelings of his parents could have been obtained by hearing or by touch as well as by sight.

2. See further Deleuze and Guattari 1973. Rigaud (1992) offers an alternate reading of the "animals" in the Wolf Man's imaginary universe, stressing that the patient's reports and associations (at least as recounted by the case history) suggest a conversion from small creatures (butterflies, a small bird), linked with the child's hatred of siblings, to large and dangerous ones (the wolves), linked with the terrible parents. In her view, the small animals seem to be "the converging point between separation and castration anxieties" (1992: 146). The theoretical connections and metaphorical associations among human biological and cultural evolution, masculinity (and the horror of femininity), "being upright," and the "visibility" of the genitals run throughout Freud's work. They reach developed (and bizarre) expression in *Civilization and Its Discontents* (Freud 1930a), but were present earlier as well. Unfortunately there is no space to consider them in detail here. For discussion in relation to intriguing examples of pictorial art, see Weinberg 1994.

3. Ironically, Freud's attempt at clarification—his effort clearly to locate clarity and unclarity—backfired. His 1919 footnote used a lengthy quotation from an essay published in 1917 by his student Reitler, who had actually located this example of Leonardo's supposed errors in drawing. But Reitler had published a misleading engraved reproduction of Leonardo's drawing, reproduced by Freud, rather than the artist's original in the royal collections at Windsor Castle (Fig. 55). In fact, the drawing does not appear to show the figures' legs below the knees at all or the male figure's supposedly strange expression. Therefore it does not really

permit an unambiguous identification of Leonardo's supposed ambiguity. Freud was interested in Leonardo's image making and well versed in the art-historical literature. He probably knew, then, about the original drawing, which had been published in facsimile in 1913 in the standard edition of Leonardo's anatomical drawings (Vangensten, Fonahn, and Hopstock 1913: 3v; compare Eissler 1961: 194–97). But if so, he avoided discussing and illustrating it in favor of the more tendentious, but more useful, reproduction. In a further addition to the 1923 edition of "Leonardo," Freud only partially clarified the matter after *this* error—or suppression—had been brought to his attention by readers of the 1919 edition. In sum, the image seems to stand for a condition of a subject's representation that Freud must secure at all costs.

4. Visualizing these complex historical processes, Darwin's diagram shows the modified descendants of a common species ancestor, A at time 0, tending to diverge to create two varieties (a-1 and m-1) by time I. (Of course, as Darwin cautions, "the [typological] breaks [between varieties and species] are imaginary," and both the absolute time lags and the degree of variation schematized in the diagram can be specified at any scale.) The modified descendants of another common species ancestor, z-1 descended from I, diverge at time II to create t-2 and z-2. And two species that are sufficiently intermediate between—that is, not too similar to—these two species, labeled E and F, leave descendants, very little modified, at time X. At this point several further varieties of the species modifying from A and I have also appeared. Simultaneously, there has been an extinction of some species in the entire environment; they have been the least successful in the competition "between those forms which are most nearly related to each other in habits, constitution, and structure." At time XIV, fifteen new species have appeared from the eleven original candidates (A–L). Importantly, they have mostly replaced their ancestors. Most of the ancestral species have been eliminated: of the eleven original species, only three (A, F, and I) have contributed any modified descendants whatsoever to the fourteenth generation. For example, in the group of species ABCD, A "supplants and exterminates" B by time I, C by time II, and D by time III. In the group of species GHIKL, I supplants and exterminates all of its competitors from GHKL by time VII. More accurately, the modified descendants of A and I (namely, a-1, m-1, and z-1) supplant and exterminate most of their competition by time I, including the *parents* A and I themselves and any *unmodified* descendants of the parents.

5. Jung was fully alert to the basic problem of the causal temporality of the emergence of a person—what Wollheim (1984) has called the "thread of life"— which Freud had continually addressed. In my view, he implicitly accepted Freud's refutation—in the Wolf Man case history—of his model of the emergence of a psyche in pure *Zurückphantasie*. The later theory of archetypes plants the system of *Zurückphantasieren* in the inherited racial past of the individual—thus making historically available to the individual the structure of predisposition for specific psychic divisions which Freud had initially wanted to identify. The real difference between the Freudian and Jungian histories, then, is that in the Freudian system the individual inherits "instincts" to feel and to want pleasure and unpleasure in certain specific ways (i.e., a *Vortrag-Nachtrag*); in the Jungian system, the individual inherits "symbols" of certain specific pleasures and unpleasures (i.e., a *Nachtrag-Vortrag*). In Freudian history, individual symbolic consciousness and significances are ultimately determined by, and lean on, "vital" or bodily instincts, needs, and desires; in Jungian history, individual vital processes are ulti-

mately determined by, and lean on, symbolic consciousness and significances. Although the Freudian and Jungian accounts are diametrically opposed, both derive—and in dialectical relationship—from attention to the same "historical" issue.

6. In *New Foundations for Psychoanalysis,* Jean Laplanche (1989: 17–37) has investigated this territory—the place of "biology" and "phylogenesis" in psychoanalysis—with his usual precision and insight, with special attention to the Freudian concept that one order of biopsychic process "leans on" another (the process of *Anlehnung*). He identifies three principal roles for "biology" in Freud's thought—biology as "hope" (namely, and specifically, for a method of biochemically treating mental illness); biology as "model" (biology provides the *Vorbild,* the vital prototype, of certain psychic processes); and biology as "origin" (the historical or evolutionary origins of human psychic and social structures). For the last, Laplanche believes that the "primal fantasy" of castration could be possible only within that human historicity—we might even call it the "historicality" or the knowledge of being-in-history—established "by the immensely important cultural discovery which introduces the human being to the idea of contradiction," that is, that the fantasy is a historical product of the evolutionary emergence of language or at least of "binary logic" (ibid.: 37). By contrast, certain other biologically founded "predispositions"—for "there can be no question of completely dismissing the notion of predisposition" (ibid.: 35)—might have greater evolutionary antiquity, such as the "mourning" which provides the biological *Vorbild* of "melancholia" (an instance of *Anlehnung*) and which can be observed regularly in nonhominid mammalian species (I extrapolate from Laplanche's comments on p. 19).

These questions have often been thought to bog down in inconclusive debates about paleoanthropological possibilities. Laplanche is profoundly interested in them (cf. Laplanche 1980a, 1980b) because he recognizes that the "last moment" of biological evolution, the "first moment" of the subject's being-in-history, somehow hands over or passes on the inaugural differentiating criterion (Laplanche calls it a "category" in the Kantian sense [1989: 31]) for the subject's primal repression, its decisive distinction of what is pleasurable (safe) and what is unpleasurable (dangerous), as well as some kind of specific biopsychical mechanism for effecting this "differencing." (Laplanche 1976 urges that the *Vorbild* of the Freudian "ego" is something like an antenna or sensitized pseudopodal surface, the membrane-ego or "skin ego" evoked beautifully by Didier Anzieu [1989] and assumed, I believe, by Bersani and Dutoit [1993].) As we have seen, this is not a trivial but in some respects the central historical question for psychoanalytic metapsychology. In *New Foundations,* Laplanche concludes that the differencing probably cannot be conducted by "biologically inscribed *mnemonic* scenarios" (1989: 35), that is, a biologically acquired memory-image of what (for previous generations) was safe and what was dangerous, what pleasurable and what unpleasurable. But a coherent positive account remains to be worked out. Needless to say, I am not concerned here with the historical and theoretical issues as they might be phrased today (cf. Davis 1995a: chaps. 1, 3, 4, 8) but only with Freud's own "mnemonic scenarios" for his theory of the phylogenetic foundation of human psychogenesis.

7. The early psychoanalysts were convinced that homosexuality and anal erotism were intimately connected—in some contexts, practically the same thing. As his letters show, the link was investigated with particular vigor by Sandor Ferenczi, probably Freud's most innovative student at this period, between 1908

and 1914. In 1908, for instance, Ferenczi noted that he had heard a speech at the Society of Physicians by an acquaintance, a Hungarian military doctor named Moritz Popper, "who wants to cure all cases of impotence through prostate massage"; heterosexual impotence was widely believed to express frustrated or (for the Freudians) repressed homosexual desires, and Popper's erotic therapy probably alleviated some of the symptoms of at least some of his patients. On the same evening, Ferenczi spoke about "psychic impotence," presumably homosexuality (Freud/Ferenczi 1993: 25 [November 22, 1908]). A few years later, in 1911, when Freud was in the middle of the Wolf Man's analysis, Ferenczi published a paper on the "intimate connections beween anal erotism, homosexuality, hypochondria, and paranoia," in which a patient "interprets his homosexual anal erotism (operations on the rectum) first hypochondriacally and feels all kinds of lethal illnesses in himself; only later is it detached by persecution mania" (ibid.: 358 [March 16, 1912]). No doubt Ferenczi's identification and analysis of homosexual anal erotism was a productive starting point for considering paranoia, a more complex and specific formation which supposedly leans on it. But in the case history of the Wolf Man, Freud cannot assume but rather must explain homosexual anal erotism. He also needs, however, to narrate temporally later formations in the Wolf Man's psychic development—his "anal erotism" in later childhood and adolescence, his paranoias, and so forth. At certain points in the logic of the case history, then, what must be explained in its own right will simply be assumed for the purposes of further explanations.

8. I have been unable, however, to identify this image. It is possible that the source, Ernest Jones (1953: 1–2), was reporting Freud family lore that was based on some kind of confusion.

VII. **Intersubjective Transformation**

1. As a metaphorical way of explaining the fragmented, often senseless language of psychotics, Freud had once asked Fliess: "Have you ever seen a foreign [e.g., German] newspaper which passed Russian censorship at the frontier? Words, whole clauses and sentences are blacked out so that the rest becomes unintelligible. A *Russian censorship* of that kind comes about in psychoses and produces the apparently meaningless *deliria*" (Freud 1985: 289 [December 22, 1897]). (For the actual practice of "Russian censorship," see Choldin 1985: figs. 6.1–6.5.) Metaphors for psychic "censorship" played a major part in *Die Traumdeutung* and elsewhere (see Anzieu 1986: 484–509), not least because Freud himself censored personal material—especially the so-called big dream, "analyzed down to the ground," which may have concerned his wife Martha and which Freud dropped from the draft of the book on Fliess's advice (Freud 1985: 316 [June 9, 1898]). A "substitute" dream for this "lost" dream was also censored, probably because it contained a potentially dangerous political allusion and other material which was too uncomfortable for Freud to publish (ibid.: 318 n. 1 [June 20, 1898]; these interpretations were offered by McGrath 1986: 259–60, 263–64). "Condemning" the "big dream" required considerable rewriting of one part of the draft of *Die Traumdeutung* (see Freud 1985: 364 [August 1, 1899]). The whole matter may have been on Freud's mind in 1910 when he began the analysis of the Wolf Man. His work was partly motivated, as we have seen, by his followers' complaints that he had never presented a completely analyzed patient's case and had left essential personal associations out of the ostensibly exemplary dream analyses in *Die*

Traumdeutung. Moreover, one of his disciples, Herbert Silberer (1910), had just published an article in which he explicitly discussed the parallel, first broached by Freud in 1897, between political and psychic censorship—and in the very context of reexamining one of Freud's own self-analyzed dreams, the so-called "Count Thun" dream, in which this double meaning seemed to appear in the dream representation.

2. In Freud's important *"non vixit"* dream, the annihilatory power of the dreamer's gaze, identified with the stare of his father and other figures of authority (Freud 1900a: 421–25; Anzieu 1986: 375–88), could be compared directly with the attentive gaze of the wolves (= parents, father) in the Wolf Man's report of his dream. Although the drawing of the dream, I have argued, immediately rendered itself legible for Freud as a replication of the primal scene of the repression of bisexuality, we saw that nothing in the Wolf Man's dream report or in the drawing intrinsically indicates that the wolves in the dream should be male. But if Freud made a connection with the *"non vixit"* dream, his existing interpretation of his own imagery might have disposed him to regard the attentive, even terrifying or annihilating, gaze of the wolves as masculine. Forging this connection might have contributed to his desire to suppress the manifestly subjective elements in his interpretation of the patient's history—for in his *"non vixit"* dream, of course, it was he, Freud, who possessed the attentive, annihilatory gaze attributed to the wolves in the Wolf Man's dream. The connection, then, would have positioned Freud as a "wolf" in relation to his patient—a metaphor that the case history both remarks and represses in other ways.

Freud's *Die Traumdeutung* contains a report of a childhood anxiety dream of Freud's—"one from my seventh or eighth year"—that in its apparent content, or at least Freud's presentation of it, replicates aspects of the wolf dream and its meaning as constructed by Freud: "[The dream] was a very vivid one, and in it I saw my beloved mother, with a peculiarly peaceful, sleeping expression on her features, being carried into the room by two (or three) people with birds' beaks and laid upon the bed. I awoke in tears and screaming, and interrupted my parents' sleep" (Freud 1900a: 583). The birds recall for Freud a boy who had told him the vulgar German word for sexual intercourse. As he says, moreover, "the strangely draped and unnaturally tall figures with birds' beaks were derived from the illustrations to Phillipson's Bible," the Freud family Bible (an edition typically used by assimilated Jews), in which Freud's father Jacob recorded his eldest son's birth and which he presented to him in 1891 as a thirty-fifth birthday present (see further Rosenfeld 1956; Anzieu 1986: 294–309; Rice 1990: 17–18, 76–77). "So it was that [the Wolf Man's] mental life impressed one," Freud wrote in the case history, "in much the same way as the religion of ancient Egypt" (119). The "religion of ancient Egypt" served not only as an explicit metaphor for the preservation, accretion, and syncretism of psychic "attributes" of vastly differing relative antiquities but also, implicitly, as a metaphor for the history of desire and repression in the infantile, childhood, or family context (see Huber 1987). We do not know whether Freud's "Egyptian bird dream" as he described and interpreted it in *Die Traumdeutung* disposed him to read the Wolf Man's dream and drawing in a particular way—the row of Egyptian gods has much the same meaning in its replicatory context as the tree of repression does in its—because it is not clear exactly when Freud decided to compare the Wolf Man's psychic history to Egyptian religion. (It may have been a comparison he explained to the patient; the Wolf Man, we recall, responded to Freud's advice that the psychoanalysis needed a symbolic resolution by giving him an Egyptian statuette.) But it is likely that Freud's "childhood anxiety dream" reported in his book on the interpretation of dreams came to mind, at least in a general way, when a patient reported his dream.

3. The best detailed historical studies of Freud's self-analysis are Sulloway 1979 and Anzieu 1986, though they are quite different in their sources and conclusions; see also Grinstein 1990 and a suggestive contemporary interpretation by Edmundson 1990. Klaus Theweleit (1994) has argued that Freud's "other" in his self-analysis—if we are not to indulge the legend of his autochthonic role in psychoanalysis—was his fiancée Martha, to whom he wrote hundreds of letters between 1882 and 1886. The other obvious candidates—for it appears to me that Freud's intersubjective self-analysis was distributed among several relationships—would be the great friend of his teenage years Eduard Silberstein (see Freud 1990) and the interlocutor who succeeded Martha, Wilhelm Fliess (Freud 1985).

4. It would take another study to show that other activities and cases—such as the "Rat Man" case (Freud 1909d)—were germane in this regard; I am not claiming that the Wolf Man case was the sole hinge in Freud's reimagination of himself. Freud had immediately identified homosexual material in his first session, in 1907, with the "Rat Man"; the notes for the meeting have survived. Like the Wolf Man, the Rat Man knew of Freud's interest in childhood sexuality, and, also like the Wolf Man, he may have immediately projected a strong, if perhaps calculated, "transference" toward him (see Mahony 1986; Ellman 1991: 291–310).

REFERENCES CITED

Works and Correspondence of Sigmund Freud

Works by Sigmund Freud

Note: For the convenience of English-speaking readers, Freud's psychoanalytic works are cited using the date and letter (e.g., Freud 1900a) assigned in the Tyson-Strachey "Chronological Hand-List of Freud's Works" (1956), followed by the volume and page number of the *Standard Edition of the Complete Psychological Works of Sigmund Freud*, translated and edited by James Strachey in collaboration with Anna Freud and with the assistance of Alix Strachey and Alan Tyson, 24 vols. (London: Hogarth Press, 1953–74) (abbreviated below as *SE*). Scientific and pre-psychoanalytic works by Freud are cited by date of publication and differentiating letters where necessary. For the standard and most accurate Freud bibliography, see *Freud—Bibliographie mit Werkkonkordanz*, ed. Ingeborg Meyer-Palmedo and Gerhard Fichtner (Frankfurt am Main: S. Fischer Verlag, 1989).

1877. Über den Ursprung der hinteren Nervenwurzeln im Rückenmarke von Ammocoetes (Petromyzon planeri). *Sitzungsberichte der kaiserlichen Akademie der Wissenschaften* [Vienna], *Mathematisch-naturwissenschaftliche Klasse* 75, Pt. 3/1: 15–27.

1878. Über Spinalganglien und Rückenmark des Petromyzon. *Sitzungsberichte der kaiserlichen Akademie der Wissenschaften* [Vienna], *Mathematisch-Naturwissenschaftliche Klasse* 78, Pt. 3: 81–167.

1884a. Eine neue Methode zum Studium des Faserverlaufs im Centralnervensystem. *Zentralblatt für die medizinischen Wissenschaften* 22: 161–63.

1884b. A new histological method for the study of nerve-tracts in the brain and spinal cord. *Brain* 7: 86–88.

1886 (and L. O. von Darkschewitsch). Ueber die Beziehung des Strickkörpers zum Hinterstrang und Hinterstrangskern nebst Bemerkungen über zwei Felder der Oblongata. *Neurologisches Centralblatt* 5: 121–29.

1886. Über den Ursprung des Nervus acusticus. *Monatschrift fur Ohrenheilkunde* NF 20/8: 243–51, 20/9: 277–82.

1891. *Zur Auffassung der Aphasien*. Leipzig and Vienna: Franz Deuticke. (See *Sigmund Freud—Zur Auffassung der Aphasien: Eine kritische Studie*, ed. Paul Vogel [Frankfurt am Main: Fischer Taschenbuch Verlag, 1992].)

1894a. The Neuro-Psychoses of Defence. *SE* 3: 41–62.

1895d (and Joseph Breuer). Studies on Hysteria [*Ueber Hysterie*]. *SE* 2.

1896a. Heredity and the Aetiology of the Neuroses. *SE* 3: 143–56.

1896b. Further Remarks on the Neuro-Psychoses of Defence. *SE* 3: 159–86.

1896c. The Aetiology of Hysteria. *SE* 3: 189–222.

1897a. Die infantile Cerebrallähmung. Vienna: A. Holder.

1897b. Abstracts of the Scientific Writings of Dr. Sigm. Freud 1877–1897. *SE* 3: 225–57.

1898b. The Psychical Mechanism of Forgetfulness. *SE* 3: 288–98.

1900a. The Interpretation of Dreams [*Die Traumdeutung*]. *SE* 4, 5.

1901b. The Psychopathology of Everyday Life. *SE* 6.

1905c. Jokes and Their Relation to the Unconscious. *SE* 8.

1905d. Three Essays on the Theory of Sexuality. *SE* 7: 125–243.

1905e. Fragment of an Analysis of a Case of Hysteria. *SE* 7: 3–122.

1908c. On the Sexual Theories of Children. *SE* 9: 207–26.

1909b. Analysis of a Phobia in a Five-Year-Old Boy. *SE* 10: 3–147.

1909d. Notes upon a Case of Obsessional Neurosis. *SE* 10: 153–318.

1910a. Five Lectures on Psychoanalysis. *SE* 11: 3–55.

1910c. Leonardo da Vinci and a Memory of His Childhood. *SE* 11: 59–138.

1910h. A Special Type of Choice of Object Made by Men (Contributions to the Psychology of Love, I). *SE* 11: 163–76.

1911c. Psycho-Analytic Notes on an Autobiographical Account of a Case of Paranoia (Dementia Paranoides). *SE* 12: 3–79.

1912b. The Dynamics of Transference. *SE* 12: 99–108.

1912x. Totem and Taboo. *SE* 13: 1–161.

1913d. The Occurrence in Dreams of Material from Fairy Tales. *SE* 12: 281–90.

1913i. The Predisposition to Obsessional Neurosis. *SE* 12: 313–26.

1914c. On Narcissism: An Introduction. *SE* 14: 69–102.

1914d. On the History of the Psycho-Analytic Movement. *SE* 14: 3–66.

1914g. Remembering, Repeating and Working-Through (Further Recommendations on the Technique of Psycho-Analysis, II). *SE* 12: 147–56.

1916x. Introductory Lectures on Psycho-Analysis. *SE* 15, 16.

1918b. From the History of an Infantile Neurosis. *SE* 17: 3–124.

1919a. Lines of Advance in Psycho-Analytic Therapy. *SE* 17: 159–67.

1919e. "A Child Is Being Beaten": A Contribution to the Study of the Origin of Sexual Perversions. *SE* 17: 177–204.

1923a. Two Encyclopedia Articles. *SE* 18: 234–62.

1923c. Remarks on the Theory and Practice of Dream-Interpretation. *SE* 19: 109-21.

1924. *Gesammelte Schriften*, vol. 8: *Krankengeschichten*. Vienna: F. Deuticke.

1925a. A Note upon the "Mystic Writing-Pad." *SE* 19: 227–33.

1925b. An Autobiographical Study. *SE* 20: 3–70.

1925e. The Resistances to Psycho-Analysis. *SE* 19: 213–22.

1926d. Inhibitions, Symptoms, and Anxiety. *SE* 20: 77–172.

1927e. Fetishism. *SE* 21: 149–57.

1928b. Dostoevsky and Parricide. *SE* 21: 175–93.

1930a. Civilization and Its Discontents. *SE* 21: 59–145.

1933a. New Introductory Lectures on Psycho-Analysis. *SE* 22: 3–181.

1937c. Analysis Terminable and Interminable. *SE* 23: 209–53.

1937d. Constructions in Analysis. *SE* 23: 256–70.

1940e. The Splitting of the Ego in the Process of Defence. *SE* 23: 273–78.

1941a. Letter to Josef Breuer [1892]. *SE* 1: 147.

1950. Project for a Scientific Psychology [1895]. *SE* 1: 283–392.

1987. *A Phylogenetic Fantasy: Overview of the Transference Neuroses* [1917], trans. Axel Hoffer and Peter T. Hoffer, ed. Ilse Grubrich-Simitis. Cambridge, Mass.: Harvard University Press.

1990a. Aphasia [1888]. In *A Moment of Transition: Two Neuroscientific Articles by Sigmund Freud,* trans. and ed. Mark Solms and Michael Saling, pp. 31–38. London: The Institute of Psycho-Analysis and Karnac Books.

1990b. The Brain [1888]. In *A Moment of Transition: Two Neuroscientific Articles by Sigmund Freud,* trans. and ed. Mark Solms and Michael Saling, pp. 39–86. London: The Institute of Psycho-Analysis and Karnac Books.

Correspondence of Sigmund Freud

Freud/Abraham 1965. *A Psycho-Analytic Dialogue: The Letters of Sigmund Freud and Karl Abraham, 1907–1926,* ed. Hilda C. Abraham and Ernst Freud, trans. B. Marsh and Hilda C. Abraham. New York: Basic Books.

Freud/Jung 1974. *The Freud/Jung Letters: The Correspondence between Sigmund Freud and C. G. Jung,* ed. William McGuire, trans. R. Manheim and R. F. C. Hull. Princeton: Princeton University Press.

Freud 1985. *The Complete Letters of Sigmund Freud to Wilhelm Fliess, 1887–1904,* ed. and trans. Jeffrey M. Masson. Cambridge, Mass.: Harvard University Press.

Freud 1986. *Briefe an Wilhelm Fliess 1887–1904,* ed. Jeffrey M. Masson with the assistance of M. Schröter, transcriptions by Gerhard Fichtner. Frankfurt am Main: S. Fischer Verlag.

Freud 1990. *The Letters of Sigmund Freud to Eduard Silberstein, 1871–1881,* ed. Walter Boehlich, trans. Arnold J. Pomerans. Cambridge, Mass.: Harvard University Press.

Freud/Ferenczi 1993. *The Correspondence of Sigmund Freud and Sandor Ferenczi.* Vol. 1, *1908–1914,* ed. Eva Brabant, Ernst Falzeder, and Patrizia Giampieri-Deutsch. Cambridge, Mass.: Harvard University Press.

Freud/Jones 1993. *The Complete Correspondence of Sigmund Freud and Ernest Jones, 1908–1939,* ed. R. Andrew Paskauskas, introduction by Riccardo Steiner. Cambridge, Mass.: Harvard University Press.

Other Works

Abeln, Reinhard. 1970. *Unbewusstes und Unterbewusstes bei C. G. Carus und Aristoteles.* Meisenheim am Glan: Hein. Monographien zur philosophischen Forschung 70.

Abraham, Nicolas, and Maria Torok. 1986. *The Wolf Man's Magic Word* [1976], trans. Nicholas Rand. Minneapolis: University of Minnesota Press.

Abrahamson, David. 1980. The Borderline Syndrome and Affective Disorders: A Comment on the Wolf-man. *Schizophrenia Bulletin* 6: 549–51.

Adler, Alfred. 1907. *Studie über die Minderwertigkeit von Organen.* Berlin: Urban and Schwarzenberg.

———. 1917. *The Neurotic Constitution,* trans. Bernard Glueck and John E. Lind. New York: Moffat, Yard.

———. 1928. Der psychische Hermaphroditismus im Leben und in der Neurose [1910]. In *Heilen und Bilden,* 3rd ed., ed. Erwin Wexberg. Munich: J. F. Bermann.

Amacher, Peter. 1965. *Freud's Neurological Education and Its Influence on Psychoanalytic Theory.* New York: International Universities Press. Psychological Issues 4, no. 4 (Monograph 16).

Andersson, O. 1962. *Studies in the Prehistory of Psychoanalysis: The Etiology of Psy-*

choneuroses and Some Related Themes in Sigmund Freud's Scientific Writings and Letters, 1886–1896. Stockholm: Svenska Bokforlaget.

Andree, Rolf. 1977. *Arnold Böcklin: Die Gemälde.* Basel: F. Reinhardt and Munich: Prestel.

Anonymous. 1740. *Plain Reasons for the Growth of Sodomy in England.* London: A. Dodd.

Anzieu, Didier. 1986. *Freud's Self Analysis* [1st ed., 1959], 2nd ed. [1975], trans. Peter Graham. London: The Institute of Psycho-Analysis and the Hogarth Press.

———. 1989. *The Skin Ego,* trans. Chris Turner. New Haven: Yale University Press.

Appignanesi, Lisa, and John Forrester. 1992. *Freud's Women.* New York: Basic Books/HarperCollins.

Asvarishch, Boris. I. 1990. Friedrich's Russian Patrons. In *The Romantic Vision of Caspar David Friedrich: Paintings and Drawings from the U.S.S.R.,* ed. Sabine Rewald. New York: Metropolitan Museum of Art/Abrams.

Bakan, David. 1958. *Sigmund Freud and the Jewish Mystical Tradition.* Princeton: Van Nostrand.

Bann, Stephen. 1991. *The True Vine: On Visual Representation and the Western Tradition.* New York: Cambridge University Press.

Berillon, Dr. 1908–1909. La traitement psychologique de l'homosexualité basé sur la reéducation sensorielle. *Revue de l'hypnotisme* 23: 44–46.

Bernardi, Ricardo. 1989. The Role of Paradigmatic Determinants in Psychoanalytic Understanding. *International Journal of Psycho-Analysis* 70: 341–57.

Bersani, Leo, and Ulysse Dutoit. 1993. *Arts of Impoverishment: Beckett, Rothko, Resnais.* Cambridge, Mass.: Harvard University Press.

Birken, Lawrence. 1988. *Consuming Desire: Sexual Science and the Emergence of a Culture of Abundance, 1871–1914.* Ithaca, N.Y.: Cornell University Press.

Blüher, Hans. 1917. *Die Rolle der Erotik in der männlichen Gesellschaft.* 2 vols. Jena: Eugen Diederichs Verlag.

———. 1922. *Die deutsche Wandervögelbewegung als erotisches Phänomen: Ein Beitrag zur Erkenntnis der sexuellen Inversion.* 6th ed. Prien (Chemsee): Kampmann und Schnabel.

Blum, Harold P. 1974. The Borderline Childhood of the Wolf Man. *Journal of the American Psychoanalytic Association* 22: 721–41.

Bonaparte, Marie. 1925. Notes on the Analytic Discovery of a Primal Scene. *Psychoanalytic Study of the Child* 1: 119–25.

Borch-Jacobsen, Mikkel. 1988. *The Freudian Subject,* trans. Catherine Porter. Stanford: Stanford University Press.

———. 1993. *The Emotional Tie: Psychoanalysis, Mimesis, and Affect.* Stanford: Stanford University Press.

Borisova, Elena A., and Grigory Sternin. 1988. *Russian Art Nouveau.* New York: Rizzoli.

Bowie, Malcolm. 1987. *Freud, Proust, and Lacan: Theory as Fiction.* New York: Cambridge University Press.

Bowlt, John. 1973. Russian Symbolism and the "Blue Rose" Movement. *Slavonic and East European Review* 51: 161–81.

Brennan, Teresa. 1992. *The Interpretation of the Flesh: Freud and Femininity.* London and New York: Routledge.

Brion, Marcel, ed. 1988. *De la peinture du paysage dans l'allemagne romantique:*

Carl Gustav Carus, Neuf lettres sur la peinture de paysage, et Caspar David Friedrich, Choix de textes. Paris: Plon.

Brivic, Sheldon. 1991. *The Veil of Signs: Joyce, Lacan, and Perception.* Urbana: University of Illinois Press.

Brooks, Peter. 1984. Fictions of the Wolf Man: Freud and Narrative Understanding. In *Reading for the Plot: Design and Intention in Narrative,* pp. 264–85. New York: A. A. Knopf.

Brown, Roger, and Richard J. Herrnstein. 1981. Icons and Images. In *Imagery,* ed. Ned Block, pp. 19–49. Cambridge, Mass.: MIT Press.

Brunswick, Ruth Mack. 1928. A Supplement to Freud's "History of an Infantile Neurosis." *International Journal of Psycho-Analysis* 9 (1928): 439–76. (Reprinted in Gardiner 1971, cited here.)

———. 1929. Note on the Childish Theory of Coitus a Tergo. *International Journal of Psycho-Analysis* 10: 93–95.

———. 1940. The Pre-Oedipal Phase of Libido Development. *Psychoanalytic Quarterly* 9: 293–319.

———. 1945. [Note updating "A Supplement to Freud's 'History of an Infantile Neurosis' " (Brunswick 1928).] In *The Psychoanalytic Reader: An Anthology of Essential Papers with Critical Introductions,* ed. Robert Fliess, p. 86. New York: International Universities Press.

Budge, E. A. Wallis. 1895. *First Steps in Egyptian.* London: Kegan, Paul, Trench, Trubner and Co.

———. 1896. *An Egyptian Reading Book for Beginners.* London: Kegan, Paul, Trench, Trubner and Co.

Burton, Robert. 1989. *The Anatomy of Melancholy,* ed. Thomas C. Faulkner, Nicolas K. Kiessling, and Rhonda L. Blair. Vol. 1: Text. Oxford: Oxford University Press.

Byock, Jesse L. 1990. *The Saga of the Volsungs: The Norse Epic of Sigurd the Dragon Slayer.* Berkeley: University of California Press.

Carotenuto, Aldo. 1982. *A Secret Symmetry: Sabina Spielrein between Freud and Jung,* trans. Arno Pomerans, John Shepley, and Krishna Winston. New York: Pantheon Books.

Carter, K. C. 1980. Germ Theory, Hysteria, and Freud's Early Work on Psychopathology. *Medical History* 24: 259–74.

Carus, Carl Gustav. 1831. *Briefe über Landschaftsmalerei, geschrieben in den Jahren 1815–1824.* 1st ed. (2nd ed., 1835). Leipzig: G. Fleischer.

———. 1841. *Zwölf Briefe über das Erdleben.* Stuttgart: P. Balz'sche Buchhandlung.

———. 1846. *Psyche: Zur Entwicklungsgeschichte der Seele.* 1st ed. Pforzheim: Flammer und Hoffmann.

———. 1847. *Friedrich, der Landschaftsmaler.* Dresden: B. G. Teubner.

———. 1853. *Symbolik der menschlichen Gestalt.* Leipzig: Brockhaus.

———. 1857. *Über Lebensmagnetismus und über die magischen Wirkungen überhaupt.* Leipzig: F. A. Brockhaus.

——— 1861. *Natur und Idee; oder das Werdende und sein Gesetz.* Vienna: W. Braumuller.

Casper, J. L. 1852. Ueber Nothsucht und Päderastie und deren Ermittelung seitens des Gerichtsarztes. *Vierteljahrschrift für gerichtliche und öffentliche Medicin* 1: 21–78.

———. 1863. *Klinische Novellen zur gerichtlichen Medicin.* Berlin: August Hirschwald.

———. 1881. *Handbuch der gerichtlichen Medicin.* 7th ed., ed. Carl Liman. 2 vols. Berlin: August Hirschwald.

de Certeau, Michel. 1981. The Freudian Novel: History and Literature. *Humanities in Society* 4: 121–44.

Chase, Cynthia. 1992. Translating the Transference: Psychoanalysis and the Construction of History. In *Telling Facts: History and Narration in Psychoanalysis,* ed. Joseph H. Smith and Humphrey Morris, pp. 103–26. Baltimore: Johns Hopkins University Press.

Choldin, Marianna Tax. 1985. *A Fence around the Empire: Russian Censorship of Western Ideas under the Tsars.* Durham, N. C.: Duke University Press.

Cioffi, Frank. 1969. Wittgenstein's Freud. In *Studies in the Philosophy of Wittgenstein,* ed. Peter Winch, pp. 197–208. New York: Humanities Press.

Clark, Ronald W. 1980. *Freud: The Man and the Cause.* New York: Random House.

Cohn, Dorrit. 1993. Freud's Case Histories and the Question of Fictionality. In *Telling Facts: History and Narration in Psychoanalysis,* ed. Joseph H. Smith and Humphrey Morris, pp. 21–47. Baltimore: Johns Hopkins University Press.

Couperus, Louis. 1891. *Footsteps of Fate,* trans. Clara Bell. London: W. Heinemann.

Culler, Jonathan. 1981. *The Pursuit of Signs: Semiotics, Literature, and Deconstruction.* Ithaca, N.Y.: Cornell University Press.

Darwin, Charles. 1859. *On the Origin of Species by Means of Natural Selection.* 1st ed. London: J. Murray.

———. 1871. *The Descent of Man.* 1st ed. 2 vols. London: J. Murray.

———. 1874–76. *Gesammelte Werke,* trans. J. V. Carus. 7 vols. Stuttgart: E. Schweizerbart.

———. 1988. *On the Origin of Species* [1876]. In *The Works of Charles Darwin,* ed. Paul H. Barrett and R. B. Freeman, vol. 16. London: W. Pickering.

Davidson, Arnold. 1987. Sex and the Emergence of Sexuality. *Critical Inquiry* 13: 252–77.

Davis, Whitney. 1994. The Renunciation of Reaction in Girodet's *Sleep of Endymion.* In *Visual Culture: Images and Interpretations,* ed. Norman Bryson, Keith Moxey, and Michael Ann Holly, pp. 161–204. Middletown, Conn., and Hanover, N. H.: Wesleyan University Press and University Press of New England.

———. 1995a. *Replications: Archaeology, Art History, Psychoanalysis.* University Park: Pennsylvania State University Press.

———. 1995b. Winckelmann's Homosexual Teleologies. In *Sexuality in Ancient Art,* ed. Natalie B. Kampen, forthcoming. New York: Cambridge University Press.

———. 1995c. Freud's Leonardo und die Kultur der Homosexualität. *Texte zur Kunst* 5/17: 56–17.

Decker, Hannah S. 1977. *Freud in Germany: Revolution and Reaction in Science, 1893–1907.* New York: International Universities Press. Psychological Issues Monograph 41.

de Lauretis, Teresa. 1994. *The Practice of Love: Lesbian Sexuality and Perverse Desire.* Bloomington: Indiana University Press.

Deleuze, Gilles, and Felix Guattari. 1973. "14 Mai 1914: un seul ou plusieurs loups?" *Minuit* 5 (September): 2–16.

———. 1987. *A Thousand Plateaus,* trans. Brian Massumi. Minneapolis: University of Minnesota Press.

Derrida, Jacques. 1978. Freud and the Scene of Writing. In *Writing and Difference,* trans. Alan Bass, pp. 196–230. Chicago: University of Chicago Press.

———. 1986. Foreword: Fors: The Anglish Words of Nicholas Abraham and Maria Torok, trans. Barbara Johnson. In Abraham and Torok 1986, pp. xi–xlviii.

———. 1987. *The Post Card: From Socrates to Freud and Beyond,* trans. Alan Bass. Chicago: University of Chicago Press.

Descartes, René. 1649. *Passions de l'âme.* Amsterdam: chez Louys Elzevier.

Deutsch, Helen. 1973. *Confrontations with Myself.* New York: W. W. Norton.

Dobrzecki, Alina. 1982. *Die Bedeutung des Traumes für Caspar David Friedrich: Eine Untersuchung zu den Ideen der Frühromantik.* Giessen: Schmitz.

Dollimore, Jonathan. 1991. *Sexual Dissidence: Augustine to Wilde, Freud to Foucault.* Oxford: Oxford University Press.

Donn, Linda. 1989. *Freud and Jung: Years of Friendship, Years of Loss.* New York: Scribner.

Edelman, Lee. 1991. Seeing Things: Representation, the Scene of Surveillance, and the Spectacle of Gay Male Sex. In *Inside/Out: Lesbian Theories/Gay Theories,* ed. Diana Fuss, pp. 93–116. New York: Routledge.

Edmunds, Lavinia. 1988. His Master's Choice. *The Johns Hopkins Magazine* 40, no. 2 (April).

Edmundson, Mark. 1990. *Towards Reading Freud: Self-Creation in Milton, Wordsworth, Emerson, and Sigmund Freud.* Princeton: Princeton University Press.

Eissler, K. R. 1961. *Leonardo da Vinci: Psychoanalytic Notes on the Enigma.* New York: International Universities Press.

———. 1971. *Talent and Genius: The Fictitious Case of Tausk contra Freud.* New York: Quadrangle Books.

Ellenberger, Henri F. 1993. Freud's Lecture on Masculine Hysteria (October 15, 1886): A Critical Study [1968]. In *Beyond the Unconscious: Essays of Henri F. Ellenberger in the History of Psychiatry,* ed. Mark S. Micale, pp. 119–35. Princeton: Princeton University Press.

Ellis, Havelock. 1897. *Studies in the Psychology of Sex.* Vol. 1: *Sexual Inversion.* London: The University Press.

———. 1901. *Studies in the Psychology of Sex.* Vol. 2: *Sexual Inversion.* 2nd ed. Philadelphia: F. A. Davis.

Ellis, Havelock, and John Addington Symonds. 1896. *Das konträre Geschlechtsfühl,* trans. Hans Kurella. Leipzig: Georg H. Wigand's Verlag.

———. 1897. *Sexual Inversion.* London: Wilson and Macmillan.

Ellman, Steven J. 1991. *Freud's Technique Papers: A Contemporary Perspective.* Northvale, N.J.: Aronson.

Fairbairn, W. R. D. 1956. Considerations Arising out of the Schreber Case. *British Journal of Medical Psychiatry* 29: 113–27.

Ferenczi, Sandor. 1916a. Introjection and Transference [1909]. In *Contributions to Psychoanalysis,* trans. Ernest Jones, pp. 35–93. London: Hogarth Press.

———. 1916b. On the Part Played by Homosexuality in the Parthenogenesis of Paranoia [1911]. In *Contributions to Psychoanalysis,* trans. Ernest Jones, pp. 154–86. London: Hogarth Press.

———. 1927. Review of Rank 1926. *International Journal of Psycho-Analysis* 8: 93–100.

———. 1955. Stimulation of the Anal Erotogenic Zone as a Precipitating Factor in Paranoia [1911]. In *Final Contributions to the Problems and Methods of Psychoanalysis*, ed. Michael Balint, trans. Eric Mosbacher et al., pp. 295–302. New York: Basic Books.

Fineman, Joel. 1987. Shakespeare's Will: The Temporality of Rape. *Representations* 20: 25–76.

Fish, Stanley. 1989. Withholding the Missing Portion: Psychoanalysis and Rhetoric. In *Doing What Comes Naturally: Change, Rhetoric, and the Practice of Theory in Literary and Legal Studies*, pp. 525–54. Durham, N. C.: Duke University Press.

Fodor, Nandor. 1945. Lycanthropy as a Psychic Mechanism. *Journal of American Folklore* 58: 310–16.

———. 1959. *The Haunted Mind: A Psychoanalyst Looks at the Supernatural*. New York: Helix Press.

Frazer, James G. 1913. *Balder, the Beautiful: The Fire-Festivals of Europe and the Doctrine of the Eternal Soul*. 2 vols. London: Macmillan (= *The Golden Bough*, 3rd ed., Part 7).

Freud, Ernst; Lucie Freud; and Ilse Grubrich-Simitis, eds. 1978. *Sigmund Freud: His Life in Pictures and Words*. New York: Harcourt Brace Jovanovich.

Freud, Martin. 1958. *Sigmund Freud: Man and Father*. New York: Vanguard Press.

Friedlaender, Benedict. 1904. *Die Renaissance des Eros Uranios*. Berlin: Verlag "Renaissance." (Reprint, New York: Arno Press, 1975.)

Frosch, John. 1967. Severe Regressive States during Analysis. *Journal of the American Psychoanalytic Association* 15: 504–505.

Galdston, Iago. 1956. Freud and Romantic Medicine. *Bulletin of the History of Medicine* 30: 489–507.

Gamwell, Lynn, and Richard Wells, eds. 1989. *Sigmund Freud and Art: His Personal Collection of Antiquities*. Binghamton: State University of New York and London: Freud Museum.

Gardiner, Muriel, ed. 1971. *The Wolf-Man by the Wolf-Man*. New York: Basic Books.

———. 1983a. The Wolf Man's Last Years. *Journal of the American Psychoanalytic Association* 31: 867–97.

———. 1983b. *Code Name "Mary": Memoirs of an American Woman in the Austrian Underground*. New Haven: Yale University Press.

Gardner, Sebastian. 1990. Psychoanalysis and the Story of Time. In *Writing the Future*, ed. David Wood, pp. 81–97. London: Routledge.

———. 1993. *Irrationality and the Philosophy of Psychoanalysis*. Cambridge: Cambridge University Press.

Gay, Peter. 1988. *Freud: A Life for Our Time*. New York: Norton.

Ginsburg, Lawrence M., and Sybil A. Ginsburg. 1987. A Menagerie of Illustrations from Sigmund Freud's Boyhood. *Psychoanalytic Study of the Child* 42: 469–86.

Ginzburg, Carlo. 1989. Freud, the Wolf Man, and the Werewolf [1986]. In *Clues, Myths, and the Historical Method*, trans. John and Anne C. Tedeschi, pp. 146–55. Baltimore: Johns Hopkins University Press.

Golynets, Sergei. 1982. *Ivan Bilibin*. New York: Abrams.

Gombrich, E. H. 1961. *Art and Illusion*. Princeton: Princeton University Press/Bollingen Series.

Gottlieb, R. M. 1989. Technique and Countertransference in Freud's Analysis of the Rat Man. *Psychoanalytic Quarterly* 58: 29–62.

Gould, Stephen Jay. 1977. *Ontogeny and Phylogeny*. Cambridge, Mass.: Harvard University Press.

Graber, Gustav Hans. 1926. Ein Vorläufer der Psychoanalyse. *Imago* 12: 513–23.

Gray, Camilla. 1962. *The Russian Experiment in Art, 1863–1922*. London: Thames and Hudson.

Greenacre, Phyllis. 1973. The Primal Scene and the Sense of Reality. *Psychoanalytic Quarterly* 42: 10–41.

Grigg, Kenneth A. 1973. "All Roads Lead to Rome": The Role of the Nursemaid in Freud's Dreams. *Journal of the American Psychoanalytic Association* 21: 108-26.

Grimm, Jakob. 1875. *Deutsche Mythologie*. 4th ed. Berlin: F. Dummler.

Grinstein, Alexander. 1990. *Freud at the Crossroads*. Madison, Conn.: International Universities Press.

Grosskurth, Phyllis. 1991. *The Secret Ring: Freud's Inner Circle and the Politics of Psychoanalysis*. Reading, Mass.: Addison-Wesley.

Grünbaum, Adolf. 1988. The Role of the Case Study Method in the Foundations of Psychoanalysis. *Canadian Journal of Philosophy* 18: 623–57.

Haeckel, Ernst. 1874. *Anthropogenie oder Entwicklungsgeschichte des Menschen: Vorträge über die Grundzuge der menschlichen Keimes- und Stammes-Geschichte*. Leipzig: Wilhelm Engelmann.

Halpert, Eugene. 1975. Lermontov and the Wolf Man. *American Imago* 32: 315–28.

Handlbauer, Bernhard. 1990. *Die Adler-Freud-Kontroverse*. Frankfurt: Fischer Taschenbuch Verlag.

Harris, Jay, and Jean Harris. 1984. *The One-Eyed Doctor, Sigismund Freud: Psychological Origins of Freud's Works*. New York: J. Aronson.

Haxthausen, August. 1856. *Transkaukasia*. Leipzig: F. A. Brockhaus.

Heller, Peter. 1990. *A Child Analysis with Anna Freud*, trans. S. Burckhardt and M. Weigand. Madison, Conn.: International Universities Press.

Hertz, Wilhelm. 1862. *Der Werwölf: Beiträge zur Sagensgeschichte*. Stuttgart: A. Kroner.

Herzer, Manfred. 1985. Kertbeny and the Nameless Love. *Journal of Homosexuality* 12: 1–26.

———. 1992. *Magnus Hirschfeld: Leben und Werk eines jüdischen, schwulen, und sozialistischen Sexologen*. Frankfurt and New York: Campus Verlag.

Herzog, Patricia S. 1991. *Conscious and Unconscious: Freud's Dynamic Distinction Reconsidered*. Madison, Conn.: International Universities Press. Psychological Issues Monograph 58.

Hirschfeld, Magnus. 1991. *Transvestites: The Erotic Drive to Cross-Dress* [1910], trans. Michael A. Lombardi-Nash. Buffalo: Prometheus Books.

Hirschmüller, Albrecht. 1989. Die Wiener Psychiatrie der Meynert-Zeit: Untersuchungen zu Sigmund Freuds nervenarztliche Ausbildung. Doctoral diss., Eberhard-Karls-Universität, Tübingen.

———. 1991. *Freuds Begegnung mit der Psychiatrie: Von der Hirnmythologie zur Neurosenlehre*. Tübingen: edition diskord.

Holt, Robert L. 1962. A Critical Examination of Freud's Concept of Bound versus Free Cathexis. *Journal of the American Psychoanalytic Association* 10: 475–515. (Reprinted with comments in Holt 1989.)

———. 1989. *Freud Reappraised: A Fresh Look at Psychoanalytic Theory*. Madison, Conn.: International Universities Press.

Huber, Gérard. 1987. *L'Egypte ancienne dans la psychanalyse*. Paris: Maisonneuve and Larose.

Jackson, J. Hughlings. 1931–32. Evolution and Dissolution of the Nervous System

[1884]. In *Selected Writings of John Hughlings Jackson*, ed. James Taylor, pp. 45–75. London: Hodder and Stoughton.

Jakobson, Roman, and Marc Szeftel. 1966. The Vseslav Epos. In *Roman Jakobson: Selected Writings*, vol. 4, pp. 301–68. The Hague: Mouton.

Jones, Ernest. 1953. *The Life and Work of Sigmund Freud*. Vol. 1. New York: Basic Books.

———. 1955. *The Life and Work of Sigmund Freud*. Vol. 2. New York: Basic Books.

———. 1957. *The Life and Work of Sigmund Freud*. Vol. 3. New York: Basic Books.

Jones, James W. 1990. *"We of the Third Sex": Literary Representations of Homosexuality in Wilhelmine Germany*. New York: Peter Lang. German Life and Civilization 7.

Jung, Carl G. 1973. *Memories, Dreams, Reflections*. Rev. ed., ed. A. Jaffe, trans. R. and C. Winston. New York: Pantheon Books.

Kaan, Heinrich. 1844. *Psychopathia Sexualis*. Leipzig: Voss.

Kanzer, Mark. 1972. Review of Gardiner 1971. *International Journal of Psycho-Analysis* 53: 419–22.

Kartiganer, Donald M. 1985. Freud's Reading Process: The Divided Protagonist Narrative and the Case of the Wolf-Man. In *The Psychoanalytic Study of Literature*, ed. Joseph Reppen and M. Charney, pp. 3–36. Hillsdale, N.J.: Analytic Press.

Kennedy, Hubert. 1988. *Ulrichs: The Life and Work of Karl Heinrich Ulrichs, Pioneer of the Modern Gay Movement*. Boston: Alyson Publications, Inc.

Kerr, John. 1993. *A Most Dangerous Method: The Story of Jung, Freud, and Sabina Spielrein*. New York: Knopf.

Kittler, Friedrich A. 1990. *Discourse Networks 1800/1900*, trans. Michael Metteer with Chris Cullens. Stanford: Stanford University Press.

Klein, Dennis B. 1985. *Jewish Origins of the Psychoanalytic Movement*. Chicago: University of Chicago Press.

Klein, Melanie. 1932. *The Psychoanalysis of Children*. London: The Hogarth Press.

Kochik, Olga. 1980. *Borisov-Musatov*. Moscow: Aurora.

Koerner, Joseph Leo. 1987. *Caspar David Friedrich and the Subject of Landscape*. New Haven: Yale University Press.

Kraepelin, Emil. 1899. *Psychiatrie: Ein Lehrbuch für Studirende und Aertze*. 6th ed. Leipzig: J. A. Barth.

———. 1904. *Psychiatrie*. 7th ed. Leipzig: J. A. Barth.

———. 1909. *Psychiatrie*. 8th ed. Leipzig: J. A. Barth.

———. 1987. *Memoirs*, trans. and ed. H. Hippius, G. Peters, and D. Ploog. New York: Springer-Verlag.

Krafft-Ebing, Richard von. 1894. *Psychopathia Sexualis*. 9th ed. Stuttgart: F. Enke.

Krüll, Marianne. 1986. *Freud and His Father* [1976], trans. Arnold J. Pomerans. New York: W. W. Norton.

Kupffer, Elisar von, ed. 1899. *Lieblingsminne und Freundesliebe in der Weltlitteratur*. Leipzig: M. Spohr.

Lacan, Jacques. 1977. The Agency of the Letter in the Unconscious, or Reason since Freud. In *Ecrits*, trans. Alan Sheridan. London and New York: W. W. Norton, Inc.

Laplanche, Jean. 1976. *Life and Death in Psychoanalysis*, trans. Jeffrey Mehlman. Baltimore: Johns Hopkins University Press.

———. 1980a. *Problématiques I: L'Angoisse*. Paris: PUF.

———. 1980b. *Problématiques II: Castration-Symbolisations*. Paris: PUF.

———. 1989. *New Foundations for Psychoanalysis,* trans. David Macey. Oxford: Basil Blackwell.

Laplanche, Jean, and J.-B. Pontalis. 1968. Fantasy and the Origins of Sexuality. *International Journal of Psycho-Analysis* 49: 1–18.

Last, Hugh. 1928. The Founding of Rome. In *The Cambridge Ancient History,* 1st ed., ed. S. A. Cook, F. E. Adcock, and M. E. Charlesworth, vol. 7, pp. 333–69. Cambridge: Cambridge University Press.

Leclaire, Serge. 1958. À propos de l'épisode psychotique que présente "L'homme aux loups." *La Psychanalyse* 4: 83–110.

Levy, Florence J. 1968–69. The Significance of Christmas for the "Wolf Man." *Psychoanalytic Review* 55: 615–22.

Lewes, Kenneth. 1988. *The Psychoanalytic Theory of Male Homosexuality.* New York: Simon and Schuster.

Lewin, Bertram D. 1957. Letters Pertaining to Freud's "History of an Infantile Neurosis." *Psychoanalytic Quarterly* 26: 449–60.

Lothane, Zvi. 1989. Schreber, Freud, Flechsig, and Weber Revisited: An Inquiry into Methods of Interpretation. *Psychoanalytic Review* 76: 203–61.

Loti, Pierre. 1887. *My Brother Yves* [1883], trans. Mary P. Fletcher. London: Vizetelly and Co.

Lubin, Arnold J. 1967. The Influence of the Russian Orthodox Church on Freud's Wolf-Man (With an Epilogue Based on Visits with the Wolf-Man). *Psychoanalytic Forum* 2: 25–48.

Lukacher, Ned. 1986. *Primal Scenes: Literature, Philosophy, Psychoanalysis.* Ithaca, N.Y.: Cornell University Press.

Lyngstrad, Alexandra, and Sverre Lyngstrad. 1971. *Ivan Goncharov.* New York: Twayne Publishers.

Macmillan, Malcolm. 1990. *Freud Evaluated: The Completed Arc.* Amsterdam: North-Holland.

———. 1992. The Sources of Freud's Methods for Gathering and Evaluating Clinical Data. In *Freud and the History of Psychoanalysis,* ed. Toby Gelfand and John Kerr, pp. 99–152. Hillsdale, N.J.: The Analytic Press.

Magid, Barry. 1992. Self Psychology Meets the Wolf Man. *Psychoanalysis and Psychotherapy* 10: 178–98.

Mahony, Patrick J. 1984. *Cries of the Wolf Man.* New York: International Universities Press. History of Psychoanalysis Monograph 1.

———. 1986. *Freud and the Rat Man.* New Haven: Yale University Press.

Marinov, Vladimir. 1991. Le détail du dessin de l'Homme aux loups non interprété par Freud. *Psychanalyse à l'Université* 16: 117–32.

Martin, Peer J. 1960. On Scierneuropsia: A Previously Unnamed Psychogenic Visual Disturbance. *Journal of the American Psychoanalytic Association* 8: 71–81.

Masson, Jeffrey M. 1982. Review of Obholzer 1982. *International Journal of Psycho-Analysis* 9: 116–19.

———. 1985. *The Assault on Truth: Freud's Suppression of the Seduction Theory.* New York: Penguin Books.

McGrath, William J. 1986. *Freud's Discovery of Psychoanalysis: The Politics of Hysteria.* Ithaca, N.Y.: Cornell University Press.

Meffert, Ekkehard. 1986. *Carl Gustav Carus: Sein Leben, seine Anschauung von der Erde.* Stuttgart: Freies Geistesleben.

Meissner, W. W. 1977. The Wolf Man and the Paranoid Process. *Annual of Psychoanalysis* 12: 23–74.

Merezhkovsky, Dmitri. 1902. *Tolstoi as Man and Artist, with an Essay on Dostoievski.* London: A. Constable.

———. 1904. *The Romance of Leonardo da Vinci,* trans. Herbert Trench. London: Putnam's Sons.

Minkina, Tat'yana. 1991. The Russian style moderne. In *The Twilight of the Tsars: Russian Art at the Turn of the Century.* London: South Bank Centre.

Moll, Albert. 1893. *Die konträre Sexualempfindung.* 2nd rev. ed. Berlin: Fischer's Medizinische Buchhandlung/H. Kornfeld.

Møller, Lis. 1991. Construction in the Case of the Wolf Man. In *The Freudian Reading,* pp. 57–87. Philadelphia: University of Pennsylvania Press.

Money, John. 1990. Androgyne Becomes Bisexual in Sexological Theory: Plato to Freud and Neuroscience. *Journal of the American Academy of Psychoanalysis* 18: 397–408.

Moran, Frances M. 1993. *Subject and Agency in Psychoanalysis: Which Is to Be Master?* New York: New York University Press.

Morris, Humphrey. 1992. Translating Transmission: Representation and Enactment in Freud's Construction of History. In *Telling Facts: History and Narration in Psychoanalysis,* ed. Joseph H. Smith and Humphrey Morris, pp. 48–102. Baltimore: Johns Hopkins University Press.

Müller, Johannes von. 1802. *Briefe eines jüngen Gelehrten an seinen Freund,* ed. S. F. C. Brun. Tübingen: J. G. Cotta.

Nägele, Rainer. 1987. *Reading after Freud: Essays on Goethe, Hölderlin, Habermas, Nietzsche, Brecht, Celan, and Freud.* New York: Columbia University Press.

Nancy, Jean-Luc, and Philippe Lacoue-Labarthe. 1992. *The Title of the Letter: A Reading of Lacan,* trans. Francois Raffoul and David Pettigrew. Albany: State University of New York Press.

Nelken, Halina. 1991. *Images of a Lost World: Jewish Motifs in Polish Painting, 1770–1945.* Oxford: Institute for Polish-Jewish Studies.

Novitz, David. 1977. *Pictures and Their Use in Communication.* The Hague: Mouton.

Nunberg, Herman, and Ernst Federn, eds. 1962–75. *Minutes of the Vienna Psychoanalytic Society.* 4 vols. New York: International Universities Press.

Obholzer, Karin. 1982. *The Wolf Man: Conversations with Freud's Controversial Patient—Sixty Years Later,* trans. Michael Shaw. New York: Continuum.

Offenkrantz, William, and Arnold Tobin. 1973. Problems of the Therapeutic Alliance: Freud and the Wolf Man. *International Journal of Psycho-Analysis* 54: 75–78.

O'Neill, John. 1989. Science and the Self: Freud's Paternity Suit (The Case of the Wolf Man). *Social Discourse* 2: 151–59.

Palombo, Stanley. 1973. The Associative Memory Tree. *Psychoanalysis and Contemporary Science* 2: 205–19.

Pankejeff, Serge. 1939. Die rechtlichen Gründlagen der Haftpflichtversicherung ("Versicherungsfall" und "Schadensabwehrmassnahme" in der Haftpflichtversicherung). *Das Versicherungsarchiv: Monatsblätter für private und öffentliche Versicherung* 5/6: 177–204.

Philippson, Ludwig, ed. 1858–59. *Die israelitische Bibel.* 2nd ed. 3 vols. Leipzig: Baumgartner's Buchhandlung.

Platen-Hallermünde, August von. 1896–1900. *Die Tägebucher des Grafen August von Platen,* ed. G. von Laubmann and L. von Scheffler. 2 vols. Stuttgart: J. G. Cotta'schenbuchhandlung nachfolger.

Popper, Karl R. 1959. *The Logic of Scientific Discovery.* London: Hutchinson.

————. 1962. *Conjectures and Refutations.* New York: Basic Books.

Praetorius, Numa [pseud. of Eugen Wilhelm]. 1904. Review of E. Gley, *Aberrations de l'instinct sexuel* (1884). *Jahrbuch für sexuelle Zwischenstufen* 6: 476–77.

————. 1906. Review of Freud 1905d. *Jahrbuch für sexuelle Zwischenstufen* 8: 729–48.

Prause, Marianne. 1968. *Carl Gustav Carus, Leben und Werk.* Berlin: Deutscher Verlag für Kunstwissenschaft.

Prichard, James Cowles. 1835. *A Treatise on Insanity and Other Disorders Affecting the Mind.* London: Sherwood, Gilbert, and Piper.

Raeburn, Michael, ed. 1991. *The Twilight of the Tsars: Russian Art at the Turn of the Century.* London: South Bank Centre.

Ralston, W. R. S. 1872. *The Songs of the Russian People, as Illustrative of Slavonic Mythology and Russian Social Life.* London: Ellis and Green.

Rank, Otto. 1926. *Technik der Psychoanalyse.* 2 vols. Vol. 1: *Die analytische Situation.* Vienna: F. Deuticke.

————. 1927. Review of Freud 1926d. *Mental Hygiene* 11: 180–82.

Reitler, Rudolf. 1917. Eine anatomisch-kunstlerische Fehlleistung Leonardos da Vinci. *Internationaler Zeitschrift für Psychanalyse* 4: 204–208.

Rice, Emanuel. 1990. *Freud and Moses: The Long Journey Home.* Albany: State University of New York Press.

Richter, Paul. 1976. On Professor Gombrich's Model of Schema and Correction. *British Journal of Aesthetics* 16: 338–46.

Ricoeur, Paul. 1970. *Freud and Philosophy: An Essay on Interpretation,* trans. Denis Savage. New Haven: Yale University Press.

Rigaud, Colette. 1992. Figures animales et pulsions fratricides. *Psychanalyse à l'université* 17: 135–48.

Ritvo, Lucille B. 1991. *Darwin's Influence on Freud: A Tale of Two Sciences.* New Haven: Yale University Press.

Roazen, Paul. 1975. *Freud and His Followers.* 1st ed. New York: Knopf.

————. 1985. *Helene Deutsch: A Psychoanalyst's Life.* Garden City, N.Y.: Anchor Press/Doubleday.

————. 1990. *Encountering Freud: The Politics and Histories of Psychoanalysis.* New Brunswick, N.J.: Transaction Books.

————. 1992. Freud's Patients: First-Person Accounts. In *Freud and the History of Psychoanalysis,* ed. Toby Gelfand and John Kerr, pp. 289–305. Hillsdale, N.J.: The Analytic Press.

————. 1993. *Meeting Freud's Family.* Amherst: University of Massachusetts Press.

Robinson, Paul A. 1993. *Freud and His Critics.* Berkeley: University of California Press.

Robitsek, Alfred. 1912. Symbolisches Denken in der chemischen Forschung. *Imago* 1: 83–90.

Rogers, L. R. 1964. Representation and Schemata. *British Journal of Aesthetics* 5: 159–78.

Romanes, George John. 1883. *Mental Evolution in Animals.* London: Kegan Paul, Trench.

————. 1888. *Mental Evolution in Man: Origin of Human Faculty.* London: Kegan Paul, Trench.

Rose, Jacqueline. 1986. *Sexuality in the Field of Vision.* London: Verso.

Rosenfeld, Eva. 1956. Dream and Vision: Some Remarks on Freud's Egyptian Bird Dream. *International Journal of Psycho-Analysis* 37: 97–105.

Rosenzweig, Saul. 1992. *Freud, Jung, and Hall the King-Maker: The Historic Expedi-*

tion to America (1909), with G. Stanley Hall as Host and William James as Guest. St. Louis: Rana House Press.

Rudnytsky, Peter L. 1991. *The Psychoanalytic Vocation: Rank, Winnicott, and the Legacy of Freud.* New Haven: Yale University Press.

Rusakova, A. 1975. *V. E. Borisov-Musatov.* Leningrad: Aurora Art Publishers.

Rycroft, Charles. 1971. Not So Much a Treatment, More a Way of Life. *New York Review of Books,* 17 October 21, pp. 8–11.

Sadger, Isidor. 1908. *Konrad Ferdinand Meyer: Eine pathographisch-psychologische Studie.* Wiesbaden: Bergmann. Grenzfragen des Nerven- und Seelenlebens 59.

———. 1909a. *Aus dem liebesleben Nicolaus Lenaus.* Vienna: F. Deuticke. Schriften zum angewandten Seelenkunde 6.

———. 1909b. *Heinrich von Kleist: Eine pathographisch-psychologische Studie.* Wiesbaden: Bergmann. Grenzfragen des Nerven- und Seelenlebens 70.

———. 1910. *Belastung und Entartung: Ein Beitrag zur Lehre vom kranken Genie.* Leipzig: privately printed.

Sadovnikov, D. 1986. *Riddles of the Russian People: A Collection of Riddles, Parables, and Puzzles,* trans. Ann C. Bigelow. Ann Arbor: University of Michigan Press.

Sarab'ianov, Dimtrii V. 1990. *Russian Art: From Neoclassicism to the Avant-Garde, 1800–1917.* New York: Abrams.

Schimek, Jean. 1974. The Parapraxis Specimen of Psychoanalysis. *Psychoanalysis and Contemporary Science* 3: 210–30.

Schrenck-Notzing, Albert von. 1895. *Therapeutic Suggestion in Psychopathia Sexualis (Pathological Manifestations of the Sexual Sense), with Especial Reference to Contrary Sexual Instinct* [1894], trans. Charles Gilbert Chaddock. Philadelphia: F. A. Davis.

Schultz, D. 1990. *Intimate Friends, Dangerous Rivals: The Turbulent Relationship between Freud and Jung.* Los Angeles: Jeremy Tarcher, Inc.

Schur, Max. 1966. Some Additional "Day Residues" of "The Specimen Dream of Psychoanalysis." In *Psychoanalysis—A General Psychology: Essays in Honor of Heinz Hartmann,* ed. R. M. Lowenstein, Lottie M. Newman, Max Schur, and Albert J. Solnit, pp. 45–85. New York: International Universities Press.

———. 1972. *Freud: Living and Dying.* New York: Hogarth Press and the Institute of Psycho-Analysis.

Segal, Hanna, and David Bell. 1991. The Theory of Narcissism in the Work of Freud and Klein. In *Freud's "On Narcissism": An Introduction,* ed. Joseph Sandler, Ethel Spector Person, and Peter Fonagy, pp. 149–74. New Haven: Yale University Press.

Senn, Harry A. 1982. *Were-Wolf and Vampire in Romania.* Boulder, Colo.: East European Monographs and New York: Columbia University Press.

Shaw, J. C., and G. N. Ferris. 1883. Perverted Sexual Instinct. *Journal of Nervous and Mental Diseases* 10: 185–204.

Shephard, Roger N., and Lynn A. Cooper. 1982. *Mental Images and Their Transformations.* Cambridge, Mass.: MIT Press.

Silberer, Herbert. 1910. Phantasie und Mythos. *Jahrbuch für Psychoanalytische und Psychopathologische Forschungen* 2: 554–56.

Silverman, Kaja. 1992. *Male Subjectivity at the Margins.* New York and London: Routledge.

Sinistrari d'Amero, Ludovicus Maria. 1883. *De la sodomie [De delictis et poenis (1754)].* Paris: I. Liseux.

Société du Salon d'Automne. 1910. *Catalogues 1902–1910.* Paris: Société du Salon d'Automne.

Solms, Mark, and Michael Saling. 1990. *A Moment of Transition: Two Neuroscientific Articles by Sigmund Freud.* London: Karnac Books.

Spence, Donald P. 1980. *Narrative Truth and Historical Truth: Meaning and Interpretation in Psychoanalysis.* New York: Norton.

Steele, Robert S. 1982. *Freud and Jung: Conflicts of Interpretation.* London and Boston: Routledge and Kegan Paul.

Stepansky, Paul E. 1983. In *Freud's Shadow: Adler in Context.* Hillsdale, N.J.: Analytic Press.

Sulloway, Frank J. 1979. *Freud, Biologist of the Mind: Beyond the Psychoanalytic Legend.* New York: Basic Books.

Swan, Jim. 1974. Mater and Nannie: Freud's Two Mothers and the Discovery of the Oedipus Complex. *American Imago* 31: 1–64.

Symonds, John Addington. 1871. *Miscellanies by John Addington Symonds, M. D., Selected and Edited, with an Introductory Memoir, by His Son.* London: Macmillan and Co.

———. 1875–86. *The Renaissance in Italy.* 7 vols. London: Smith, Elder and Co.

———. 1883. *A Problem in Greek Ethics.* London: privately printed.

———. 1891 (?). *A Problem in Modern Ethics.* London: privately printed.

———. 1893. *Walt Whitman: A Study.* London: Routledge and Sons.

———. 1969. *The Letters of John Addington Symonds,* ed. Herbert M. Schueller and Robert L. Peters. Vol. 3: *1885–1893.* Detroit: Wayne State University Press.

———. 1984. *The Memoirs of John Addington Symonds: The Secret Homosexual Life of a Leading Nineteenth-Century Man of Letters,* ed. Phyllis Grosskurth. New York: Random House.

Theweleit, Klaus. 1994. *Object-Choice (All You Need Is Love . . .): On Mating Strategies and a Fragment of a Freud Biography,* trans. Malcolm Green. London: Verso.

Tögel, Christfried. 1989. *Berggasse—Pompeji und Zurück: Sigmund Freuds Reisen in die Vergangenheit.* Tübingen: edition diskord.

Tuke, Daniel Hack. 1891. *Prichard and Symonds in Especial Relation to Mental Science, with Chapters on Moral Insanity.* London: J. and A. Churchill.

Tylor, Edward Burnett. 1903. *Primitive Culture.* 4th ed. London: J. Murray.

Ulrichs, Karl Heinrich. 1898. *Forschungen über das Rätsel der mannmännlichen Liebe* [12 vols. of 1864–79], ed. Magnus Hirschfeld. Leipzig: Max Spohr. (Reprint, New York: Arno Press, 1975.)

Vangensten, C. L.; A. Fonahn; and H. Hopstock, eds. 1913. *Leonardo da Vinci, Quaderni d'anatomia,* vol. 3. Christiana: J. Dybwad.

Vasari, Giorgio. 1991. *The Lives of the Artists* [1568], trans. Julia Conway Bondanella and Peter Bondanella. Oxford: Oxford University Press.

Viderman, Serge. 1977. *Le céleste et le sublunaire: la construction de l'espace analytique deux.* Paris: PUF.

Wachtel, Andrew B. 1990. *The Battle for Childhood.* Stanford: Stanford University Press.

Wallace, Edwin R. 1983. *Freud and Anthropology: A History and Reappraisal.* New York: International Universities Press. Psychological Issues Monograph 55.

Warner, Marina. 1989. Signs of a Fifth Element. In *The Tree of Life: New Images of an Ancient Symbol,* ed. Roger Malbert. London: South Bank Centre.

Weber, Samuel. 1982. *The Legend of Freud.* Minneapolis: University of Minnesota Press.
Weinberg, Jonathan. 1994. Urination and Its Discontents. In *Gay and Lesbian Studies in Art History,* ed. Whitney Davis, pp. 225–43. Binghamton, N.Y.: Haworth Press.
Wernicke, Carl. 1967. The Symptom Complex of Aphasia [1874], trans. Norman Geschwind. *Boston Studies in the Philosophy of Science* 4.
Whitman, Walt. 1882–83. *Specimen Days and Collect.* Philadelphia: R. Welsh.
Winckelmann, J. J. 1778. *W.s Briefe an seine Freunde in der Schweiz,* ed. L. Usteri. Zurich: Orell, Gessner, Fuesslin, und Compagnie.
———. 1784. *Johann Winkelmanns [sic] Briefe an einen Freund in Liefland,* ed. J. F. Voigt. Coburg: Rudolph Ahl.
Winer, Robert. 1993. Echoes of the Wolf Men: Reverbations of Psychic Reality. In *Telling Facts: History and Narration in Psychoanalysis,* ed. Joseph H. Smith and Humphrey Morris, pp. 140–59. Baltimore: Johns Hopkins University Press.
Wittgenstein, Ludwig. 1966. *Lectures and Conversations,* ed. Cyril Barrett. Oxford: Basil Blackwell.
Wollheim, Richard. 1984. *The Thread of Life.* Cambridge, Mass.: Harvard University Press.
Wundt, Wilhelm. 1913. *Elemente der Völkerpsychologie: Grundlinien einer psychologischen Entwicklungsgeschichte der Menschheit.* 2nd ed. Leipzig: A. Kröner.
Zenkovsky, Serge A. 1963. *Medieval Russia's Epics, Chronicles, and Tales.* New York: Dutton.
Zipes, Jack. 1982. *Rötkäppchens Lust und Leid: Biographie eines Europaischen Märchens.* 1st ed. Cologne: Eugen Diederich.

INDEX

Abraham, Karl, 24, 29, 62, 206
Abraham, Nicolas, 17–20
Adler, Alfred, 2, 26, 30, 114, 206, 209, 221–22, 224–25

Beardsley, Aubrey, 5, 211
Bilibin, Ivan, 188–89, 192
Biology. *See* Phylogenesis
Bisexuality, xvi–xviii, 15, 16, 113, 141, 152–53, 157, 209, 211, 222, 234, 239. *See also* Fliess, Wilhelm; Homosexuality; Primal scene; Sexuality
Blüher, Hans, 232
Böcklin, Arnold, 97, 107, 108, 109
Bonaparte, Marie, 45
Bonstetten, C. V. von, 115
Borisov-Musatov, V. E., 10
Brand, Adolf, 232
Breuer, Josef, 65, 231
Brunswick, Mark, 3
Brunswick, Ruth Mack, 3–5, 8, 16–17, 18, 19, 26, 38–40, 51, 153–56, 202–203, 215–19
Budge, E. A. W., 82
Burton, Richard, 193

Carus, Carl Gustav, 58–59, 97–99, 177
Casper, Johann Ludwig, 121, 123
Charcot, Jean-Martin, 89, 226
Couperus, Louis, 126

Dakyns, Henry Graham, 118
Darwin, Charles, xxi, 157–61, 165, 172, 236. *See also* Phylogenesis
Deleuze, Gilles, 93
Derrida, Jacques, 90
Descartes, René, 93, 94
Deutsch, Helen, 8–9
Dostoevsky, Fyodor, 197, 199
Drosnes, Leonid, 24–26
DuBois-Reymond, Emil, 25

Edelman, Lee, 149, 150
Egypt, ancient, 8, 82, 85, 239
Eitingon, Max, 63, 196
Ellis, Havelock, 119, 121–23, 232–33
Eulenburg, Prince Philipp zu, 119

Ferenczi, Sandor, 1, 22, 23, 24, 26, 31, 61–62, 102, 103, 114, 133–34, 135, 137, 138, 172, 206, 208–209, 210, 221, 231, 233, 237–38
Fish, Stanley, 184, 194, 204
Flechsig, Paul, 135
Fliess, Wilhelm, 65, 67, 68, 78, 82, 96, 97, 99, 106–108, 109–14, 132, 208–10, 222, 231–33, 234, 238, 240. *See also* Bisexuality; Freud, Sig(is)mund, relations with students
Fodor, Nandor, 187–90, 191
Frazer, James George, 193
Freud, Alexander (brother), 110, 179, 182
Freud, Amalia (mother), 177
Freud, Anna (daughter), 9
Freud, Martha (fiancée and wife), 210, 238, 240
Freud, Martin (son), 177, 200
Freud, Sig(is)mund, dreams and parapraxes of, 27, 73–75, 89, 106–14, 208, 238–40
—, homosexuality and, xviii–xix, 15–16, 51, 101–103, 108, 113–14, 123–40, 141, 199–213, 221, 224, 231–33, 233–34, 240. *See also* Fliess, Wilhelm; Homosexuality; Intersubjectivity
—, patients of and/or case studies by: "Emma," 75–77, 81, 105; "Dora," 68, 234; "Little Hans," 124–26, 127, 128, 132, 137; "Rat Man," 2, 240; Frau Marton, 234; Philipp Stein, 133–34, 135, 137, 138; Daniel Paul Schreber, 24, 124, 128, 133, 135, 137–39, 167, 206, 234. *See also* Abraham, Karl; Abraham, Nicolas; Ferenczi, Sandor; Pankejeff, Serge; Sadger, Isidor; Vinci, Leonardo da
—, personal life of, xxi, 101–103, 177–82, 192–94, 199–204, 231–32, 238–40. *See also* Fliess, Wilhelm
—, relations with students, 27–28, 30, 114, 130, 208–10, 231–32. *See also* Adler, Alfred; Ferenczi, Sandor; Jung, Carl Gustav; Rank, Otto; Stekel, Wilhelm
—, scientific and psychological studies by, xxii–xxiii, 45, 72–104, 123–31, 161–65, 222–24, 226–27, 229–30, 240. *See also* Neurology; Sexuality
Freud Archives, 9

WHITNEY DAVIS, Professor of Art History at Northwestern University and Director of Northwestern's Alice Berline Kaplan Center for the Humanities, is the author of *The Canonical Tradition in Ancient Egyptian Art; Masking the Blow: The Scene of Representation in Late Prehistoric Egyptian Art;* and *Replications: Archaeology, Art History, Psychoanalysis.* He is the editor of *Gay and Lesbian Studies in Art History.*

Lightning Source UK Ltd.
Milton Keynes UK
UKHW020933060821
388083UK00012B/563